ROME 476

David Parker Essays

Volume Three

Waterside Productions
2055 Oxford Ave
Cardiff, CA 92007
www.waterside.com

Printed in the United States of America

ISBN-13: 978-1-960583-48-2 paperback edition
ISBN-13: 978-1-960583-49-9 ebook edition

The author would like to thank the following authors and publishers for their permission to reprint:

Excerpts from Cosmos by Carl Sagan. Copyright © 1980 by Carl Sagan. Reprinted by permission of Random House.

Excerpts from Thoughts. Governor Jerry Brown, copyright © 1976, by Edmund G. Brown. Used by permission of Jerry Brown. All rights reserved.

Excerpts from Insider Trading and the Stock Market by Henry Manne. Copyright © 1966 by Henry Manne. Reprinted by permission of Simon & Schuster/The Free Press.

Excerpts from "Has Economic Analysis Improved Regulatory Decisions?" Journal of Economic Perspectives, 23, no. 1, (Winter 2008) by Robert Hahn and Paul C. Tetlock used by permission from Robert Hahn and Paul C. Tetlock.

Mike Locukovich cartoon reprinted by permission of Mike Luckovich and Creators Syndicate, Inc.

Rome fell in 476.
With it Western civilization, civil
rights, scientific and technological
progress. Followed by the Dark Ages.
One thousand years.

Why did Rome fall?
Because its soldiers didn't lift a finger
to stop the Huns.
Why? Those soldiers hadn't been paid.
Why? All tax revenue went to service
interest on the debt.

CONTENTS

CHAPTER 1: PODCAST NOTES

CHAPTER 2: JOURNAL OF LAW AND BUSINESS

CHAPTER 3: LETTERS TO THE EDITOR

CHAPTER 4: FOUR ESSAYS

CHAPTER 5: SHORT ESSAYS

1

PODCAST NOTES

A. DAVID PARKER

CLASSICAL LIBERAL

I'm a classical liberal. All my friends are romantic liberals, progressives, well-meaning people who would like to see the world come together as a community to plan their society, spend whatever it takes, solve the nation's social and economic problems. They are Dionysus: from the heart; compassion. I am Apollo: reason.

Progressives, life doesn't work that way. *Every* nation, *every* economic system has problems. Except, ultimately, those problems are personal, not solvable by government.[1] There are no species in nature where some members tell others what to do. All societies, humans included, evolved spontaneously, as if **led by an invisible hand**, according to Adam Smith (*Wealth of Nations*) and F.A. Hayek (*The Constitution of Liberty*). Survival is encoded in our genes; morality is encoded in our genes; instinct—living cells for millions of years pursuing their self-interest to survive—created human society better than anything humans can possibly create by design. There is no need for government. To the declaration, "I'm going to live in harmony with nature," Nietzsche responded (approximately): "Who do you think you are? You can't live any other way."

---

[1] On that platform, in 1976, Jerry Brown ran for president: government cannot solve all our problems; It is not in the American character to ask government to do so. Edmund G. Brown Jr., *Thoughts, Governor Jerry Brown* (San Francisco: City Lights Books, 1976).

***

America, an advanced industrialized economy, not a village, experiences globalization, capitalism, racism, economic discrimination. Except, those problems exist in every advanced economy. America at least is a free society, where citizens choose how they earn a living, whom they associate with, whom they vote for. Unfair, but minorities must not let their reality hold them back. Minorities experience social and economic discrimination everywhere. In Indonesia, pogroms kill 100,000 Chinese at a time (jealous of their economic success); in Europe, six million Jews (for the same reason); in Africa, for 1,000 years, slavery destroyed the lives of millions (two-thirds went east, one-third went west). The solution, however, always the same, is to obtain an education, pursue a career, pursue your self-interest to survive, turn to your own community, move away from a bad situation. In America, if you are Black and trained as an architect and no one will hire you, work for a Black architect, work for Black clients. If you're good, the market will beat a path to your door—as did the market to the Negro Baseball League, where players were better than those in the National League.

Progressives, money can't solve social and economic problems. Stop spending![2] Overheard in a Brooklyn barber shop (by one of the musicians in my band): "If you can solve a problem with money, you don't have a problem." The richest nation in the world, awash in cash, America willingly funds the War on Poverty—except that poverty, 15 percent in 1964, is still 15 percent. The needle never

---

[2] This author taught at Bret Harte Elementary School in San Francisco for 20 years. An academically low-performing school, yet nothing was left upon which to spend money: kindergarten and first-grade classrooms each had private bathrooms; schoolyards were separated by age so that older students wouldn't bother younger ones; the school had a library and full-time librarian, an auditorium with a stage and professional lighting, a full-size gymnasium (open to the neighborhood at night and weekends) and a full-time gym teacher; it had a large kitchen with two commercial ovens and three cooks (until the district closed all school kitchens to bring in preheated processed government surplus—which the kids, hungry, threw in the garbage); plus, classrooms were large in size, teachers were excellent (all volunteered to be at that school) with an unusually high ratio of male teachers and an unusually high number of resource teachers providing one-on-one instruction. Bret Harte remained the lowest-scoring elementary school in the district.

2

moved (on average).[3] Remove those programs today and poverty jumps to 22 percent, immediately.[4] The War on Poverty made Americans dependent.[5]

From 1970 to 2000, funding for public education doubled due to the Elementary Secondary Education Act. Immediately, test scores plummeted and have not returned. Today, only 36 percent of *all* American students are proficient in reading and math.[6]

Government intervention in any market destroys that market. Government intervention in health care turned health insurance into prepaid health care—why health insurance costs three times what it would: it's no longer insurance. Before Medicare, health insurance was the price of auto insurance (or life insurance, or property insurance)—$200 a month, for a young person, $50 a month (in 2022 dollars). Remove government, and the cost of health care will drop 66 percent.

Government builds low-income housing. Cheaply, unaesthetically, designed to congregate low-income people all in one place. It's absolutely unnatural—why low-income housing usually reverts to slums. Open that housing to everyone; that won't happen.

Free markets are a force of nature. Government's one duty is to remove, not add, inhibitions to their movement. Government's duty is to protect, not provide life, liberty and property.

***

Our Founding Fathers got it right: if we want a pluralist society, limit the size of government. Maximum individual freedom in exchange

---

[3] U.S. Census Bureau, *Historical Poverty Tables: People and Families—1959-2021*, https://www.census.gov/data/tables/time-series/demo/income-poverty/historical-poverty-people.html.

[4] Charles Murray, *Losing Ground: American Social Policy 1950–1980* (New York: Basic Books, 1984), p. 65.

[5] The U.S. has spent $23 trillion on the War on Poverty, three times what the U.S. has spent on all wars it ever fought—with nothing to show.

[6] The National Assessment of Educational Progress (NAEP), *The Condition of Education 2020*, U.S. Department of Education, https://nces.ed.gov/programs/coe/pdf/coe_cnb.pdf.

for maximum personal responsibility. Until 1933, America represented just that: social, political and economic freedom; what French political scientist Alexis de Tocqueville most admired about our new nation—how responsible citizens were.

James Madison, principal author of the Constitution, asked, "Why do we need government?" He finally conceded that not all men are angels, that we need government (a neutral third party) to protect life, liberty and property, to protect social, political and economic freedom. *Protect, not provide.* Madison also said we had better guard the guard: checks and balances in government—an elected legislature, an executive, a judiciary for legal review.[7]

In 1933, President Franklin D. Roosevelt reversed checks and balances. He fired the guard, fired the Supreme Court. He threatened to add six justices who would rubber-stamp everything he asked—and got his way. Dictatorship. In 1933, with the four-year depression over (1929–1932), anxious to implement the programs he campaigned on in 1932, Roosevelt reversed the end of that depression. He turned it into the Great Depression, which continued unnecessarily for another eight years, when no depression in the history of the U.S. (or the world) ever lasted more than four years.[8] Now we are stuck with progressivism, with a $2.8 trillion yearly budget deficit, a $30 trillion national debt, $100 trillion in unfunded liabilities—all paid for by taxes on the middle class. Worse, by borrowing.

The opposite, conservatism, holds that the laws of money, business and economics are so timeless that government intervention in the economy can only be counterproductive. It's why, for example, the 2008 recession lasted ten years rather than two.

If the U.S. can't abide by its Constitution, a one-page document, a simple set of general rules, the U.S. has no chance. To the Founding Fathers, freedom meant freedom *from* government. To

---

[7] Alexander Hamilton, James Madison, and John Jay, *The Federalist Papers: A Collection of Essays, Written in Favour of the New Constitution* (New York: J. & A. McLean, 1788), Federalist, no. 51.

[8] After 90 years of debate, all economists today, Nobel economist Paul Krugman included, agree: Roosevelt caused (not ended) the Great Depression.

progressives, society has moved forward from that idea, hence, "progressivism." To progressives, the U.S. Constitution is rule of thumb, not rule of law.

A San Francisco Conservative

I'm a San Francisco conservative. Well, not that conservative; I'm a member of the ACLU. It is my intuition about political economy that compels me to write: to tell progressives they are wrong. The New Deal, the Great Society, the Affordable Care Act, Biden's Family Planning Act, *all* seek to solve the nation's problems by spending money. Those programs, however, are all paid for by the poor and middle class, not the rich. Jeff Bezos hasn't paid tax in 20 years. It's why the rich aren't complaining: they're not paying. They're laughing at Ocasio-Cortez's "Tax the Rich" written in blood on the back of her designer dress.

The indifference of the rich, an amorality bordering on immorality, compels me to write, to tell progressives to stop trying to solve the nation's social and economic problems through the political process: spending money, regulating business.

I have 150 years' experience; I know what I'm talking about:

- 40 years a teacher, inner-city public schools, plus 10 years a volunteer;

- 40 years a professional musician: 20 years Berkeley Symphony Orchestra, 20 years Dave Parker Sextet;

- 50 years professional real estate investment: industrial, office, large residential;

5

- 35 years reading and writing in political economy: post-university 35,000 hours concentrated study.

I predicted these events:

- In 2008—(at the beginning of the financial crisis)—that the financial crisis would take ten years to resolve, and that growth and interest rates would remain low for the next ten. My suggestion that government allow the economy to self-correct (austerity), that the recession would then last no more than two years, was printed in *The Economist* as a Letter to the Editor alongside a similar letter from the economic advisor to the prime minister of England.

- In 2010—(at the beginning of the Euro crisis) —that there would be no euro crisis. As Greece defaulted on its sovereign debt, as Europe panicked, I said the euro wouldn't drop one cent, that Germany would never allow it. With its unmatched productivity, with the value of the euro high (yet much lower than would be the deutsche mark), Germany controls the economies of Europe.

- In 2015—when Donald Trump announced his candidacy for president, everyone laughed. I spontaneously responded, "He won!" On the eve of the 2016 election, with some polls showing Hillary 90 percent, all polls a majority, I announced, "He won!"

- In 2020 I could not predict a Trump victory (although I thought he might win). Rather, I said he deserved to lose—because he used the office for personal gain, misled the nation with respect to COVID-19, and did not fulfill his campaign promises. I said that Donald Trump, like Arnold Schwarzenegger, governor of California, was not a trained politician—why neither could control the legislature.

Still, intuition tells me not to underestimate Donald Trump. His latest project, Truth Social, a media platform to challenge Twitter and Facebook and take their customers, whether it fails or not, is brilliant. In 2015, as a lifelong Democrat, in favor of universal health insurance, Trump planned to run as a Democrat—until the Clintons told him they wouldn't allow it. So, he ran as a Republican. He didn't care. He told the Republican candidates, "Move over," and they did. Don't underestimate someone who can do that. Read *Art of the Deal* and you'll understand how Trump negotiates: from an extreme, even fraudulent, position, to get the other side to compromise; *then* he compromises.

In 2016, citizens voted for Trump because there was a national consensus that neither political party had any intention of solving the problems *all* Americans care about:

1. High cost of health care
2. Poorly performing public schools
3. Lax law enforcement

Citizens lied in the polls. Thus, Donald J. Trump. The *J* stands for genius.

***

- In March 2022, the Fed started raising interest rates. All economists predicted recession. But, when *all* economists predict something, guaranteed it's not going to happen.

- In 2023, I predicted the demise of the Democratic Party, that within 30 years it will become the nation's minority party, a conscience to the nation, a reminder not to overlook the less fortunate, but the Senate, the House, the presidency, and six of the nine Supreme Court Justices will be Republican. Black, Latin, and blue-collar voters, culturally conservative, taken for granted by the nation's well-meaning well-educated coastal elites, are increasingly voting Republican.

- In 2013, I predicted that Bashar al-Assad of Syria would win, would bomb his own people into submission. In 2022, Putin is doing the same, bombing his own people, Ukraine, into submission. He may win, but I won't predict it.

My 150 years' experience translates into ability to correctly state a problem. The solution, then, is usually obvious; it's in the statement.

FOUR SIMULTANEOUS CAREERS

This "in-the-moment" San Francisco conservative simultaneously lived four professional careers. A gambler's instinct—good judgment, a sense of when to move, when not to move—allowed me to combine those four careers.

Teaching

I would wait for a student to say something—which sometimes took several weeks—then incorporate that remark as a focal point of the semester's work. At *that* moment, I had the class: the lesson was now about something that really interested them.

Example: "Mr. Parker, you just got back from two weeks of winter vacation. What's with this 'I'll be leaving in two weeks for two weeks in Paris'?" Implied: "What are we paying you for?" Another student then walked up to my table (without permission), flipped out a wad of 20-dollar bills, tossed a couple over to me, and said, "Get me one of those little Eiffel Towers!" Both students were ten years old. So I tell them about my apartment in Paris, teach them a French song; I have their attention all year long. Every day they ask a new question. No one misses class. I promised them all an Eiffel Tower.

Jazz

A waiter drops some plates on the floor: *crash*! I point to the drummer and say, "Cymbal!!" To the trumpet: "Trill!!" Sax: "Play something!" We're off and running.

Business

Deals are made, not found. They're in the streets. An agent sent me a solicitation letter to purchase 22 units. I called. "Let's make an offer." He says, "No, no, the seller is really difficult. I just wanted to keep my name in front of you." I said, "No, no, make an appointment with the seller at his office. I'll do the talking. I'll make the deal." I said, "Mr. Seller, the market is down, lenders aren't lending, interest rates are high, vacancies are up." (True or not, you gotta shake the seller up a little.) "Mr. Seller, you just inherited the property. I'll pay your price,[9] use my connections to get a loan, and you carry back the balance."[10] He said, 'Fine." Too easy. I then suggested, "Why don't you loan me an additional $100,000 from your proceeds? I'll pay you 5 percent interest for ten years." He said, "Fine." There were three agents in the room. Their jaws fell open. Had I let them speak, worse, told them ahead of time what I would say, they never would have allowed it—a leveraged buyout. I had to remind them: deals are made, not found.

Writing
I do not write from an outline (which drives my editor nuts). I write spontaneously, three to five hours a day—waiting for the sentence I need, which often comes at the end of the day, the last sentence. But that's what it takes, the downside of spontaneity: waste, yes, but I found sentence number one for the next day, which often generates a whole paragraph. By the end of the writing project, with so much editing, the work eventually comes together as if it had an outline. My writing is art.

***

The ability to make judgment calls in the moment connected my four careers: teaching, jazz, business and writing. Plus the ability to delegate. In business, the best CEOs delegate. It's the key to running a large business, nay, several businesses at a time. What those CEOs have in common is that many are dyslexic. According to Cass School of Business in London, 35 percent of the world's great CEOs have dyslexia.[11] They can read, but they don't. Rather, they listen and

---

[9] Always give full price to someone who just inherited an asset. Having no idea how the underlying fortune that made that asset possible was created, they are, then, so afraid of someone stealing that asset, they will never lower their price.

[10] Paying the price ten years later, when the note is due, compensates for overpaying at the beginning.

[11] AMA Staff, "New Research Reveals Many Entrepreneurs Are Dyslexic," American Management Association, January 24, 2019, https://www.amanet.org/articles/new-research-reveals-many-entrepreneurs-are-dyslexic/.

make judgment calls. Having learned since childhood to choose classmates to help them, by age five they have already made hundreds of judgment calls as to whom they can count on, whom they can't. Having observed the teacher, listened to what he or she said, observed body language, remembered what the teacher kept repeating, those dyslexics filled their answer sheets with sentences that catered to that teacher's sensibilities. Flattered, the teacher overlooked that the student really didn't answer the question.

Timing, delegation, knowing the most underlying truth—*these* are the keys to operating a large business; the reason for Andrew Carnegie's success. Carnegie knew, for example, never to stop production—especially during an economic downturn—because that is when you grab market share from those who can't hold on. It was not through monopolistic practices or union busting that Carnegie made his fortune. It was by relentlessly picking up market share until he owned every steel mill.

Consider these dyslexic heads of industry: Richard Bronson, Virgin Airlines; Ted Turner, CNN and many other industries; William Hewlett, Hewlett-Packard; Kinko's; Federal Express; Charles Schwab.

The ability to make important decisions *in the moment* is why the world's great industries, militaries and governments are usually headed by one person. Few individuals have the deep experience to make judgment calls at that level.

Consider these uneducated heads of industry: Henry Ford and Thomas Edison. *Their* success lay in persistence.

B. Business and Economics

The Corporate State

Brer Rabbit says to Brer Fox, who finally caught him, "Oh, please, please, please, please, whatever you do, don't throw me in thet briar patch!"

Of course, country Fox throws crafty Rabbit into the briar patch.[12]

Today, large corporation Brer Rabbit pleads with progressive government Brer Fox, "Oh, please, please, please, please, whatever you do, don't regulate me!" Progressive fox, of course, is unaware that crafty rabbit *wants to be regulated.* Why? Because massive regulation, Sarbanes–Oxley/Dodd–Frank, is so expensive, millions of dollars just in legal fees per year, that only large corporations with their low, long-run average costs (economies of scale) can afford to comply—then gobble up the small firms that cannot.

Having created monopolies, a nation without competition, government now orders those few monopolies to do its bidding: raise prices above market and give the excess profit to government (as taxation). Government then distributes that money to every citizen— as complete social services: health insurance, pension, education, college education, unemployment insurance, cultural access to the nation's great theaters, concert halls, fine restaurants and tourist attractions.

Those ten surviving corporations have what they want: monopoly; government has what it wants: high tax revenue (to pay for public services); citizens have what they want. Except, to receive those public services, citizens gave government what government really wanted: their political freedom. In sum, the corporate state.

Conceived by Otto von Bismarck in Germany, 1870, the "corporate state" is how strong-arm governments remain in power:

---

[12] *The Chandler Stories,* like *Huckleberry Finn* (America's second-greatest novel), are no longer taught in the nation's public schools. With their rural 1850s Southern dialect, those authors are politically incorrect.

National Socialism. In the 1920s, communism—socialism from the Left: Lenin, Stalin. In the 1930s, fascism—socialism from the Right: Hitler, Mussolini. Today, Putin, Xi. The abbreviation for National Socialism is NAZI.

***

The very purpose of a firm is to incorporate elements of production under one roof. It's cheaper than jobbing those elements to other companies (or other countries). In economics, theory of the firm.

Firms also incorporate to obtain liability protection for their owners—from lawsuits that would otherwise extend to owners' personal assets: home, pension, children's college funds. In England, corporations are "limited liability companies," Ltd; in France, "sociétés anonymes," S.A.; in the U.S., "incorporated," Inc.

The goal of every business is to produce a well-made product. And provide income to owners and employees. Except, in a competitive market economy, profit is zero: efficient-market hypothesis, the notion that as new firms rush in whenever profit rises above zero, that competition returns profit to zero. Throw a dart at the stock market page: the return is the same for all firms. The moment any firm's profits rise, professional investors rush in and buy. When traffic backs up on the freeway, the moment one lane begins to move, cars jump in such that there was no profit in changing lanes. Karl Marx's greatest error: the idea that there is profit to distribute to workers (if they owned the means of production). Error also because workers are not interested in running a business, a difficult skill to acquire. They care about their paycheck —plus, unions would never let workers forgo their weekly paycheck for a percentage of the firm's yearly net income, even if that amount were twice their salary.[13] Asking workers to run a business is like asking stagehands to play in the orchestra—what citizens in

---

[13] Unions have convinced workers not to fall for that trap: "Put in a day's work; get paid!"

communist countries traded their political freedom for: a dream. Then, watched their nation return to the Middle Ages.

***

What about B corporations—corporations that devote a portion of their profit to worthy causes? Again, Marx's error: there is no profit to distribute. Corporations would have to raise the price of their products—and risk being driven out of business. No free lunch. Milton Friedman was correct when he said firms should stay focused on earning a profit. In a competitive economy, they should not get sidetracked with charitable work. Of the top 100 firms on the Dow Jones Industrial Average in 1961, three exist today. If they wish to contribute, as individuals, employees and owners should choose charities and causes of *their* choice, not the firm's choice.[14]

THE FIVE LAWS OF ECONOMICS

There are only five laws of economics. None evident, all counterintuitive. Abstracted from a universe beyond our grasp, the subject of economics is difficult.

Law One: Comparative Advantage
Nations should produce according to their comparative, not absolute, advantage.

The wise merchant-philosopher, Solon, told 6th century Athens: Stop farming! You have the best farmers but the worst soil. You're wasting your time. Produce olive oil (anyone can plant olive trees), put it in painted pottery (created by your excellent artists), and ship it everywhere (in your highly developed shipping industry). *That* is your comparative advantage. You know how to farm, but

---

[14] Firms contributing to causes: marketing. Firms diversifying their employee base: marketing. Firms adjusting to climate change: marketing.

farming is your *absolute* advantage (which isn't an advantage). Greece earns ten dollars an hour producing and shipping pottery, whereas farming nations in the region earn one dollar an hour. Continue farming, and Athens loses nine dollars an hour, a stiff opportunity cost, whereas Athens' trading partners, at one dollar an hour, lose nothing. They're not competing with Athens; they're not losing the opportunity to paint and ship pottery.

Comparative advantage is the ability to produce a good or service at a lower opportunity cost than another person or country.

Athens followed Solon's advice. Genius. It allowed 5th century Athens to flourish. No longer producing everything themselves, Athens now traded for everything. Throughout the Mediterranean, goods and services were produced at their lowest price, standard of living rose for *all* nations. Athens became rich.[15]

The region's best artists and businesspeople flocked to Athens. Trade and commerce developed to an extraordinary level. And then, by miracle, Athens developed the notion of individual rights, Western civilization, the idea that the rights of the individual precede those of the state.[16]

Everything we know today about art, architecture, science, mathematics, literature, poetry, philosophy, politics, and democracy started or was outright discovered in 5th century Athens. Everything around you, every building, road, theater, museum, university, scientific research facility, institution of democracy you owe to 5th

---

[15] If imposing tariffs destroys the benefit of producing according to comparative advantage, why do nations do it? Because populist politicians win elections saying they will protect jobs by imposing tariffs on foreign goods, and progressive politicians win elections by saying they will spend whatever it takes to cure the nation's problems—which guarantees that *all* citizens will pay higher than market prices for *all* goods and services. In other words, when nations lose jobs, it is because they no longer have the comparative advantage. Or, throwing money at social problems is never the solution.

[16] Western civilization means that the needs of the community do not precede the rights of the individual. If you live in the West and disagree with that, leave. You have no business trying to turn the West into something else. That philosophic leap, East to West, was an evolutionary step forward for humankind.

century Athens (plus modern government to 1st century Rome and contemporary social, political and economic freedom to 18th century Britain, Scotland, France and America).[17]

Law Two: Marginal Utility Theory

Another economic principle based on relativity is marginal utility theory: the notion that all economic decisions are based on an individual's perception at a moment in time—in relation to how much of something that individual already has. Marginal utility means that all decisions, economic or not, are subjective.

As Solon told Athenians to forget what they did in the past, so, too, marginal utility theory says forget about what happened in the past. At a moment of decision, "at the margin," the past is irrelevant. If you flipped a coin 50 times and it came up heads 50 times, what are the odds the next flip will be tails? An irrelevant question. At the next flip, the odds are what they were at *each* of those 50 flips: 50–50.[18]

Marginal utility is the amount of added utility gained from an additional unit increase in consumption of a particular good.

Related, the principle of diminishing marginal utility says that the greater the consumption of some good or service, the smaller the increase in utility from an additional unit consumed.[19]

Value (of anything) is determined "at the moment." Why? Because value is subjective, different for everyone. The value of a

---

[17] Postmodernist multiculturalists, wishing to create inclusiveness, preach that 5th century Athens, 1st century Rome, 18th century Age of Enlightenment, i.e., Western civilization, is only one of the world's many cultures—and that public schools better teach those other cultures and economic systems, socialism, for example, which today they do. It bodes badly for the free world.

[18] A minority population debating whether to leave a country where they have been badly treated is still making a decision at a moment in time. To stay because they feel their nation owes them something, reparations, is a mistake (unless they really believe they're going to get a big check) if their future is better elsewhere.

[19] A restaurant offers another pizza "on the house." "Oh, no more, please. I can't eat another bite." The pizza has no value to that diner (unless he can sell it, in which case it has exchange value).

glass of water, removed from a moment in time for a particular person, is unknowable. Value is not objective.

At home (with running water), a glass of water has little value. In Death Valley, 110 degrees, empty thermos, dying of thirst, that glass of water is worth the diamond ring on your finger. Twenty-five hundred years ago, Aristotle couldn't figure out this famous "diamond–water paradox." Two hundred fifty years ago, Adam Smith couldn't figure it out. In 1871, Carl Menger did: value is not objective; value is *subjective*, in relation to how much one has "at the moment." It's different for every human being.[20]

Law Three: Price Is a Function of Supply and Demand

When demand for products rises and supply doesn't, price rises. Pent-up demand for goods and services from consumers (demanders) not spending during COVID-19 lockdowns (2020 and 2021), along with supply backed up from producers (suppliers) closing their factories, caused prices to rise in 2022. That's not inflation! That's supply and demand.

Inflation is government increasing a nation's money supply at a rate faster than the rate of increase of the nation's population.[21] Government payments to citizens suffering loss of income during COVID-19, by printing money but not asking citizens to repay it via a permanent line-item on their federal 1040 income tax return for 20 years, cause inflation. Producers, believing the nation's price rise stems from a genuine increase in demand, increase production—

---

[20] Income inequality exists because every human being values money differently. The notion of economic justice is pure nonsense. Had Karl Marx understood marginal utility theory, he would have remained an economist, and 100 million people wouldn't have died fighting for or against communism. He wouldn't have written the *Communist Manifesto*. Unfortunately, Marx thought the value of a good or service was the value of the labor and material that went into its production: "labor theory of value." Absolutely wrong. Value is a function of supply and demand. Adam Smith was correct about everything he wrote except that he, too, believed the labor theory of value, the one thing Marx took from him (instead of everything else), believing that the higher the product's price, the higher labor should be paid, that workers should be paid well enough to purchase what they produce, that a worker making Cadillacs should be paid three times a worker making Fords, even though the work is exactly the same.

[21] Increase the money supply 3 percent when the population increased 2 percent: inflation!

until they realize the rise in price was not from a genuine increase in demand, then, fire their workers. Recession.

American health care is a perfect example. Medicare gives citizens (patients) a level of health care way beyond what they're asking for.[22] Remove citizens from negotiating price, as Medicare does, and the market disappears. Government intervention in health care killed that market—why health insurance in the U.S. today is simply prepaid health care. Citizens pay between $1,200 and $2,000 a month for health insurance, when prior to Medicare and Medicaid, health insurance was the price of auto insurance, about $200 a month ($50 for a young person). Americans would be better off receiving that $1,200 to $2,000 differential each month in cash, paying $200 for health insurance, and depositing $400 into a medical savings account to pay for routine care. After a $5,000 deductible, insurance would kick in (although $400 a month multiplied by 12 is $4,800). Health insurance would return to what it once was for: major medical.[23]

The law of demand states that the quantity of a good demanded rises as its price falls (and drops as its price rises).

When government intervenes in a market, hands out huge sums of money for COVID-19 relief, hands out enormous health coverage, consumers will be indifferent to what things cost. Remove consumers from price negotiation, the market fails—why socialized health care costs three times what it should.

---

[22] The last six months of life alone may cost $500,000. If that means wiping out your personal savings, leaving nothing for your children or grandchildren, most Americans would not spend that money. But, since it's paid for, who cares? My father always checked the bill at the restaurant, yet walked into a hospital during his last years and declared, "Take care of me. I don't care what it costs!"

[23] Do the math. Keep that $12,000–$24,000 differential every year. At the end of your 40-year career, you will have $480,000–$960,000 in cash in the bank. You could have bought a couple of apartment buildings. When you retire, with those loans paid off, the rent is your pension, $60,000 a year (6 percent on a one-million-dollar building). Plus, had you been allowed to keep your 15 percent Social Security contribution (7½ percent + 7½ percent) $7,500 a year if you earned $50,000 a year over a 40-year career, there's another $300,000.

Law Four: The Law of One Price

There is one price in the world.

Competitive markets guarantee there is only one price in the world: its lowest. With profits pushed to zero, what competitive markets do (efficient market hypothesis), the degree to which the price of a particular good or service is higher in one country is the degree to which that country's government intervenes in the market. Price is higher because risk of doing business there is higher.[24]

Entrepreneurial compensation is another matter. CEO salaries of $100 million a year (also for nonprofit corporations) in efficient markets are still at their lowest. An expense to a firm, a reduction in profit, those salaries are carefully calculated: as a percent of the increased revenue (or stock price) a particular individual personally generates. Professional athletes' salaries are similarly determined. Remove Steve Curry from the San Francisco Warriors' lineup and the extent to which attendance drops, ticket prices drop, revenue from radio and television broadcasting drops—*that's* Curry's salary: 50 percent of the drop. Fifty million dollars.

The notion of "one price in the world" is part of a larger concept, the idea that rates of return on capital are timeless: for 4,300 years, since Babylon, 1–2 percent on savings (what banks pay for deposits); 2–3 percent on mortgage lending (what borrowers on real estate pay for a loan); 3–5 percent on venture capital (what investors

---

[24] Most of the world's currencies (2022) are undervalued—because the dollar is too strong. On the Big Mac index (created by *The Economist*), a Big Mac costs £3.69 in Britain and $5.15 in the U.S. The implied exchange rate is 0.72 (3.69/5.15). The difference between this and the actual exchange rate, 0.83, suggests that the British pound is 13.8 percent undervalued [0.72/0.83 = 86.2 percent]. Undervalued would mean that Britain is intervening in its economy, but since *all* the world's currencies are undervalued compared to the dollar, it means the U.S. government is intervening in its economy—increasing the nation's interest rate. The rate of return on U.S. treasuries (2022) is now twice that of the euro, three to four times that of the yen. To purchase U.S. treasuries, the whole world is competing to acquire dollars, hence, its price is pushed up.

The Economist created the Big Mac index as a fast way to compare the price level of a common good or service (or a similar basket of goods and services). The index is based on the theory of purchasing-power parity, the notion that in the long run, exchange rates should move toward the rate that would equalize the price of an identical basket of goods and services in *any* two countries.

pay for money, higher because risk is higher). Those rates are a function of the time value of money, what the market will pay for the use of capital.[25]

In Babylon, where property lines were recorded on clay tablets, owners could borrow against their real estate. Those mortgages were then sold on the secondary market (collateralized mortgage obligations), what Fannie Mae does: purchases mortgages that banks make to homeowners—which puts money back into the banks for them to make more loans. President Bill Clinton pressured Fannie Mae to purchase loans from borrowers who didn't really qualify: subprime loans. Clinton thought every working American with good credit should have a home (what a progressive would think). When borrowers defaulted on those loans (what a conservative would predict), that created the 2008 financial crisis, which lasted ten years. As Franklin Roosevelt caused the ten-year Great Depression (in 1933, forcing the New Deal onto the nation when the depression of 1929–1932 was over), Bill Clinton caused the Great Recession (pressuring banks to make bad loans when it wasn't necessary). Both presidents, progressives, wanted government to help the less fortunate. Conservatives and the Supreme Court warned them not to.

In efficient competitive markets, where profit is driven to zero, timeless rates on savings, mortgage lending and venture capital are not really rates of return; they are the *time value of money*, what demanders of capital will pay to use capital over a period of time. Capital is surplus production, not gold or currency. Gold and currency represent capital; they facilitate the purchase of goods and services, they replace barter, they are a store of value, but they are not capital.

Nations, then, that accumulate gold or currency (more than needed for daily money transactions) create inflation, not wealth.

---

[25] There is so much capital in the world today that the price of capital is low (which, worldwide, pushes up asset prices: real estate, stock, art, future capital projects). In competitive markets, where profit is driven toward zero (entrepreneurial compensation is something else), where material prices can be high, not even value-added projects make sense—why today's investors are simply looking to preserve capital, why banks in Switzerland charge depositors to hold their money, why Chase Bank in the U.S., with $500 billion in cash, no longer accepts new depositors.

Inflation, an inconvenience to the market, causes an increase in the price level in *all* markets, not an increase in value. To the contrary, price increases from inflation wipe out the value of a nation's savings (retired persons living off their savings) by raising the price of all goods and services. Adam Smith wrote *Wealth of Nations* to say just that (among other great things). It was his warning to Europe that what Spain was doing, robbing the New World (in the 16th and 17th centuries) of all its gold, was a worthless endeavor: it simply created inflation throughout Europe. With all its gold, Spain was, then and now, the poorest nation in Europe.

Law Five: Say's Law
When an economy is in recession, governments should stay back. Markets self-correct faster than anything done through interference.

Recessions are the result of an overextension of credit.—Jean-Baptiste Say (1803). Always, producers borrow too much, overproduce, then, when the inventory doesn't sell, lay off their employees. Recession.

How long? Until there is demand again for that inventory, one, because old goods wore out, two, because there was natural population growth of 2 percent. Automatically, the economic cycle restarts. Production rises, employees are rehired.

Government, however, cannot stimulate an economy to pull it out of recession by infusing it with cash (unless it infuses enough to pay for a world war). Government stimulation during COVID-19 lockdown (approximately the cost of World War II) was not to cure a recession but to prevent one.[26]

Government cannot stimulate an economy. Producers know that money given to consumers, not earned, can easily be withdrawn. If not confident, producers will not resume production. The Keynesian argument that money thrown into an economy will have a multiplier effect, that every $10 will generate $7.50 worth of new

---

[26] Why is it okay for government to hand out $3 trillion so citizens can stay home to binge-watch television, not care where their next paycheck comes from? Worse, that the $3 trillion was borrowed with no intention of paying back. Where's *that* clause in the Constitution?

demand, thus new production, new employment, is false.[27] Consumers will hoard that $10. They don't know how long the recession will last. This liquidity trap, the Ricardian equivalence, i.e., human nature, is market reality.

Market reality is that in a free economy, suppliers, not demanders, make the decisions. A free economy, a supply-side phenomenon, resumes only when producers start producing. What they produce in surplus to their own needs is itself the definition of capital, surplus production, that which gives producers something to trade for other things. Barter, except that in a modern economy, capital is traded for money.[28] In this sense, producers, as suppliers, are automatically demanders—because it is only they who have the means to trade, which is what an economy is: trade.

Say's Law: Supply creates its own demand.

Implied: there is always demand, recession or not, if the price of labor and materials is flexible.[29]

Conclusion

These five laws of economics, five laws of nature, are not to be toyed with. Let government intervene in the economy to lessen the impact of creative destruction—the natural phenomenon of whole industries disappearing because of new technology or better ways of doing things—and that nation's economy will be left behind.

---

[27] Keynesians argue that the multiplier effect works its way through the entire economy. If the marginal propensity to consume is .75, the multiplier is four times. An increase of $10 to the economy will generate $40 of new production (in the same way as a decrease in the economy of $10 generates $40 in lost demand). Keynesian progressives advocate throwing money at all societal problems. Believing national economies are inherently unstable, but that governments *are* stable, Keynesians believe that government is a powerful vehicle for remedying instability. If the nation's government has no savings, it needs only borrow. U.S. citizens see nothing wrong with the nation's $30 trillion national debt.

[28] The free trade of capital, capitalism, is economic freedom—as the free trade of ideas, free speech, is social freedom.

[29] Union inflexibility prolongs recovery from recession.

The U.S. has the comparative advantage in high technology. All Americans, therefore, should work in that industry. Then, trade for everything else. Solon. The standard of living of America and all its trading partners will rise enormously (as it did in Athens).

Reality: Six percent of the U.S. workforce is qualified to work in high technology—the only ones who made the effort to do so.[30] And because progressive domination of public education has turned that institution into a center of inclusiveness (where no one fails because academic standards were lowered), Americans today no longer compete. U.S. Department of Education test scores show that only 36 percent of the nation is "proficient" in reading and math,[31] why 70 percent of tech employees in Silicon Valley are foreign-born.[32]

The American Revolution was fought to create a nation based on maximum individual freedom—coupled with maximum individual responsibility.[33] In 1933, Franklin Roosevelt reversed that. A progressive decided that government interference in the economy was a good idea—without realizing the U.S. would become a nation of dependent citizens (Social Security, Medicare, Affordable Care Act), with enormous regulation of business (Sarbanes–Oxley, Dodd–Frank), with government agencies controlling citizens and the economy (the EPA, the Department of Education), today's aristocracy, although historically, all of this is specifically what Americans fled—as do today's immigrants.

---

30 U.S. Bureau of Labor Statistics, "Beyond the Numbers," May 31, 2018, bls.gov/opub/btm/volume-7/high-tech-industries-an-analysis-of-employment-wages-and-output.htm.

31 National Center Education Statistics, U.S. Department of Education, "The Nation's Report Card," National Assessment of Educational Progress (NAEP), https://www.nationsreportcard.gov/mathematics/nation/achievement/?grade=4 [see also grade=8, and substitute reading for mathematics]. Not just public schools, all schools.

32 Ethan Baron, "H-1B: Foreign Citizens Make Up Nearly Three-Quarters of Silicon Valley Tech Workforce, Report Says," *The Mercury News*, January 1, 2018, updated May 8, 2018, https://www.mercurynews.com/2018/01/17/h-1b-foreign-citizens-make-up-nearly-three-quarters-of-silicon-valley-tech-workforce-report-says/.

33 Alexis de Tocqueville, in *Democracy in America*, was absolutely amazed at how responsible Americans were. Nothing like that existed in Europe.

China and Russia are having a field day exploiting a nation whose schools no longer teach a core curriculum, no longer teach love of country, nor the history and culture of British and American democracy. Rather, American schools today praise failing students (to encourage them) and cater to identarian politics.

Having "progressed" from the Founding Fathers, from the U.S. Constitution, America today is a nation without principles.

And then, my five laws of economics mean precisely that it makes no difference what country, what culture, what ideology holds sway, whether a nation upholds principles or not—those laws cut right through. Those who understand them profit from them. Impossible under communism, but those who grabbed all the industries in Russia in 1989 had prepared for that day long before. *They* are the ones who would have owned those industries.

BUSINESS INSIGHTS

1. If you want great financial success, don't go to college. Great athletes, great artists, great thinkers, many did not. Those years, 18 through 22, are your most mentally fertile. Einstein, sitting in a patent office, made his great discoveries. To make a great fortune, play professional sports, develop great ideas; it takes ten years of concentration. There's a lifetime for study afterward.

Andrew Carnegie.

2. Income and wealth are two separate matters. Income is to live on, wealth is to acquire—if one's economic goal is financial independence.[34]

---

[34] Not everyone has that goal.

Without business or financial training, wealth can be acquired by saving half your salary, then purchasing, with leverage, every year for ten years, an incoming-producing asset. Buy the house next door. Next year, the house next door, or the corner grocery, or a fleet of trucks. If you live in an expensive city, get a partner—your spouse, a family member—and buy half a house.

Cut your expenses. Everyone in America lives way over their means.

- Don't commute. Live around the corner from where you work. Work those two extra hours at time and a half.
- Share rent with a roommate, or bring in a second family. (Easier when you're young.)
- Share an automobile, share the Internet.
- If a loaf of bread costs five dollars (which it does in San Francisco), buy a bag of oats for five dollars and make 50 loaves.
- Eat at home.
- Don't fly.
- Other expenses? Don't pay them; get a loan.

Difficult to pull off? Start thinking about it.

3. Other People's Money (OPM)

OPM is the most underlying truth in investment.

When you purchase an asset, get the bank to loan the full amount. Easier during an economic downturn, when, for example, mortgages on real estate are probably more than the value of the property. If you have enough cash reserves to hold it, banks will give you those properties. They don't want foreclosures on their books.

Or, purchase real estate with the seller carrying the entire purchase price in a promissory note. If the seller wants some cash, get a new first loan for 50 percent of the purchase price, and have the seller carry the balance. The leveraged buyout.

Difficult to pull off? Start thinking about it.

Take investors as partners. Let *them* put up the money; you put up the deal, for example, an option-to-purchase.

4. Own the real estate where your business is located.

In a downturn in the economy, the rent you pay still pays off the loan. That's not a loss, it's an investment.

In a downturn in the economy, move into your place of business; rent out your residence.

Advice: pay off the mortgage on your home.[35]

The young owner of Chez Panisse restaurant in Berkeley, California, Alice Waters, asked her father for startup money. He said absolutely not—unless you have an option to buy the property. Waters postponed her business until she got that option—which is why California's most famous restaurant never charged high prices (and still offers low-price meals for locals): because Waters earned a fortune from the increase in value of the underlying real estate. Upon opening, immediately, her restaurant brought a stream of food merchants who located nearby. Together, that drove up the value of all properties in the area.

Georgia Pacific paper company loses money every year. They couldn't care less. They own the forest where the paper comes from —half the state of Georgia.

McDonald's makes hamburgers. That's not their business. McDonald's is in real estate—the largest single owner of real estate

---

[35] Thanks to progressivism (perhaps no thanks), in 1934, Franklin Roosevelt created the Federal Housing Authority (FHA), which allowed banks to make long-term loans of up to 90 percent of a home's value, with payments people could afford—a perfect example of liberal versus conservative reasoning. Yes, everyone could afford a home—because they were only putting 10 percent down—but then demand for homes doubled, as did price. Meaning, in 2022, a $125,000 home sells for $250,000. Loan payments on $225,000 (250,000 x .90) are $1,208 a month, $435,000 over 30 years at 5 percent interest per annum. Instead of saving $12,500 a year for ten years, then paying $125,000 cash, today's home buyer pays $685,000 ($435,000 in payments + $125,000, the doubled house price). All government programs are a tax on the middle class.

in the world (and in the very best locations). The restaurants are franchises.

One of my tenants in San Francisco opened a restaurant. Twice, during two economic downturns, to keep her restaurant afloat, she refinanced her personal residence. Twenty years later, she sold the restaurant for what she had paid. Her rent, however, paid off my mortgage. Thank you.

5. Don't become a B corporation.

Don't become a corporation that focuses on giving back a portion of your profit or, at great expense (not compensated by a higher price for your product), cuts emissions of CO_2.

In a competitive market, where profit is driven to zero (efficient market hypothesis), you will be driven out of business.

6. Don't stop production!

Andrew Carnegie did not make his fortune as an aggressive monopolist or by union busting. Like the fox (who knows a lot of things) and the hedgehog (who knows one big thing), Carnegie, hedgehog, knew, no matter what the economy, *not to stop production*. In a downturn, produce at cost, but don't stop. Customers who need your product will come to you. Their previous supplier couldn't hold on. At every downturn, Carnegie would buy a failing mill. Within ten years, he owned them all.

7. Spend money to make money.

Saving money by cutting costs, or worse, cutting corners, to keep your price down in a competitive economy, is a limited, uncreative business model.

Spending money by adding costs to create a better product than your competitors is an expansive creative business model.

8. Own your supply chain.

McDonald's, vertically integrated, owns the wheat and potato farms, the cattle, the underlying real estate.

One hundred years ago, Henry Ford made the parts he needed (or owned the factories that made them)—and he "owned" his labor. A notorious racist and anti-Semite, he hired Black workers and paid them really well—five dollars an hour, almost minimum wage today. So grateful for their jobs, those workers never struck, never unionized, never quit. Supply: guaranteed.

Would Ford have been caught empty-handed because of COVID-19? No.

GLOBALIZATION

"Globalism failed to deliver the economy we need." Rana Foroohar, associate editor for the *Financial Times*, printed in the *New York Times International*, October 17, 2022.[36]

No person in business could make such a statement. Globalization, free trade, liberalism, neoliberalism are not dead; they are how an economy works. It's what human beings do: trade.[37]

Laws of money, business and economics are timeless. The law of one price, timeless, means that for any good or service there is only one price in the world—which means that any intervention in the economy will distort that price as markets counter by increasing the price of *all* goods and services. The price of a McDonald's hamburger is the same everywhere in the world, but in countries where it is higher, governments intervened. The intervention forced a rise in the nation's foreign exchange rate that lowered the value of

---

[36] Rana Foroohar, "Globalism Failed to Deliver the Economy We Need," *New York Times*, October 17, 2022, https://www.nytimes.com/2022/10/17/opinion/neoliberalism-economy.html.

[37] A sculptor in a village in Kenya may find no one to pay $1,000 for his sculpture. Place it on worldwide Instagram; it may be bid up to $10,000.

the nation's currency, which forces citizens to pay more for that McDonald's hamburger.

Foroohar says neoliberalists thought globalization would counter bad economic policies by populist leaders, that it would keep them in check. Ironically, the opposite happened: jobs were outsourced, unemployment rose. Populism was fuelled; there's some truth to that. But then Foroohar mocks supply-side capitalism, the notion that it is producers, and producers only, who create the trickle-down economy. Of course they do—*they* are the ones at risk, the ones who create a product, employ workers, pay them. In a competitive economy, interference by government, a cost to producers, is always countered with lower wages and a rise in product price.

The Soviet Union collapsed because its government replaced producers—without having first learned (through trial and error) how to manage large enterprises. It collapsed because it replaced trained musicians with their stagehands, so to speak.

Owners of factories left. Their lives' savings confiscated, producers had no incentive to remain, to help the young USSR maintain some semblance of a market economy (why China quickly called them back). Too much was wrong. With citizens no longer spending their own money, instead spending money distributed by the state, producers lost confidence. That money could easily be withdrawn or wildly increased (whenever a politician needed to win an election) or hoarded (in anticipation of worse to come). Hoarding, the Ricardian equivalence to government-supplied money, creates a liquidity trap. Any one of these is enough to bring an economy to a halt. Russia's creative industrialists left.[38]

***

---

[38] Ayn Rand, *Atlas Shrugged* (New York: Signet, 1957).

"Neoliberalism philosophy is tapped out." Because, according to Foroohar, during every economic downturn, companies fail.[39]

Of course, they fail. They didn't prepare for the downturn. Lacking capital reserves, they can't hold on—as happens at every mayhem caused by creative destruction.[40] Of the top 100 corporations on the Dow Jones Industrial Average in 1961, three are there today. General Motors, Ford and Chrysler are not. Tesla, worth more than the three of them combined, replaced them. In 30 years, people will ask: "What's Facebook?"

"Globalization failed to deliver the economy we need."[41]

Who's "we"? Coastal liberals? Most of the nation? Hillary Clinton's "deplorables"?

"How can we make sure that economic globalization doesn't run too far ahead of national politics?"[42]

We can't. Government doesn't control nature, government *is* nature: human nature.

SpaceX to the Moon

It's been 50 years since man walked on the moon. A project made possible because the National Aeronautics and Space Administration (NASA) was given unlimited resources. As in the 1940s, when the U.S. military was provided all it needed to fight World War II, so too, in the 1960s, to fly to the moon, NASA was provided all it needed.

Will Congress again provide NASA with all it needs? Knowing that government programs cost more than equivalent programs managed by the private sector, will Congress once again offer 5

---

[39] Foroohar, "Globalism Failed."

[40] "Only when the tide goes out do you discover who's been swimming naked."—Warren Buffet

[41] Foroohar, "Globalism Failed."

[42] Foroohar, "Globalism Failed."

percent of the federal budget so that NASA can again employ a 200,000-member workforce? That Congress currently offers NASA only 0.5 percent says it all. No. Aware that the War on Poverty already cost $23 trillion, three times more than all wars America ever fought, Congress is not going to write that check.

America *will* return to the moon, but in partnership with the private sector, with Elon Musk's SpaceX's *Starship*. A private sector industrialist, light years ahead of any government vision, Musk did not create *Starship* to go to the moon (except for some tourist revenue). *Starship* was created to go to Mars.[43]

The only way man will explore the universe is via the private sector.[44]

If NASA went to the moon in the 1960s to regain America's honor after the shock of the Soviet Union's 1957 Sputnik launch, is that why we're going to Mars, a space race?

***

Government agencies don't pay enough to attract creative talent; they are not, therefore, a creative environment. Nor do they operate like creative businesses, where funding decisions at least include a cost-benefit analysis. NASA grants contracts (Boeing, Lockheed Martin) on a cost-plus basis, knowing but seemingly not caring that costs will spiral out of control. Musk runs SpaceX like an airline. He uses the same planes over and over. The Space Shuttle was reused, but NASA threw away its launch and booster rockets (and almost everything else). NASA, since 1972, completed only a dozen launches, with no launches in the last 11 years. SpaceX completed

---

[43] Musk's plan is to colonize Mars—melt the ice caps for water and CO2, create oceans, plant trees. No government thinks that big. (If solar radiation makes Mars unlivable for humans, so strong that we'd have to live underground protected by three-foot thick steel walls, that could be a consideration.)

[44] The only way mankind will clean up the environment on Earth is via the private sector, creative entrepreneurs removing CO2 from the atmosphere. (It's too late to cut emissions; the damage is done.)

31 launches in 2021 alone and through 2022, 100 booster landings, without a failure![45]

> After the Russian invasion of Ukraine and the Western sanctions that followed, Dmitry Rogozin, former head of the Russian space agency Roscosmos, signaled a looming end to the U.S.–Russia space partnership. "If you block cooperation with us," he tweeted in February [2022], "who will save the ISS [International Space Station] from an uncontrolled deorbit and fall into the United States or Europe?" Elon Musk answered that call, replying with the SpaceX logo.[46]

***

The argument against going to space is that those billions of dollars would be better spent ameliorating problems on Earth. Global warming, for example.

False objection. Most of those billions of dollars go to launching satellites—which aid in telecommunications, GPS, and are important in lowering the cost of sending up satellites. Plus, what those billionaires and even government spend is a small percentage of their cash. Billionaires and government, both, give tremendous amounts to social and economic causes. Let 'em have a little fun.

---

[45] Eric Berger, "We Are Going to the Moon," *Reason* magazine, December 2022, https://reason.com/2022/11/15/we-are-going-to-the-moon/.

[46] Fiona Harrigan, "So Long, Soyuz: Russia Is Leaving the International Space Station," *Reason* magazine, December 2022, https://reason.com/2022/11/15/so-long-soyuz/.

Over $264 billion has been invested in the space sector, $25.9 from space billionaires Richard Branson, Jeff Bezos, Elon Musk.[47] Social spending is $1.3 trillion *per year*.[48]

Pleadings about the "problems here on Earth" assume that spending for anything other than poverty and climate change shows a lack of concern for humanity. Bezos might as well withdraw the $10 billion he donated in 2020 alone to fight climate change, the $100 million he donated to José Andrés' World Central Kitchen to relieve global hunger.[49] Elon Musk should do likewise with his support of Doctors Without Borders, of educational charities and environmental groups, to whom in 2022 alone he gave five million Tesla shares. Musk said that 99 percent of resources available for solving problems *should* do just that, but that 1 percent for space, for extending life beyond Earth, can also be done.

According to Bernie Sanders' socialists, space billionaires Branson, Bezos and Musk have so much discretionary income precisely because they aren't paying their share of taxes. Before we allow them to dabble in space, they should pay up. Well, before we force them to pay up, we better decide what "their share" is. To encourage their creativity, will we allow them to keep 10 percent of what they earn? Or is even that too much?

Progressive reformers argue that if billionaires were properly taxed ("from each according to his ability to each accord to his needs"), tax money under government, i.e., citizen control would be so much more wisely spent. That's not what Andrew Carnegie thought. Carnegie believed that only those who earn money are

---

[47] According to *Space Investment Quarterly*, as reported by Katherine Mangu-Ward, "The Case for Space Billionaires," *Reason* magazine, December 2022, https://reason.com/2022/11/15/the-case-for-space-billionaires/.

[48] "What is Spending on Welfare?" USgovspending, https://usgovernmentspending.com/us_welfare_spending.

[49] *Op cit*, p.26.

qualified to spend it. Politicians throwing taxpayer money at societal problems is not philanthropy.[50]

It's waste.

***

As is terraforming the galaxy—changing whole planets to suit our ends. Arrogant vandalism.

As was immigration to the New World.

Why? Because our species is not capable of living on a continent, let alone a planet, without trashing it. Not to terraform, then, is to buy the argument that humanity deserves to perish until it can demonstrate an ability to live in harmony with itself, with other species, with the environment. Eco-nihilism.

Which ignores Darwin. Survival of the species means not letting humanity be destroyed by an asteroid or a super volcano. Terraforming is our moral duty. As Europeans brought smallpox to the New World, which killed native Americans, humanity will bring tons of bacteria to wherever it goes. Don't worry about it: our Milky Way galaxy is huge (and there may be no one else out there anyway).

We can't risk annihilation on Earth. We must build our exact biological conditions elsewhere—spread humanity throughout the universe. Elon Musk suggests nuking the Martian north and south poles to release CO2 to thicken and warm the atmosphere, to flood the planet's basins with water. Ronald Bailey mentions also, in *Archives of Microbiology*, 2019, "two Irish biologists described how developments in synthetic biology could create organisms that would survive on Mars and begin transforming its surface and atmosphere [using our ability to create DNA synthetically]," and states that a team of space scientists in *Acta Astronautica* explain how material

---

[50] Carnegie spent his last 50 years carefully giving away his fortune for *permanent*, not temporary, needs: libraries, concert halls, institutions of peace (throughout the world). Carnegie would not understand today's charities, which give cash to the homeless so they can purchase drugs.

from the Martian moons could be used to create an artificial magnetosphere to protect the planet's surface from radiation.[51]

> While humanity's greatest immediate challenge is to survive the next century or two, our greatest achievement will be eventually greening the universe and bringing it to life.

> —Andrea Owe, Environmental philosopher[52]

***

The 1967 Outer Space Treaty (OST), whose core goal is peace, written at the height of the space race, states that astronauts "shall be regarded as the envoys of mankind," that stationary weapons of mass destruction in space are not permitted and that "national appropriation" is forbidden.

In a world of peace, of nations united, that's beautiful law. In a world of psychopathic rulers, unenforceable. In a world where man was not meant to live in peace, where all religions have their Adam and Eve story, in which God punishes everyone forever by telling them they are on their own, such law is unenforceable.

The Outer Space Treaty is simply the failures of the League of Nations, the United Nations, the New Deal, the War on Poverty repeated. Unenforceable.

No appropriation? What does that mean? Nations can't own a slice of the moon, a piece of junk? Without property rights, private developers, the only ones with the ability to do something with the moon, will never go there.[53]

---

[51] Ronald Bailey, "Why We Should Terraform the Galaxy," *Reason* magazine, December 2022, https://reason.com/2022/11/15/terraform-the-galaxy/.

[52] Bailey, p. 31.

[53] Don't count on government. The only thing governments do well is fight wars—civil wars, world wars—and then only because they are given unlimited resources, plus the ability to draft anyone and everyone, then place the best persons where needed. Central planning from Plato's *Republic*. (Continued on next page)

Without property rights, individual entrepreneurs will never invest in space exploration. Monetizing spaceships with moon tourism is easy; bringing back gold and uranium is not—which means it won't happen without property rights. With property rights (as explained in John Locke's *Second Treatise on Civil Government*, the basis for America's Declaration of Independence and Constitution), citizens have a natural right to what they produce: their art, their crops, what (with permission) they mine from the ground.

No one has the right to land as far as the eye can see. Indigenous people anywhere (including Europeans 1,000 years ago) have a right to land they are working and to land deemed sacred, but the transition of ownership of land from lesser-developed to higher-developed civilizations has never been gentle: survival of the fittest.

Even if land transfer in the U.S. had been respectful, ownership would be exactly as it is today. With their larger vision, the higher-developed civilization would have offered two to three times what the native population thought their land was worth. Black reparation land, Latino ranch land, Native American reservation land—most owners would have sold it. As in the 1920s, every owner of land from Owens Valley to Los Angeles sold their land to William Mulholland—who understood Los Angeles' population of 100,000 inhabitants in 1900 would increase to millions.[54]

***

The Federal Communications Commission (FCC), miraculously, has a market-driven approach to regulating telecommunications in space, i.e., satellites. As long as no harm is done, it doesn't interfere.

(Continued from previous page) In the 1960s, NASA was given unlimited resources, but never again—unless Earth is attacked by aliens. Space exploration belongs to the private sector.

[54] Donald Trump paid $1 million for condos worth $500,000 to create Trump Tower at Columbus Circle in NYC. Mark Zuckerberg purchased all the land surrounding his homes in San Francisco and Palo Alto. He paid $5 million for parcels worth $1 million.

Communicating with one another, entertaining, watching out for each other, satellites come in peace.

Not China. Chinese state-owned companies are rushing to create copycats of innovative U.S. companies to close the gap, and so, continue to develop and test anti-satellite weapons (while generating orbital debris that threatens peaceful use of space by other operators—which attracts strong rebuke from U.S. officials). A good case, then, for U.S. leadership in space. A good case for fighting World War III now: get it over with. Or, build up our defenses.

Understood, again, miraculously, is that neither should the Federal Aviation Administration (FAA) overly regulate commercial space flight—that the young industry needs freedom to develop naturally, to figure things out. The FAA surveys the new space industry to ensure public safety during commercial launches and reentry, but also encourages, facilitates and promotes commercial space transportation. Amazing, regulatory agencies working with those they supervise.

***

False arguments:

1. Sunk costs are recoverable.

We're so invested in the ISS, in various missions to space, the new Space Force, that our human predilection to rescue sunk costs by continuing (even doubling down) to spend prevents us from abandoning wasteful endeavors. Space exploration should be done by robots.

2. The world will become a better place.

Will humans in the future live flourishing lives? Will morality improve?

No. It would have happened by now. The West's mushrooming social, political and economic 18th century liberal freedoms helped create prosperity, but the West is prosperous for the same reason that undemocratic China, Japan, Taiwan, Singapore and South Korea are prosperous: they experienced an industrial revolution.

3. Should we go to Mars?

No. Mars may have the ability to have oceans and greenery, but that process may take 500 years.

The moon is right here. If things go wrong, Earth will send someone.

4. Humans are destroying the earth through environmental damage.

That will end. Nuclear energy via fusion and high-density energy storage will stop pollution. The immediate solution, however, is to remove CO_2 from the atmosphere. Technology has always solved man's problems.

C. POLITICS

WOKE

MAGA: Make America Great Again. Stick to the nation's principles, the U.S. Constitution.

Woke: take a stand, challenge injustice and racism.

Two good ideas in America promoted by bad people: the nation's most Left and most Right. Each cancels the other. Each distorts those ideas.

Each would employ government to enforce its wishes—without an informed grasp of the economic consequences.

Both act as if unaware of what the Founding Fathers created—a nation of maximum individual liberty, maximum individual responsibility. Both are unaware that the degree to which a nation constrains social, political or economic freedom is the degree to which it constrains all three.

Economies that produce in abundance become wealthy, whether socialist, communist, fascist, free market, European socialist, communist with Chinese characteristics. Still, the degree to which those nations' governments intervene in their economies is not only that by which they lower their social and political freedom but by which they create a corporate state, a state run by a handful of monopolies, national socialism.[55]

In 1933, Franklin D. Roosevelt intervened in the economy. He took a depression that had run its course, 1929–1932, and turned it into the deepest depression the world has ever known, the Great Depression of 1933–1941. Today, 80 years later, all economists, *New York Times* opinion writer Paul Krugman included, agree. Roosevelt turned a nation of maximum individual freedom (why the Supreme Court vetoed *everything* he asked) into a nation of maximum individual dependence—with everyone today dependent on government for education, health care and pension (not to mention housing and food), and all of it paid for by borrowing.

In 2008, Barack Obama intervened in the economy to prevent the Great Recession from turning into a second Great Depression. He had the U.S. Treasury bail out the banks—which was the right thing to do because it saved the nation's financial system and because that loaned money was repaid.[56] The loans, plus the Federal Reserve's lowering of interest rates to 0.01 percent, ended the

---

[55] National Socialism abbreviated is NAZI.

[56] The Government bailout during COVID-19 (2020–2021) was not a loan; it was a handout. Worse, it offered relief to people and businesses who were mostly underfinanced, already failing. Joe Biden is trying to waive student debt (2022) with a handout (paid for by borrowing), as House Speaker Nancy Pelosi traveled to Taiwan against State Department advice: to bolster the Democratic Party desperately attempting not to lose both the House and Senate in the 2022 midterm election. Pure politics.

recession by 2013 (although without government intervention it would have ended by 2011).

Except, the Fed kept rates at 0.01 percent until 2022. Realizing this had created spiraling inflation, it intervened again to raise interest rates. But in relation to truly high demand (from savings accumulated during two years of COVID-19 lockdown) and an escalating lack of supply (from excessive factory lockdown during COVID-19), the Fed forgot about those underlying forces: that high prices in 2022 were really a function of supply and demand, *not inflation*. Why, then, do we always look to government to solve our problems?

In 1995, Bill Clinton rewrote the Community Reinvestment Act to put pressure on banks to issue mortgage loans in low-income neighborhoods. Then he pressured Fannie Mae to purchase those subprime loans, which had been made to borrowers with good credit but who otherwise didn't qualify. That started a chain reaction throughout the entire financial industry, leading to the 2008 financial crisis. One more example of government intervention in the economy ruining markets.

Government intervention in the economy, 1933 and 2008, progressive economic policy, caused and prolonged those two crashes. Just as MAGA and Woke try to tell people what to do, citizens should know that any intervention in their lives prolongs the underlying social, political or economic self-correction process.[57]

Populist MAGA politicians saying anything to get elected would have the U.S., in the name of protecting American jobs, put up tariffs to prevent the entry of foreign imports. But protecting dying industries violates the most fundamental economic law of comparative advantage.[58]

---

[57] Affirmative action corrects for past abuse. Cost: racism prolonged. Why? Because minority candidates who benefit from affirmative action are usually not at the level of the persons who would have got the position (although the law says they must be). Minority students at UC Berkeley, for example, have received notes on their desks: "You're taking the place of someone more qualified."

[58] In 2009 the cost per job saved was at least $900,000. See Gary Clyde Haufbauer, "U.S. Tire Tariffs: Saving Few Jobs at High Cost," … (Continued on next page)

Woke would have anyone they disagree with barred from speaking in public, especially on a college campus. According to *New York Times* opinion writer David Brooks, Woke has succeeded: conservative professors on college campuses have been reduced to 1.5 percent.[59] There are more, but, afraid to lose their jobs, they don't speak. McCarthyism.

***

At a party of "progressive" friends, a woman pulled from her purse a card she always kept there and read aloud:

> The loneliness of a Black among whites;
> The loneliness of a Jew among gentiles;
> The loneliness of a gay among straights.

I added:

> The loneliness of a conservative among liberals.

Dead silence. Not on their radar.

***

France's government, schools, employers—all are forbidden to ask about race, ethnicity, religion or gender. *Laïté.*

To unite the nation and instill love of country, French schools teach a core curriculum of French history and culture.

American schools do the opposite. Instead of a core curriculum focusing on the history and culture of British and American

---

(Continued from previous page) ... working paper, http://ideas.repec.org/cgi-bin/htsearch?q=hubauer+%27US+TIRE+TARIFFS (a research division of the Federal Reserve Bank of St. Louis).

[59] David Brooks, "The Future of Nonconformity," *New York Times*, July 24, 2020, https://www.nytimes.com/2020/07/23/opinion/substack-newsletters-writers.html.

democracy—5th century Athens, 1st century Rome, the 18th century's Age of Enlightenment, arguably the three greatest periods in human history, the source of Western civilization, an evolutionary step forward for mankind, the idea that the rights of the individual precede those of the state—American schools focus on current events: civil rights protests, systemic racism, privilege, worse, to foster inclusiveness, the crises, cultures and countries from which their parents fled.

All cultures excel in some areas, but an aural culture, African, Latin or Native American, cannot compete with an advanced industrialized economy. Darwinism, the stronger mindlessly crushing the weaker, is why conquering cultures don't respect the cultures they conquer. That elephant in the room is studiously avoided by progressive liberals who see themselves as sharing the aspirations of society's marginalized. Hypocrisy. Alone at night in New York City trying to hail a cab, Barack Obama, a highly cultivated individual, might not be noticed.

***

"They won't know you, the you that's hidden somewhere in the castle of your skin." West Indies author George Lamming, in *Castle of Your Skin*, could be Ralph Ellison, in *Invisible Man*.

No one, however, has a lock on that feeling. Living in San Francisco, this author, canceled by friends and family for espousing conservatism, feels that loneliness. A teacher for 40 years in the city's inner-city schools, where talk in the lunchroom (from Black personnel) was "Why must we follow so many directions from those white central office personnel when we, college educated, are perfectly capable of running our own schools?," reminding them of *Brown v. Board of Education*, paid a price.

Fact: European immigrants to America (educated or not) are from an advanced civilization: 5th century Athens, which produced everything you see around you—every building, road, library, research institution, concert hall, everything you know about math, science, architecture, art, poetry, literature, drama, politics, psychology, philosophy (from a city of only 100,000 individuals during a 100-year period 2,500 years ago), plus 1st century Rome, which produced modern law and government, plus 18th century Age of Enlightenment, which produced contemporary notions of social, political and economic freedom in Britain, Scotland, France and America. That foundation is what American schools should be teaching. There's no time for other cultures.

***

Equality before the law is the only thing Frederick Douglass and Martin Luther King asked.[60] In other words, forcing American schools to focus on the bad things America has done (without pointing out the list is very short in comparison to the good things and that the list of good things other nations have done is very short in relation to the bad things they have done) will not eliminate systemic racism. It will fuel it. Making white children feel guilty for the nation's past sins, coming home from school asking their parents, "Did America do anything good?" will not end racism.[61]

Stop talking about it![62]

Stop talking about it? Cancel free speech? Cancel those who say things no one wants to hear? That's the New Left with their new definition of tolerance: the duty to refrain from saying what others don't want to hear (political correctness)—a tyranny of the majority that would prevent conservative speakers from even entering a college campus.

Contrast the Old Left. Mario Savio, UC Berkeley, 1964, who led a strike to prevent the university from censoring world news, from

---

[60] King also advocated for universal basic income but had the good sense, during the 1960s civil rights protests, to limit his demands to what was achievable: equality before the law.

[61] In San Francisco, that last straw broke the camel's back. It led a very liberal city to recall three members of the Board of Education.

[62] Woke is evangelical religion. American blue-collar historian Eric Hoffer would have added, "Religions don't need a God. They need a devil."

trying to provide a safe space. Students wanted to hear what was going on. They wanted to know about Vietnam and Jim Crow. They didn't want protection; they didn't want a safe space.

The Old Left agreed with Supreme Court Justice Felix Frankfurter that ideas should not be censored. In a Jeffersonian democracy, it is understood that citizens can and do think for themselves. That when expressed, bad ideas, like the canary in a coal mine that stops chirping, are a warning to the world.

Why do students today, the New Left, think universities should once again shield them from hurtful ideas? To respond to bad ideas, students need to hear them first or they will be unqualified to take a leadership position—what they're being trained for—or develop into mature human beings.

***

In *Woke Racism*, John McWhorter refers to Ta-Nehisi Coates' *Between the World and Me* (required reading, according to McWhorter, for millions of undergraduates), wherein Coates states he has no sympathy for the white cops and firemen who died at the World Trade Center on 9/11: "They were just menaces of nature. They were the fire, the comet, the storm, which could—with no justification—shatter my body."[63]

What about students who do not want to hear what Coates just said? Where's their safe space?[64] What about students who feel sympathy for the spouses and children of those who died (from inhalation of dust and dirt) and who love their country? Why is it okay to hurt those students? Does Coates really believe Black people are treated better elsewhere in the world?

---

[63] John McWhorter, *Woke Racism: How a New Religion Has Betrayed Black America* (New York: Portfolio, 2021).

[64] Stop talking "safe space." Coates is entitled to having his ideas heard, but then so, too, should conservative professors who teach the classics.

***

The stunt pulled by the illiberal left is their assertion that they are the champions of the marginalized. I do not doubt many are sincere, just as the leaders of the Catholic church were sincere in the Inquisition. Religious fundamentalists of all sorts are sincere. But thinking you know best does not qualify for making a better world. Unless you are willing to debate your ideas openly, you are by definition an authoritarian conservative.

—Tor Hundloe[65]

HOMELESS

We forget, so we take for granted what a city is: a place of commerce, historically, the marketplace to which farmers and artisans brought their wares. Tired of commuting, threatened in travel, they erected residences above their stalls: the beginning of a town. The Industrial Revolution added manufacturing; towns became cities. Everything is there: food, clothing, shelter, schools, churches, stores, factories, culture, entertainment. Parents and children came home at noon for dinner. No need for expensive public transportation: everyone lived, walked and worked in their neighborhood; the very charm of European cities.

Politically progressive cities have forgotten these roots. Their focus on social issues (care for the marginalized), on quality-of-city-life issues (bicycle lanes, parks, pedestrian malls) runs counter to what a city is: a place of commerce. Activity that supports commerce—truck and automobile circulation, parking, loading zones, factories—must not be restricted in favor of residential use.

Because they forgot, progressive cities evolved into humane centers of lax law enforcement, homelessness and crime—which,

---

[65] Letter to the Editor, "The Working Class," *The Economist*, September 18, 2021, https://www.economist.com/letters/2021/09/18/letters-to-the-editor.

45

however, chase business away. And because progressives dislike firearms, progressive cities take little interest in how their police departments operate. Externally and internally unmonitored, they attract trigger-happy violent personnel. San Francisco, New York, Los Angeles, Minneapolis, the nation's most liberal cities, have the largest homeless populations and the most vicious police departments.

***

Progressives' misunderstanding of cities is an extension of progressives' misunderstanding of government—whose sole purpose is to protect, not provide social, political and economic freedom. With zero faith in America's historical commitment to market solutions, progressives simply do not understand that social and economic problems are **not solvable by government**, not solvable through the political process, not solvable by throwing money at them. The New Deal, the War on Poverty—neither had an effect on the nation's poverty rate.[66]

Because progressives never state the problem correctly, namely, that the homeless come to town to lie down and die, they never state the obvious solution: the homeless should leave; keep moving. Cities must tell them there is city-provided housing, food, clothing and medical attention on the outskirts of town—at unused factories and military bases.

Enforce the law.

---

[66] Poverty was 15 percent in 1964, and, on average, remains 15 percent. U.S. Census Bureau *Historical Poverty Tables: People and Families, 1959-2021*. The War on Poverty, the Elementary and Secondary Education Act (ESEA), also caused the nation's SAT scores to drop 25 percent and, with Medicare, the price of health insurance to triple.

JERRY BROWN

I'm a San Francisco conservative. I feel very alone. Am I? In 1976, when he ran for president, California Governor Jerry Brown, also a San Francisco conservative, said this:

> I think there is a sense in America that it is a democracy. The whole Jeffersonian ideal was that people are temporarily in government. Government is not the basic reality. People are. The private sector. And government is just a limited power to make things go better. Now we're inverting that, and government is all-pervasive. Every time you turn around, there's government. I think that's not part of the American character. I'd like to reverse that [process]. I think it's an uphill battle, given technology, mobility and information flow. To put government on a smaller scale and still make it work is a pretty good trick if you can do it.
>
> Government isn't a religion. It shouldn't be treated as such. It's not God; it's humans, fallible people, feathering their nests most of the time.
>
> [Government] well may be the agent [that harnesses the skills and abilities that are otherwise unutilized, of the individual], but the question is: Who is the principal manipulating the agent? Unfortunately once this relationship of agency is created, it takes on a life of its own. The idea that government has some omnipotence or omniscience is completely absurd and counter to all the thinking that went into this country. There are many things that cannot be solved. There are many things that lie beyond or beneath government.[67]
>
> What we're doing now is creating needs, we're producing needs, faster than we are producing the means to satisfy them. So we're really producing consumption at a high rate.[68]
>
> A lot of the money going in [social services] is trying to do the impossible. You've got to focus on individual accountability. You just can't get everything without pain

[67] Brown, *Thoughts,* p. 44.

[68] Brown, p. 45.

and suffering or without having to pay a price. . . . There is no such thing as a free ride.[69]

What I am concerned about is the proliferation of government programs, under the guise of doing something that they don't do. We have manpower training programs that were supposed to put people to work. All they did was put manpower trainers to work, not manpower trainees.

We have the law enforcement administration that has spent billions, supposedly reducing crime. It hasn't done that at all. We have an economic development administration in the Commerce Department that supposedly develops the country economically. It has done nothing of the kind. So there is bankruptcy of many of these social programs that have been part of the Great Society, been part of the whole New Deal, Fair Deal, Great Society tradition. We have to re-examine them, see them for what they are when they don't work and find ways in which the Federal Government, through setting a national direction, that the multi-national corporations, that the unions, that all of us are going to have to get behind.

Just because it's a problem doesn't mean the offered solution is going to do anything about it. And that's one of the great mistakes of the last 15 years, people think they come up with some great scheme cogitated in some intellectual atmosphere and think that the real world is going to change because of it. And I'm always skeptical of that approach unless you can show me that the thing is going to work in the street.[70]

Some history:

Fifth century Athens, 1st century Rome, 18th century Age of Enlightenment started well, then got too big, less face-to-face, less personal, more mystical, less rational, less disciplined, less courageous, more corrupt, less connected to individual responsibility, thus, to reality, to the reality of human nature.

---

[69] Brown, p. 45. "From each according to his ability, to each according to his needs." Let Marxism be government policy, and everyone will show why *their* needs are more important than yours. Human Nature. The Soviet Union fell because everyone showed need, no one showed ability. Russia is still suffering from that legacy.

[70] Brown, p. 46.

The ideal:

Limited government: government as a check on reality (when society wanders toward Utopia, which can be installed only by force);[71] and government as a check on social, political and economic freedom, a neutral third party to protect life, liberty and property—so that individual citizens don't take the law into their own hands. Government exists to protect, not provide. This nation was founded on that thought.

> No matter how much money, rhetoric and sermonizing we generate, it almost seems the problems keep out-running the program solutions. And that has to give any liberal pause . . . The conclusion to all this is that merely because there's a problem doesn't mean we retain the ability to find the solution.[72]

"If you can solve a problem with money you don't have a problem." Problems are personal, not societal. *All* minorities experience discrimination. But they learn to go around it. They turn within, to their own community. Then, wait. If you have something to offer, the market will come to you. Money knows no color. Blacks created their own baseball league. The market eventually realized those players were good (if not better than players in the white baseball league). The Brooklyn Dodgers wanted the pennant so badly they broke the racial barrier. That's how it works. Respect: the only cure for racism.

> The liberalism of the '60s is dead. The fact that there's a problem doesn't mean that more government will make it better. It might make it worse. The interventionism that we've seen in our society is analogous to Vietnam. With our money, power and genius, we thought that we could make the people over there like us. Then we did the same thing to our cities. When problems don't go away we

---

[71] As God created the Garden of Eden, by force, so, too, will man create Utopia. Nowhere in the world have communist governments ever been elected, but once in place, entrepreneurial leaders, the *sine qua non* of an economy, leave. Not a formula for success.

[72] Brown, p. 55.

escalate the attack until someone gives up. I'm rethinking some of that escalatory social interventionism. Inaction may be the highest form of action.[73]

As a Democrat in California, the 1976 Jerry Brown could never be elected today.

> I went over it [the budget] word by word, comma by comma; I want you to understand my philosophy . . . The economic uncertainty now facing the people of California requires that new state spending be held to a minimum. . . . The first test of all of us, and government is no exception, is to live within realistic limits. We will maintain a prudent surplus. There will be no general tax increases. The realities of the present economy [1974 recession from the oil embargo] make unwise any more than the minimal expansion of state programs.[74]
>
> I do see the need for restraint in government spending. Government is becoming not only the employer of last resort but in many cases the spender of first resort. And the burden is being carried by the average person [this podcaster's constant theme: the middle class pay all taxes] and we have to do everything we can to trim our sails to the prevailing winds. And I personally think that we can redirect government effort without escalating the cost. I think it is a very healthy and salutary thing for government in many areas to become leaner and more dedicated rather than somewhat more excessive and more affluent and really more diffuse.[75]

---

[73] Brown, p. 56.

Yet Jerry Brown also said, "As a matter of principle, that this country has a world role to play; that we cannot retreat from that responsibility. And that involves the Near East, it involves a strong economic and military presence, and that is something I think a lot of people, especially the liberal side of the spectrum, are not willing to face up to." p. 43.

"We are living within an illusion that one can reduce our defense appropriations; we can limitlessly expand our social services." p. 43.

[74] Brown, pp. 58–59.

[75] Brown, p. 59.

National Will and the Power of Ideas:

> I think that [national will] in many ways is the lesson of Vietnam. We were beaten not because we lacked technology, not because we didn't have the hardware, not because we didn't have the systems analysis at the Pentagon; we lost because we lacked the political will to carry out a particular objective . . . I think that there's a real lesson in Vietnam that applies to the domestic situation. The Viet Cong or the North Vietnamese, whatever combination of people you want to refer to, were able to beat the most powerful country in the world, at least in a material sense, because they had the vision and they had the morale and they had the will to fight and to win.[76]
>
> That's why they won. Many problems depend on an intangible like that: on dedication, on a principle, on a philosophy or an idea. An idea is more powerful than anything else. If that idea is grounded within the structure of a people, there is no stopping it—if it fits with the time. That is what I see: here we are at the top; we are now faced with a position of "Where do we go?"[77]

Realpolitik since World War II has been to stop the spread of communism. Keep losses to a minimum, 50,000 lives in Vietnam, for example. In Korea, Vietnam, Iraq, Afghanistan, we did not fight to win. As in World War I, as in the Civil War, without strategy, soldiers simply fired at each other. If one soldier was left standing, that side won. That side moved forward ten yards and dug a new trench.[78]

> The reason why everybody likes planning is because nobody has to do anything.

---

[76] In 5th century Athens, a small band of Greeks defeated the mighty Persian army; in 1776, a small group of American colonists, without a military, defeated Britain, Europe's most powerful military; in 2022, a small country, Ukraine, may defeat a large country, Russia. National will and the power of ideas.

[77] Brown, p. 60.

[78] Progressivism: civil war without strategy. Throw money at a project and see if anything is left standing.

> All there is to planning is thinking ahead intelligently.
> Planning has become a whole world by which planners
> pad payrolls in the public sector but do very little to
> provide a vision for where we ought to be going.
>
> They speak in the alphabet soup [acronyms]. Planning
> is just wheel spinning. It proliferates options at the highest
> level of abstraction such that no one can perceive that very
> little is being said.[79]

In other words, no accountability.

Economics:

Unfortunately, nowhere in *Thoughts* does Governor Brown
advance an economic argument. In 1974, two years earlier, with
similar reasoning, F.A. Hayek won the Nobel Prize in economics for
The Constitution of Liberty, in which he argued that as the universe
is so beyond our grasp, so too is an economy, a product of billions of
people making billions of decisions a minute, and that a free
economy is an absolute necessity: it's the only way producers can
determine real prices, real supply and demand—not to waste
valuable resources, human and natural—the only way to encourage
entrepreneurial creativity, to produce at a high level, for a high
standard of living.

The first requirement for creating a free economy is for the
state to stay away. Private sector planning, yes, government
planning, no. At the fall of the Soviet Union, 1989, Soviet planners
were asked, "How did you know what to produce, and how much,
and how much to charge?" Those planners responded, "We guessed.
We looked to the West and copied what you did as best we could."
Like Cuba, the Soviet Union did create equality, but at a price:
national prosperity at the level of the Middle Ages.

---

[79] Brown, p. 62.

RED AND BLUE

At the beginning of the Revolutionary War, Thomas Jefferson declared that America would be fighting for something that exists nowhere else in the world: a nation with no king or queen, a nation where every citizen, regardless of wealth or social status, has the vote, a nation with government so small you won't see it, a nation whose government will protect but not provide life, liberty and property (social, political and economic freedom), a nation that will guarantee maximum individual freedom in exchange for maximum individual responsibility. At the start of the Revolutionary War, Jefferson shouted, "If you're afraid of this, you're afraid of democracy; leave!" Thousands did. They fled to Canada.

The split today in American politics, red and blue, is still over this fear of democracy. Conservative red says there's nothing to fear; liberal blue says there's everything to fear, that we have progressed from the radicalism of our Founding Fathers, hence, progressivism. Conservatives say government should be very limited; liberals say that it should be what it is today, enormously expanded. Reds say our Founding Fathers got it right; blues say that a bunch of white misogynist slaveholders could not possibly have gotten it right (and have persuaded the nation's public schools to teach just that). Blues have no respect for what the Founding Fathers achieved—a constitutional government with power so dispersed (federalism) that no one group of citizens will have enough power to force another group to do something against its will. In 1933, the New Deal, absolutely opposed by the Supreme Court, absolutely reversed that vision, outright reversed the liberal principles upon which this nation was founded.[80] Today's gridlock in Congress is *still* the reaction to that act: literal interpretation of the Constitution. In other words, do we or do we not live by a set of principles?

---

[80] According to Justice Benjamin Cardozo, to get the New Deal approved, President Franklin Roosevelt literally frightened the Supreme Court into submission, threatening to cancel the court (as in their country, fellow 1930s megalomaniacs Mussolini, Hitler and Stalin did), by adding six justices of his personal choosing who would do his bidding. Checks and balances in government replaced by dictatorship.

Government is now so large that it is forced to operate through agencies, a fourth branch of government, "the administrative state": Environmental Protection Agency (EPA), Department of Education, Office of Immigration, to name three—in violation of the nation's founding Lockean principle: *only Congress shall pass laws.* Because only Congress is elected and is accountable to the people. Meaning, Congress must not, nay, can not, delegate that power. But Congress *does* delegate that power. Why? Because the first job of any politician is to get reelected, and that means not attaching your name to controversial legislation—why Congress says to the EPA, "*You* set standards for the nation." To the Supreme Court, "*You* make law," *Roe v. Wade.* But there is nothing in the Constitution that indicates that judges are qualified to declare that a fertilized human egg is or is not human, that abortion is or is not murder.

Social Security is an administrative agency. Every year it takes 15 percent of every citizen's personal income, then demands that Congress supplement that tax with additional borrowing from the U.S. Treasury (as an addition to the national debt).[81] Like the Affordable Care Act, Social Security is legal because the Supreme Court calls it a tax. True also for Medicare, with a 2.9 percent taking plus additional borrowing from the Treasury.[82] We do this because progressives are so afraid of economic freedom they will never let citizens vote to discontinue Social Security, or Medicare—afraid each taxpayer will realize he or she would retain 17.9 percent of their yearly income (15 percent plus 2.9 percent), $6,981 a year for as long as they work (if earning $39,000 a year, the mean U.S. per capita income), more if they earn more, which most Americans do. As they did in 1776, progressives today should flee to Canada. Or Europe, where citizens willingly pay 50 percent of their income in

---

[81] *Tax Policy Center Briefing Book, Key Elements of the U.S. Tax System,* Tax Policy Center, Urban Institute and Brookings Institute. Social Security benefit payouts exceed taxes paid in. This deficit is serviced by borrowing, first from the Social Security Trust Fund, then from the Treasury. *Taxpolicycenter.org/briefing-book/what-are-social-security-trust-funds-and-how-are-they-financed.*

[82] Patricia A. Davis, "Medicare Financial Status: In Brief, Estimated Date of HI Trust Fund insolvency," Congressional Research Service, October 21, 2021, pp. 6–7, *sgp.fas.org/crs/misc/R43122.*

annual taxes (25 percent annual income tax, plus 25 percent value-added tax).

***

Liberals and conservatives in Congress, both, spend taxpayer money on social and economic programs—the New Deal, the War on Poverty—because it gets them elected (and eases their consciences) without appreciating that it hurts those receiving aid more than it benefits them, for one, trapping them into dependency. Why else would politicians have allowed Mayor John Lindsey to bankrupt the city of New York in the 1970s by throwing huge sums of money at social and economic problems? The ultimate in hypocrisy, elite government bureaucrats (and private charities) built housing, hospitals and schools that *they* would never use. Tolstoy, *Anna Karenin.*

***

We take our Constitution for granted. We ignore Article 1, Section 8, which lists 18 original governmental powers (12 additional powers are set forth in the body of the Constitution). We ignore the fact that although the preamble to the Constitution states that our government is designed to promote the nation's general welfare (among other things), the Founding Fathers never meant create a department of welfare. Madison wanted those words, "promote the general welfare," deleted because they would come back to haunt. Red and Blue. The phrase is interpreted by progressives to be the essence of the Constitution, their justification for social security. By distorting the Enumerated Powers Clause, progressives have destroyed, for one, the market for health care. Health insurance is no longer insurance—it's prepaid health care and in violation of the Interstate Commerce Clause, which forbids states to block sales from other states, e.g., the purchase of health insurance from Pennsylvania by someone in New Jersey, where the cost is three times higher.

Since 1933, politics in America has been a battle between the conservative and progressive interpretation of the Enumerated Powers Clause. To conservatives, if the nation can't abide by a simple set of rules, the U.S. Constitution, written on *one* page, it doesn't deserve to exist. To progressives, if the nation can't move forward from that simple set of rules, created 250 years ago, it doesn't deserve to exist.[83]

> I detest ideologues, Left and Right; I am a pragmatist. It's more important to get something done."
>
> —Barack Obama[84]

---

[83] Progressives ask government to do for citizens what citizens can only do for themselves: go to work, go to school. Progressives do not understand that to pay for their programs, their inflationary spending raises the cost of *all* goods and services, thus lowering the nation's standard of living—hurting those at the lower end of the economy whom they think they are helping. Nor do they understand that only an advanced industrialized economy can afford the current 20 to 50 percent inefficiency from citizens transferring personal responsibility to the state, nor do they remember what Karl Marx said: that all nations must pass through capitalism before arriving at communism.

In other words, as GDP expands, government expands, and nations sneak into socialism, as Europe has since World War II and the U.S. since 1933. Except, socialist nations cannot later return to limited government without a catalyst, a crisis, a huge economic collapse as in Greece in 2010, which led, unbelievably, to the correct solution—a cut in social security payments, in half, or, the rise to power of a megalomaniac populist demagogue.

Collapse is possible whenever governments provide a safety net for business and regulate business. A genuine moral hazard, it encourages business to take risk. Smaller firms cannot afford the millions of dollars a year (just in attorney fees) to comply, for example, with Sarbanes–Oxley, Dodd–Frank. Larger firms with lower long-run average costs can then buy up those smaller firms, creating the corporate state, a nation run by a handful of monopolies.

And there is risk whenever governments force corporations into "shareholder capitalism," where small investors have a large say (about giving back to the community, about producing without an environmental imprint). That nonmarket distraction places large firms (and the nation) at risk, forcing them to no longer concentrate solely on producing their product. Milton Friedman is correct: in a competitive economy, firms should concentrate only on making a profit. Individuals within the firm, private citizens, will donate to charity (or the firm, if it aids in their marketing). It's not for government to make national economic policy. It's not for government to tell an artist how to paint, worse, what to paint. It's for the market.

[84] As remembered by this author from a conversation between Barack Obama and John McCain during the 2008 presidential primary.

Lacking in principle, Obama's quote is an awful thing to say—even if most Americans are not ideological. Americans are a center-right nation, not much interested in politics, not on the verge of civil war. The media makes it look that way. The parties are extreme, the people are not.

ROE V. WADE

The strongest argument in favor of the U.S. Supreme Court upholding *Roe v. Wade* (2022) is that for 50 years, it has been settled precedent: a woman has a right to privacy, thus, to an abortion. That is both a really bad and really good argument. Bad, because originally, *Roe v. Wade* was 1970s judicial activism: courts rather than Congress making law for the nation. Bad, because the court rationalized its decision on a false premise: that abortion is a constitutional right. Bad, because only Congress shall make law— not courts, not the president, not administrative agencies—because only Congress, elected, is accountable to the people.[85]

Law is formalization of custom, what a particular society does without questioning—in a democracy, the election of its legislators. In this sense, precedence *is* custom, except that law written within the last 50 years is too recent. And then, new law should first be debated in Congress.

Was *Roe v. Wade* settled law? Three justices of the Supreme Court had this to say:

> Samuel Alito: *Roe* must be overruled. It was egregiously wrong, the arguments exceptionally weak and so

---

[85] John Locke, *Second Treatise of Government* (Pantianos Classics, first published 1689), p. 123: "The legislature cannot transfer the power of making laws to any other hands: for it being but a delegated power from the people, they, who have it, cannot pass it over to others."

damaging that they amounted to an abuse of judicial authority.[86]

Clarence Thomas: A state may permit abortion, but nothing in the Constitution states that a state must do so. The decision is notoriously incorrect.[87]

Sonia Maria Sotomayor: Women have a constitutional right to an abortion.[88]

To come to its 1973 decision, the Supreme Court latched on to "the right to privacy," a right nowhere specifically stated in the Constitution (although it is in the penumbras of the Constitution).[89] The Enumerated Powers Clause of the Constitution, Article 1, Section 8, lists powers granted to the federal government. All other powers are reserved for the states. *That* reservation is what made it possible for the 13 original colonies, practically separate countries, to come together to create the "united states" of America. Federalism. Nine unelected lawyers making law for the nation is not what those colonies envisioned. For the Supreme Court to uphold *Roe v. Wade* simply on precedence is far removed from federalism— as was the declaring of precedence to justify *Planned Parenthood v. Casey* (1992), which reaffirmed *Roe*. According to Justice Kavanaugh, "precedence on precedence."

To say abortion should be legal because the consequence of an illegal abortion may be death to the birthing person is the worst application of law, in defiance of what lawyers and legal scholars know (and warn against): "the use of hard cases to make law," for example, a single mother with three children being evicted from her

---

[86] Supreme Court overturns Roe v. Wade, ending right to abortion upheld for decades, NPR, June 24, 2022, https://www.npr.org/2022/06/24/1102305878/supreme-court-abortion-roe-v-wade-decision-overturn

[87] Dobbs v. Jackson Women's Health Organization, 19–1392, https://www.supremecourt.gov/opinions/21pdf/19-1392_6j37.pdf

[88] Dobbs v. Jackson Women's Health Organization, 19–1392, https://www.supremecourt.gov/opinions/21pdf/19-1392_6j37.pdf

[89] The notion of viability (when it's okay to abort) was not rationalized in the 1973 decision, nor, to Clarence Thomas, was due process (the right to life of the fetus).

home with no place to go because she can't pay rent must not be allowed to stay (unless a charity pays on her behalf). Otherwise, the owner of that home, an 80-year-old single woman who saved all her life to buy that little home, herself now counting on that income to survive, will be evicted from where she now lives because *she* can't pay the rent.

***

Both the passage and the overturning of *Roe v. Wade*, a product of America's cultural wars, were unprincipled compromises on a morally difficult issue. Congress, always afraid to pass legislation on difficult issues (afraid of not being reelected), legalizing or illegalizing abortion, for example, has no right to delegate that responsibility to the Supreme Court (or to unelected government agencies). It is for the states to decide. If your state passes legislation you can't live with, move to another state! Like the Mormons, create your own state, but don't force your policies on the nation as a whole. That ends up politicizing the judiciary.

Judicial activism, replacing Congress with courts, academics replacing legislators, risks an emotional reaction: citizens shouting, "The Supreme Court is a body of white misogynist racists," or the nation turning to a populist demagogue.

Completely forgotten is that the U.S. Constitution was designed to be general, to account for anything that might arise.[90] The Founding Fathers went out of their way to make sure that was the case—by enumerating the powers of federal government: print money, raise a navy, protect patents, protect interstate commerce, then allowing everything *not enumerated* to be decided by the states. Abortion, gay marriage—the states should decide. If your state

---

[90] "Originalism in interpretation of the U.S. Constitution is the closest thing we have to a publicly shared state of legal principles." Beware of politics. "Originalism, which has the potential to transcend our moral disagreement, is a method of evaluation, not a party platform." William Baude, [law professor University of Chicago], "Why Conservatives Shouldn't Give up on Originalism," *New York Times*, July 7, 2020, https://www.nytimes.com/2020/07/09/opinion/supreme-court-originalism-conservatism.html.

passes an unacceptable law, move to another state. As markets circumvent economic regulation, so too, citizens, voting with their feet, circumvent political regulation. At the Constitution's signing, both Madison and Hamilton argued against a separate Bill of Rights —because future generations would use that list to say those are the only rights citizens have, when in fact, the Constitution (a one-page document) was designed to be general, to ensure that individual rights were limitless. The right to an abortion is one such right (or not).[91]

THE HIDDEN COST OF PROGRESSIVISM

With the U.S. Constitution, the Founding Fathers created a nation of maximum individual freedom, maximum individual responsibility, very limited government. Classical liberalism. Having fled anti-democratic European aristocracy and class structure, Americans did not want government in their lives. The Fathers believed Adam Smith was correct when he stated that individuals independently pursuing their self-interest to survive, without planning, naturally organize society. The invisible hand of nature.

In 1933, with progressivism, America flipped that vision. Freedom now meant freedom *with* government. President Franklin Roosevelt turned government from a neutral third party whose purpose is to protect life, liberty and property, to government as an active third party whose purpose is to *provide* (at least guarantee) life, liberty and property—the nation we have today, with most citizens to some degree dependent on government.

Meaning: every individual or family earning $50,000 a year is paying a hidden tax of at least $38,100 a year *over and above* federal and state tax income tax.

---

[91] Jane Roe, the pseudonym for Norma McCorvey, in the 1980s was very active in the abortion rights movement. In the mid-1990s, becoming friends with the head of an anti-abortion group and converting to Catholicism, she turned into a vocal opponent of the procedure. *History.com/topics/womans-rights/roe/v/wade.*

Examples:

1. Government has so regulated the market for health care that the market no longer exists. American health insurance costs two to three times what it costs in any other country. Why? Because it is no longer health insurance: it's prepaid health care.

    American health insurance, private or government, pays for all procedures. Citizens no longer bargain hunt for themselves; they don't care; it's paid. For nothing else in their life are they this indifferent to price. Health insurance in New Jersey, for example, costs three times that of Pennsylvania. Why? Because government, in complete violation of interstate commerce laws, forbids citizens from purchasing health insurance in another state (let alone in another country).

    Before Medicare, the cost of American health insurance was $200 a month (in 2022 dollars), $50 a month for a young person—the price of auto insurance, property insurance on a one-million-dollar home, life insurance. Citizens may pay $600 a month, but their employer is contributing another $1000 a month. The employer doesn't care; it's a tax write-off.

    Eliminate government from health care, and the price will fall. Ask your employer to give you what he is paying on your behalf. It's really your salary. That $800 a month times 12 is $9,600 a year. Hidden tax 1.

2. Social Security takes 15 percent of your income. You pay 7½ percent, your employer 7½ percent, but it's your money; your employer would otherwise have given you his share. Except 10 percent a month is sufficient. Placed in a safe investment where interest is compounded, that 5 percent differential on $50,000 income is $2,500 a year. Hidden tax 2.

3. In 1964, President Lyndon Johnson stated unequivocally that there would be no increase in taxes for the War on Poverty. A gullible nation now knows that this "war" cost $23 trillion, and now knows that poverty, 15 percent in 1964, on average, has remained 15 percent and is today paid entirely from taxation (worse, by borrowing). Nine hundred billion a year (15 percent of the federal budget) divided by 150 million taxpayers is $6,000 a person. Hidden tax 3.

4. In 1890, schools were private. Progressives decided to amalgamate them into today's unified school districts. But once a huge enterprise becomes a government project, it is then open not only to rent-seeking but to politicization. Political pressure in the 1970s forced public schools to concentrate on equal outcomes for all students. Not possible without lowering standards—why many parents pulled their children and sent them to private schools at a cost of $20,000 to $40,000 a year per child. If just one child per family attends private school at $20,000 a year—over and above the property taxes that family pays (even if they're tenants)—that's hidden tax 4.

Tax 1: Health Insurance

Government distorted premium	$1,000 a month	
Less normal market premium	- 200 a month	
Difference is a tax	$800 x 12 =	$9,600

Tax 2: Social Security

15 percent of $50,000 yearly income	= $7,500	
Less the normal rate of 10 percent	- 5,000	
Difference is a tax	2,500	$2,500

Tax 3: War on Poverty   6,000

Tax 4: Private School   20,000

Total: $38,100

Actually, there's more. Government regulation of any business causes that business to raise its prices (to maintain a minimum profit), a hidden tax, and farm subsidies and tariffs on foreign goods are a hidden tax. The real total is beyond anyone's imagination.

Solution:
Reverse all legislation since 1933 (except that which reinforces civil rights). It was never necessary. Without government intervention, markets naturally self-correct.

In other words, remove government from every aspect of our lives—the vision of the Founding Fathers.

Let citizens keep that $38,100 a year. Call it universal basic income.

We're a Jeffersonian democracy. We believe citizens can and do think for themselves—why no one in the U.S. is deprived of the vote, regardless of wealth or social status. (Thank you, Mr.

Jefferson.) Still, progressive elitists would have us follow Plato's *Republic*, would have the nation's most capable citizens placed in charge, and, in keeping with the *Republic*, prefer (secretly) the masses not vote for the nation's leaders. Dictatorship.

Arguments for Doing Nothing:
If you're wealthy or poor, you don't care what government does; you're not paying. The middle class pays all taxes.

If you're a large corporation, you don't care either. With your low long-run average costs (economies of scale), you can afford the millions of dollars in legal fees to comply with government regulation. Smaller firms cannot, which allows the big corporations to buy them up as they fail. With the few remaining corporations, you have the corporate state: Bismarck, Mussolini, Hitler.

As long as the U.S. has *less* regulation than Europe and Asia, the U.S. will have a competitive advantage. As prices rise (in response to regulation), U.S. prices will always be lower.

As long as the U.S. retains more social, political and economic freedom than Europe and Asia, the U.S. will always attract the world's most independent and entrepreneurial immigrants— precisely what allowed the U.S. to go to the Moon in 1969: German scientists. It's what keeps the U.S. at the forefront of high technology, information technology, artificial intelligence, biological engineering, quantum computing: 71 percent of Silicon Valley is foreign-born. With American public schools among the lowest in the industrialized world, with foreign students speaking English as a second language outscoring American students on the SAT and taking admission spots at American universities, the U.S. has nothing to worry about.

THE DEMOCRATIC PARTY IS FINISHED

The Democratic Party cannot win the nation, which is moderate to conservative, which does not buy such leftist claptrap as, "Everything for free, tax the rich." The Democratic Party decided, therefore, to increase its base by adding tens of millions of Latino voters, who they confidently feel will be their puppets. The reason Democratic presidents open the southern border.

Big mistake!

American policy under President Joe Biden (2022), without principle, is trout fishing: catch-and-release. ICE agents risking their lives to apprehend illegal immigrants are ordered to release them.[92]

In his campaign for governor of Texas, Republican George W. Bush defeated incumbent Democrat Ann Richards, a well-liked moderate, by asking Latino voters, "Why are you voting Democratic when, in fact, you are a conservative culture, and you are patriotic? You appreciate being in America. You're offended when you hear and see liberals bashing the nation. The Democrats are just using you."

George Bush won that election. (It didn't hurt that he campaigned in fluent Spanish.)

President Lyndon Johnson reportedly said, "Just give 'em [Blacks] a few dollars in poverty programs, and we'll have 'em voting Democratic for the next two hundred years."

That worked. But it's backfiring. By ignoring middle America's "deplorables," taking Black and Latino voters for granted, catering to the nation's coastal elites while ignoring the nation's blue-collar workers who are turning Republican, Democrats, within 30 years, will be the nation's minority party—a conscience of the nation reminding it not to lose compassion for the less fortunate, but no longer in power.

---

[92] The U.S. Immigration and Customs Enforcement (ICE) is a federal law enforcement agency under the U.S. Department of Homeland Security. ICE's stated mission is to protect the United States from cross-border crime and illegal immigration that threaten national security and public safety.

Less fortunate? The bottom 5 percent of this nation live better than 95 percent of the rest of the world: with hot and cold running water, modern sewerage, heating and air-conditioning, and high standards in building construction. Plus, public schools, public transportation, Social Security and health care. Immigrants have been heard to say: "A country where the poor are overweight is the country for me."

The House, Senate, presidency, a majority of the Supreme Court, within 30 years will be Republican. In such a nation, Left–Right, Red–Blue, liberal–conservative will no longer be an issue. With their proclivity for aristocracy in government, progressives will be seen as reactionary, as having "progressed" from what the Founding Fathers believed: maximum individual liberty, maximum individual responsibility, literal interpretation of the Constitution, very limited government.

The Democratic Party, taking Black, Latino and Jewish votes for granted, declares that Republicans are on the wrong side of history.

But Republicans now are also jumping aboard the immigration reform wagon, welcoming illegal immigrants. They vote Republican!

***

The Democratic Party is finished because the nation is waking up to who Democrats really are: romantic liberals, progressives who want freedom *with* government—rather than what the Founding Fathers, classical liberals, envisioned: freedom *from* government.

Interested in social and economic justice rather than social and economic freedom, Democrats believe they are fighting white privilege and racism, why people of color should vote Democrat—without acknowledging that people of color are not all of one mind, that what the Democrats are doing is racist. Add the fact that the nation's teachers' unions, 95 to 99 percent liberal, support elementary, high school and college teachers telling students that America is a racist nation built on the back of slavery, and that they too, young students, are responsible for the bad things America has done—because they benefit from that history. All of that is going to backfire.

And Democrats do not help their cause by continuing to believe that the New Deal, the War on Poverty and the Affordable Care Act are successful government programs—without ever checking facts—why it leads Democrats to favor President Joe Biden's Green New Deal (2023) without understanding its hidden socialist agenda: government provision of basic human services. Saikat Chakrabarti, the chief of staff of Congresswoman Alexandria Ocasio-Cortez (AOC), stated it this way:

> The interesting thing about the Green New Deal is it wasn't originally a climate thing at all. Do you guys think of it as a climate thing? Because we really think of it as a how-do-you-change-the-entire-economy thing.[93]

That too will backfire. Should the nation's schools return to teaching the history and culture of British and American democracy (social, political and economic freedom, individual responsibility—what the Founding Fathers envisioned, what de Tocqueville admired), the nation will return to what it really is: moderate—whose silent majority votes Republican.

D. EDUCATION

PUBLIC EDUCATION

We have public education in America because Thomas Jefferson thought our new democracy so-fragile citizens would lose it if they weren't vigilant in protecting it—if not educated, they wouldn't

---

[93] Ryan Saavedra, "AOC's Chief-Of-Staff Admits Green New Deal About Implementing Socialism," *Daily Wire*, July 11, 2019, https://dailywire.com/news/aocs-chief-staff-admits-green-new-deal-about-ryan-saavedra.

guard it. Jefferson, therefore, created the world's first public funding of education. Families that couldn't afford to send their children to school now could. *The state funded but did not administer the schools.* Freedom to the Founding Fathers was freedom *from* government, not, as for progressives, freedom *with* government.

Jefferson demanded a core curriculum of reading, math and history—subjects that enable citizens to recognize threats to democracy, politicians not telling the truth (Lyndon Johnson, for example, telling the nation the War on Poverty, a huge expenditure, would not be paid for by new taxes (which it is); worse, that poverty was a problem solvable by spending money). Duped citizens were certainly paying for that war, now funded entirely by borrowing. America has spent $23 trillion on the War on Poverty, three times more than all American wars combined.[94]

Duped also because American public schools dropped their core curriculum. Running scared, school districts today allow "current" political forces to shape curriculum. In a world safer and more stable than at any time in living memory, why do schools no longer play a reassuring role as to the well-being of the nation? Why are students taught they have the great misfortune to have been born into a country racist to its core, that its founding documents are a lie, that democracy hangs by a thread? What happened to civics?

Children are not taught that America has been and is a force for good, that the world counts on the world's most free and prosperous nation to come to its defense. In her introductory press conference (2022), the first thing Supreme Court nominee Ketanji Brown Jackson said was, "The United States of America is the greatest beacon of hope and democracy the world has ever known."[95] Rather, children are learning that the world is counting on *them* to deliver it from its problems. That *they*, therefore, must prepare for leadership; for example, confront their psychological problems by writing

---

[94] Michael Tanner, "Spotlight on Poverty and Opportunity," Cato Institute, January 23, 2019. (World War II, the most expensive war, cost $4 trillion.)

[95] Dan McLaughlin, "Judging Judge Jackson," National Review, March 3, 2022, https://www.nationalreview.com/magazine/2022/03/21/judging-judge-jackson/.

honest essays about their problems, about how, even unknowingly, they are racists. Parents and teachers are creating a generation of unhappy and overwhelmed children. Psychiatrists are having a field day. American Academy of Pediatricians, in October 2021, declared that child and adolescent mental health today is a "national emergency."[96]

Teacher colleges are teaching Paulo Freire's *Pedagogy of the Oppressed*, Howard Zinn's *A People's History of the United States*, and Nikole Hannah-Jones' *The 1619 Project*. Civics classes are teaching "action civics," political activism rather than political knowledge—how government works, how law is written. Teaching students that they must be engaged and participate in the political process to learn civics, conservatives smell a leftist agenda.

To engage students without first instilling love of country, telling them to dismantle time-tested institutions and ideals because they are inherently racist, brings joy to information-controlled Russia and China (far more racist than the U.S.). They hope America never returns to its core curriculum, the history and culture of British and American democracy.

Once parents understand what the nation's public schools are really teaching, they pull their children. During COVID-19, observing classes on Zoom with their children, parents witnessed (for the first time) what teachers taught. Shocked, their confidence shaken, some joined the alternative of homeschooling, which the U.S. Census Bureau reports increased from 3.3 percent pre-pandemic to 11.4 percent in the fall of 2020.[97] That's lower now (2022), but enrollment in private and Catholic schools is up. And there is new interest in classical studies (what this author advocates), historically what American schools taught—the three great moments

---

[96] American Academy of Pediatrics, "AAP-AACAP-CHA Declaration of a National Emergency in Child and Adolescent Mental Health," October 19, 2021, https://www.aap.org/en/advocacy/child-and-adolescent-healthy-mental-development/aap-aacap-cha-declaration-of-a-national-emergency-in-child-and-adolescent-mental-health/.

[97] Casey Eggleston and Jason Fields, United States Census Bureau, *Census Bureau's Household Pulse Survey Shows Significant Increase in Homeschooling Rates in Fall 2020*, March 22, 2021, https://www.census.gov/library/stories/2021/03/homeschooling-on-the-rise-during-covid-19-pandemic.html.

in Western civilization: 5th century Athens, 1st century Rome, 18th century Age of Enlightenment.

Politics, religion, multiculturalism—these are for parents to teach. Adolescents are so impressionable, so willing to believe their teachers, that educators should be forbidden to offer personal political opinions. Teachers: explain both sides; students: draw your own conclusions.[98]

***

Schools should not emphasize, as does critical race theory, that racism shapes all American laws. Racism may be embedded, as it is in every country, but It is not inherent nor implied in the Constitution. Our Founding Fathers, aware of their limitations, aware that slavery was evil, kept slavery out of the Constitution. From Frederick Douglass, in the 19th century, to Clarence Page, an essayist for the *PBS NewsHour,* in the 20th century: the U.S. Constitution is not a slaver document; the Founding Fathers truly did rise to the occasion.

Consider the Founding Fathers who had just finished fighting the Revolutionary War, where many died. Where those who signed their names to the Declaration of Independence had, by that act, signed their own death warrant to be hung from the gallows for insurrection should they, a nation of farmers with no military experience who took on the world's greatest military, lose. Exhausted, they were not ready to fight a civil war against those with whom they had just fought.

Racism is *not* built into the Constitution. Read it for yourself. On display in Washington, DC (and at every public library), it's a one-page document of general and timeless principles for representative government. It worked perfectly then, and it works perfectly today. The nation's public schools should teach the Constitution, make students proud to be American, proud of the arguments in defense of the Constitution, *The Federalist Papers*, and

---

[98] The essence of a Jeffersonian democracy is that every citizen be given the vote regardless of wealth or social status, *because* Jefferson believed citizens can and do think for themselves. The American Revolution was fought for that.

make students read Alexis de Tocqueville's *Democracy in America,* where he screams at Americans to get rid of slavery, then praises us for what we achieved, stating that Americans are the most responsible citizens on Earth, even in the back woods reading newspapers and arguing politics, that nothing like that existed in Europe, or anywhere.

Public schools must stop making young Americans feel bad about their country. It's unconscionable that students come home announcing to their parents, "I hate America! Did white people do anything good?"[99]—when, in fact, the U.S. is the only decent large nation in the world. Not only are China and Russia laughing at us, so too is France. In 2021, its Education Minister publicly warned the French not to let American "woke liberalism" invade French life, that French schools and government agencies never ask citizens to identify their race, religion, ethnicity, or gender, reminding the French that French schools exist to instill students with love for French history and culture, what the French believe unites them.

Similarly, American schools should focus on the history and culture of British and American democracy, not on other cultures, not on redressing social wrongs—as if low test scores are a legacy of slavery, colonialism or educational Eurocentrism. Low test scores are a legacy of low academic standards—standards lowered to achieve equal outcome, an idea that would have infuriated Frederick Douglass and Martin Luther King Jr., both of whom asked that America focus only on equality before the law, not on preferential treatment.

Underlying Truths about Education

1. Education provides the ability to succeed in life, but that is not the purpose of American public education. American public schools exist to provide students, future citizens, the ability to recognize threats to their democracy.

---

[99] Responding to those remarks, San Francisco voters recalled three school board members in 2022.

2. Classroom management, maintaining order in a classroom of socially and economically deprived students, is not teaching. Once teachers realize that management has replaced teaching, they quit: 50 percent of new, young, enthusiastic, well-prepared teachers in three years, 75 percent in five years.[100]

3. All learning is self-learning. Teachers facilitate and motivate learning, but it is students who do the work.

    All learning occurs between ages zero and three. Children from socially deprived homes enter kindergarten with a 2,500-to 4,500-word deficit, which increases through grade twelve.

4. To raise test scores, overnight, school districts need do only one thing: bring back their best students and teachers. Then, raise academic standards and institute a core curriculum focused on the history and culture of British and American democracy. It is unconscionable that the U.S. is the only country without a core curriculum, a nation unique among nations in being founded on a set of ideas and values rather than shared ethnic identity. America's core curriculum has been obliterated by multiculturalism and identarian politics, where the focus is on injustices to particular groups rather than on the values and good deeds of the nation. Take those values for granted, and the nation loses them.

Public schools should offer a report card that reflects a student's level of achievement. An eleventh-grade report card would look like this:

---

[100] California Commission on Teacher Credentialing and National Center for Education Statistics, updated January 20, 2022, https://www.ctc.ca.gov/.

5.

Subject	Grade Level	Grade
English	6	C-
Math	4	B
PE	11	B+

Students, thus, will work at their own pace. Students of the same age stay together—through elementary and middle school, kindergarten through eighth grade, receive an honest report card (shown above)—but admittance to high school, grades nine through twelve, will require that students be at grade level in all subjects. Those not at grade level would attend trade school or leave (with the right to return should *they* realize they would benefit).

The problems of American public schools are not due to a lack of funding. They are due to too much funding. America spends more than optimal, twice what any other nation spends. From 1970 to 2000, nationwide spending per pupil doubled, yet test scores fell 25 percent.[101]

Why? Because that additional funding was spent on additional programs, which cut into core curricula. Diminished marginal utility of the funds. Had the school day been extended two to three hours, test scores wouldn't have plummeted.

6. Test scores are a fraud on the public. Raising a school district's test scores to 50, the national average, has no meaning. If we were a nation of geniuses, 50 would be the national average; a nation of morons, 50 would be the national average. With 36 percent of today's fourth and eighth grade public school students proficient in reading

---

[101] Kena, G., Musu-Gillette, L., Robinson, J., et al., "The Condition of Education 2015 (NCES 2015-144)," U.S. Department of Education, National Center for Education Statistics. Washington, DC, http://nces.ed.gov/pubsearch.

and mathematics, *that* is the national average, 50; failure.[102]

Superintendents know but never acknowledge this. Pretending to be CEOs whose pay is contingent upon the rise of their company's stock, superintendents want their compensation contingent upon the rise of their district's test scores—a meaningless achievement.

EQUALITY

Stop talking economic equality! It's nobody's business. Inequality is inherent in a dynamic market economy. In *any* economy, the top 1 percent own most of the nation's wealth. Russia, China, the United States.

Think relative, not absolute poverty.[103] In America, the bottom 5 percent live better than 95 percent of the rest of the world, with hot and cold running water, modern sewage, heating and air conditioning, high standards in building construction, public schools, state-of-the-art health care, subsidized housing, food stamps, public transportation, welfare. Employment! A market economy *always* has a labor shortage (except during a downturn). China has a labor shortage;[104] Cuba has a labor surplus. Cuba has equality: everyone is poor. The trade-off for equality (possible only by force) is loss of political and economic freedom. Freedom is not free.

Freedom and opportunity, however, are what bring immigrants to America. Population in 1790, four million; in 1990, 250 million; 2020, 330 million. Twice that of Japan, America today is the third largest country in the world. People are born in other countries but to

---

[102] Kena et al., "The Condition of Education 2015."

[103] Stop viewing media. Reporting on catastrophes is their *sine qua non*. Economic inequality, poverty, houses on fire, Black crime—*that's* what holds viewers' attention long enough to view the next commercial (without which that broadcasting service is out of business). What's in the news is a small percentage of what's actually happening.

[104] China is kicking itself for having adopted a one-child policy.

America they come. Big difference! A self-selected population asking only to be responsible for their lives, to have the vote regardless of wealth or social status, America is a Jeffersonian democracy.

Inequality is a nonissue: people have different values. Take two sets of parents: One sacrifices to send their children to private schools. Their children may get ahead, but those parents work long hours and are not home when their children return from school. The other set wants to spend time with their children while they are young. Those parents work less; they can't afford private school; their children may earn less. Economic equality is no one's business.

Tax the rich? Taxes are paid by the poor and middle class. Jeff Bezos hasn't paid tax in 20 years. Apple, with its huge beautiful space station in Cupertino, California, is headquartered in Ireland; its cash, $200 billion, is headquartered on Jersey Island, a tax haven in the English Channel. Alexandra Ocasio-Cortez's "Tax the Rich!" is naïve. Outside communism, nations cannot redistribute wealth. Individual entrepreneurs, producers in a supply-side economy who alone make the economy, when threatened, take their wealth out of the country. Turn production over to the workers, who want nothing more than a paycheck, and the economy crumbles.

Redistribute money to solve a nation's social and economic problems, that money becomes the source rather than the cure of those problems. Problems are personal, not something government can solve, certainly not with money, of which there is no shortage. The world, awash in cash, has trillions of dollars searching for viable capital projects. Finding none, that cash is pushing the price of existing assets (real estate, stock, art) way beyond their worth.

Senator Bernie Sanders advocates European socialism, e.g., Denmark. But Denmark says, "Don't look at us; we're dismantling that whole experiment."[105] Like Sweden, Denmark discovered that

---

[105] In a speech at Harvard's Kennedy School of Government, Danish Prime Minister Lars Løkke Rasmussen declared: "Denmark is far from a socialist planned economy. Denmark is a market economy." Matthew Yglesias, "Denmark's Prime Minister Says Bernie Sanders Is Wrong to Call His Country Socialist," *VOX*, October 31, 2015, https://www.vox.com/2015/10/31/9650030/denmark-prime-minister-bernie-sanders.

socialism creates a less dynamic economy, thus, unemployment and shortage of goods and services. In socialist nations, unemployment is covered over with social services—which is why, during the 2008 financial crisis, quasi-socialist France experienced 25 percent unemployment without anyone realizing it, while the U.S. experienced 10 percent with everyone acutely aware. During the 2013 recovery, French unemployment dropped to 15 percent, the U.S. to 3 percent. Plastered over the Paris Metro was the advertisement: "50,000 jobs in the U.S. Come!"

Plymouth Rock, 1610, Governor William Bradford divided property evenly. His order: no one could sell their lot to another nor let another farm their lot. Good farmers could not expand; those who did not want to farm had to farm. Good farmers simply jumped the fence and farmed outside the fort, a perfect example of how markets circumvent regulation. Bradford canceled the equality rule.

If Blacks, Latinos, and Native Americans had been treated well —no slavery, no theft of land, no social or economic discrimination —everything would be exactly as it is today. With their larger vision, Europeans and Americans would have bought their land, bought those 40 acres, bought those California ranchos, would have paid two to three times what its owners thought they were worth. In the 1920s, Mulholland bought all the land from Owens Valley to Los Angeles. He knew the 100,000 population would someday be in the millions. In the 2000s, in New York City, Trump bought all the apartments at Columbus Circle. He paid $1,000,000 for apartments worth $500,000 that are today worth $10,000,000. Aural cultures simply cannot compete with advanced industrialized economies, with civilization based on the genius of 5th century Athens (the basis today, still, of all art, architecture, math, science, biology, poetry, drama, literature, philosophy); the genius of 1st century Rome (modern law and government); and the genius of 18th century Age of Enlightenment (today's notion of social, political and economic freedom).

Bolstered by the Industrial Revolution, Europe and America created everything you see around you: great cities, great technology, sophisticated government, civil rights. All a product of

Western civilization, itself an evolutionary step forward for mankind.[106]

E. FOREIGN AFFAIRS

PUTIN

> There is indeed no moral turpitude at present shown by a man's acting what at present appears to him to be good; but ignorance or error, tho' at present invincible [not exposed], may be a strong evidence of a prior culpable negligence, which may discover a depravity of temper [mind].

—Francis Hutcheson, 1787[107]

Putin.

Let's back up. To inaugurate a political-economic system that has no historical precedence, communism—which confiscated private property, the life's work of its owners, because revolutionaries knew in their hearts they had the bigger picture, that society would thank them later—implies enormous culpability,

---

[106] Jews living in Paris in the 1940s, American Indians in the 1700s and 1800s, the Aztecs of Mexico in the 1500s and 1600s, they didn't see it coming. Ignorance is no excuse. Native peoples of North and South America (or Africa), à la Jared Diamond (*Guns, Germs and Steel*), claim their land was geographically removed from Europe and Asia. Too bad. Had those peoples shown an interest, they would have built boats and sailed around. They would have found Europe and Asia and said, "Oh shit! Unless we get our act together, we're history," (based on how they treated peoples *they* conquered).

[107] Francis Hutcheson, *A Short Introduction To Moral Philosophy, In Three Parts— Containing The Elements of Ethics, And The Law Of Nature* (Whitefish, MT: Kessinger's Legacy Reprints (Kessinger Publishing), 1787), p. 104. John Locke, David Hume and Francis Hutcheson had an enormous influence on the writing of Adam Smith.

enormous depravity of mind.[108] Think Lenin, Mao, Castro, Pol Pot. Today: Assad, Erdogan, Putin, Xi.

Depravity of mind? Think Emanuel Kant: man is the goal of betterment, not the means. No one has the right to sacrifice some people for the betterment of others. Communism's favorite slogan, "the end justifies the means," is absolute immorality.[109]

**

Read the classical authors. Their ideas are still the most underlying. Aristotle, Thucydides, Cicero—the classical authors were interested in what we're interested in, except their arguments are better.

George Santayana, Harvard University professor in 1905, said, "Those who do not remember the past are condemned to repeat it." The idea is neither classical nor true. Why? Because those who do know history are also condemned to repeat it. Think Ukraine.

> Conscience. [W]ithout this sense we could discern no moral qualities. But when this is presupposed, our reason

---

[108] Karl Marx wrote *The Communist Manifesto* in 1848. Two years later Frédéric Bastiat wrote *The Law*, the counter-arguments. Still true, still in print. In 1917, 1949, 1959 and 1976, communist revolutionaries saw no need to first try Marx's ideas on a sample population. Advocating for Barack Obama's Affordable Care Act, Congresswoman Nancy Pelosi proclaimed, "It's going to be very, very exciting. Congress *has* to pass the bill so that you can find out what is in it, away from the fog of controversy." March 9, 2010, at the Legislative Conference for the National Association of Counties.

[109] *The Financial Times* (April 24, 2022) printed my Letter to the Editor:
Janan Ganesh writes that "[n]o grand theory can explain the Ukraine crisis." (Opinion, April 13). Oh yes it can! Assad in Syria, leaders in the Middle East, the great Singaporean statesman Lee Kuan Yew, Lenin, Stalin, Che Guevara: "The end justifies the means."

In a clash of civilizations all sides will claim the theory—although the world would do better to forget teleology (evidence of design in nature) and remember Adam Smith: society, without planning, without government, with individuals simply pursuing their self-interest to survive (by producing goods and services), as if led by an invisible hand, will organize itself better than anything that can be done by design. That, too, is elegant theory. As is Immanuel Kant: man is the goal of betterment, not the means.

will shew what external actions are laudable or censurable according as they evidence good or evil affections of soul.

Conscience is . . . man's judgment concerning the morality of his actions; or his judgment about his actions as to their conformity or contrariety to the law.[110]

We know the difference between right and wrong. To Hutcheson, we generally have the power to alter our inclinations.

Ignorance is either about matter *of law* or matter *of fact*. This division takes place chiefly in positive laws [laws based on what we do, not what we wish we did]: for in the law of nature if the fact, or natural tendency and consequence of actions, beneficial or pernicious to society, are known, this it self makes the laws known.[111]

Humans know. A species in nature, we know instinctively why Age-of-Enlightenment philosophy is true: it's based on natural law. John Locke, the Declaration of Independence, the U.S. Constitution, all base their arguments on natural law, positive law, on what humans actually do to survive: produce goods and services, communicate, trade. According to political economist Adam Smith, humans pursuing their self-interest is precisely how society organizes itself: naturally, spontaneously, as if led by an invisible hand—better than anything humans could ever do by design. Looking to nature—where there are no species with leaders who tell others what to do—the Founding Fathers felt they could create a nation based on maximum individual freedom.

Maximum individual freedom, however, comes with maximum individual responsibility. Replace individual responsibility with government responsibility, and the nation dies—as the U.S. is dying, a nation today where everything is paid for by borrowing: social security, health care, national defense. If the interest rate on the national debt, $31 trillion, is low, risk is low, but when the interest

---

[110] Hutcheson, *A Short Introduction To Moral Philosophy*, p. 101.

[111] Hutcheson, p. 104.

rate is high, risk is high.[112] Think Rome. Rome fell in 476 because Roman soldiers didn't lift a finger to stop the Huns from sledgehammering the city to smithereens. Why? They hadn't been paid. Why? All tax revenue went to pay interest on the national debt.

***

Does natural law really exist? It isn't written anywhere. God may have written the Ten Commandments, but that's all he wrote—ten sentences saying essentially, "Believe in Me, and don't hurt each other." So, as God created *his* universe (too busy to do any more writing), humans created *their* universe—by trial and error. No plan. It is why, in a state of nature, humans can assume they have a right to their own life: they created it![113]—why no community or leader has a right to anyone's life (unless they commit murder), or anything individuals produce: their art, their clothes, the home they built, the crops they planted (by extension, the land those crops are on), their property, their income. The Founding Fathers understood this—that the purpose of government is to protect life, liberty and property, protect social, political and economic freedom, not provide it.

A weakness in the above argument is that Westerners take individual liberty so seriously that they can't imagine alternatives like Eastern civilization, which values community, aesthetics, spirituality, internal contradiction. Pretending that they, too, believe individual freedom is a universal right, Easterners know how to trap Westerners.

The perfect example: Henry Kissinger's negotiation to stop the war in Vietnam. Meeting Western negotiators on their turf, Paris, France, speaking French and English, wearing western clothing, North Vietnamese negotiators blinded Kissinger into negotiating in good faith—with Kissinger never realizing the North Vietnamese,

---

[112] $30 trillion is a lot of money. At 0 percent interest, government can borrow forever. At 8 percent interest, $2.4 trillion consumes most of the nation's $3 to $4 trillion annual tax revenue. The U.S. may have to sell Louisiana back to the French.

[113] Humans didn't create life, but, as a figure of speech, they create their own life.

stalling for time, had no intention of striking a peace treaty, had every intention of winning the war. And did.[114]

Putin is North Vietnam. Wearing a western suit, pretending to negotiate while sending 300,000 troops to the border of Ukraine, calling it a military exercise, introducing false issues (that Russia needs Ukraine as a buffer against eminent attack by NATO), the West falls for it. A liar, a trickster, not a Westerner, Putin negotiates as Russia does, as does the Middle East: in bad faith.

That simple? Both the West and the East can get stuck in their worldview. *Both* can get stuck in realist foreign policy—forgetting that life is not a chess game. Putin says Russia needs Ukraine as a buffer against Western aggression, but his real motive is his personal desire to restore a greater Russia, a grand mystical vision (in which he, strongman, pulls the strings). And then, Ukrainians, a rural superstitious people with no history of democracy, for the first time united in the consciousness of their history—pawns in Stalin's farm policy, 1932–1933 (11 million purposely starved to death), pawns in Hitler's world war, 1941 (6.85 million purposely murdered), now, pawns in Putin's megalomania—have decided to fight back: to win. Who knew?

Perhaps the war in Ukraine will awaken Europe from its "holiday from history." *New York Times* opinion writer Ross Douthat also wonders if Europe will try again to be a great nation-state and pull itself up from what the East sees as Western decadence,[115] from what this writer sees as the Achilles' heel of contemporary Western civilization: self-centeredness coupled with socialist ideals—what allows citizens to delegate individual responsibility to the state.

> [T]he essence of every dictatorship and the logic of every dictator—the need to assert his own solipsism [self-centeredness], a sense of the living populated world as a

---

[114] Henry Kissinger, *Whitehouse Years, Vol. 1* (Boston, MA: Little, Brown and Company, 1979).

[115] Ross Douthat, "They Predicted the Ukraine War. But Did They Still Get It Wrong?," *New York Times*, March 10, 2022, https://www.nytimes.com/2022/03/09/opinion/ukraine-russia-invasion-west.html.

still-life painting, a *nature morte*, in which the meek china plates on the table won't scream out if you smash them.

But to my mind, this [Ukraine] is a special case: there is, behind the movement of Russian military vehicles, a genuine fear of the existence of an Other, a desperate desire to crush the Other, to reform it, ingest it, draw it in, gulp it down, swallow it.

—Maria Stepanova, Russian poet and writer[116]

Must we stick to realist foreign policy (in 2022)—in which Ukraine cedes Donbas and Crimea, demilitarizes itself, promises never to join NATO—in which both sides try to see things from each other's perspective, then compromise? Realist foreign policy misses how Stepanova sees Putin: as impenetrable darkness. She sees no interlocutor, no one to speak with, as the West is sucked into the black hole of another's consciousness.

Correct, but not complete. The West, including Ukraine, has not seriously considered the Russian perspective. Russia needs a port on the Black Sea. It took Crimea, a state with almost no ethnic Ukrainians, because it was always part of greater Russia. Russia is taking Donbas (2022) because historically, Donbas was never part of Ukraine. Donbas, an indefensible plain, was added in 1918 at the creation of the Soviet Union—with no thought that a Russian-speaking Ukraine would ever ask to leave the Soviet Union. Nikita Khrushchev was Ukrainian; it never occurred to him. [117]

So, yes, according to Henry Kissinger, there will be a negotiated settlement. Russia will keep Crimea and withdraw to pre-

[116] Maria Stepanova, "The War of Putin's Imagination," *Financial Times*, March 19, 2022 [beautifully translated by Sasha Dugdale], https://www.ft.com/content/c2797437-5d3f-466a-bc63-2a1725aa57a5.

[117] Mario Loyola, "What Is the Ukraine Endgame?" *National Review*, June 9, 2022, https://www.nationalreview.com/magazine/2022/06/27/what-is-the-ukraine-endgame/.

February 23, 2022 lines. Not appeasement, because Russia didn't gain.[118]

Yet, NATO must stand firm, or China will take it as a signal that China can invade Taiwan. Ambiguity is the key. To Kissinger, the U.S. can't support Ukraine with boots on the ground because if Putin, with a nuclear arsenal, feels threatened, he may do something reckless. And Xi, who every day tells his people that China's foreign policy is to take back Taiwan, to save face, should not be pushed too hard. The U.S. must not directly declare a line in the sand, declare that the U.S. will defend an independent nation.[119] U.S. presence in the region (and support for Ukraine) is enough for China to believe that it better not act recklessly.

Ambiguity, not appeasement. Strongmen can never be satisfied. They never become more peaceful, their nations more prosperous, their policies more in compliance with Western freedoms. Ambiguity, because there are limits to the U.S., Europe and NATO shaping the world to their liking: think Korea, Vietnam, Iraq, Afghanistan. In 1991, Saddam Hussein annexed Kuwait, and the world rejected Iraq's use of force to change national borders. The world? Not Putin—why today he is gambling he can take Ukraine. Putin calls his invasion simply a response to a genuine existential threat—to be eliminated by incorporating Ukraine's territory and killing its leaders and supporters.[120] He didn't expect Ukrainians to fight back, nor the degree to which the U.S., Europe and NATO covertly help. Putin, then, is a reminder to the world what brutal authoritarian rulers seek to do to their neighbors: conquer them,

---

[118] Henry Kissinger in discussion with Judy Woodruff, PBS *NewsHour* (July 7, 2022). Although, to Mikhail Khodorkovsky, once Russia's richest man, imprisoned ten years by Putin, now a dissident, Kissinger's stance is a concession (because Ukraine *will* give up some of Donbass). "Kissinger doesn't realize that you don't find agreement with a gangster when you're talking from a position of weakness. He doesn't realize that, for Putin, a war is just a normal way of getting his electoral ratings up. He has started wars four times." Henry Mance Interview, "Mikhail Khodorkovsky: Putin has embarked on a route that is going to lead to his demise," *Financial Times*, June 18, 2022, https://www.ft.com/content/8b58a54e-6b0b-49c7-bfff-6189affa4449.

[119] Mance, *Financial Times*, June 18, 2022.

[120] It makes no sense to claim that Ukraine is an integral part of the historic Russian Empire and then treat it like a conquered colony.

subjugate them, and if that fails, lay waste to them, kill as many of their people as plausible.[121]

Some Underlying Truths

To appease autocrats is to encourage them and encourage the rise of more autocrats. We're appeasing Putin in Ukraine (2022) because we fear nuclear war (as we appeased Hitler because we feared World War II).

Ukraine may lead to nuclear war. Russian military doctrine allows the use of nuclear weapons in the event of an existential threat to the nation.[122]

Ukraine must fight Russia—and NATO, the EU, and the West must support Ukraine. Putin must be countered, Russia made to pay enormous reparations. Otherwise, Putin and other psychotic autocrats will wage war whenever they want. They only understand brute counterforce. Ukraine had the third largest nuclear arsenal, yet gave it up at the fall of the Soviet Union for a guarantee over its sovereignty.[123] But Russia still invaded Ukraine, then arbitrarily decided NATO was not purely a defense organization.[124]

Realpolitik (Kissinger) is not about fighting to win. It's about fighting not to lose—a losing strategy: Korea, Vietnam, Iraq, Afghanistan. Winning a war *is* a chess game (certainly for Putin): a game where pieces are mercilessly sacrificed, even the queen (i.e., whole populations), where winning decisions are often intuitive. Ukraine must fight to win.

---

[121] Todd Lindberg, "Is Ukraine Saving the West?," *Commentary Magazine*, July/August 2022, p. 34.

[122] Gideon Rachman, "Divisions in the West Threaten Ukraine," *Financial Times, June* 14, 2022, https://www.ft.com/content/611c29a9-2d98-4f01-ba5f-3e3020c709e3.

[123] Alex Levak, "A Kyiv refugee's plea for solidarity in face of attack," Letters, *Financial Times,* March 9, 2022, https://www.ft.com/content/74bd5e5e-b084-4289-9333-c7d16064b9b3.

[124] NATO did not expand eastward. Eastern Europe turned westward. Putin is frightened that Russia will also turn westward. To prevent that he must stop Ukraine. To keep himself in power he is distracting Russian citizens by creating a war.

Authoritarian governments become more paranoid and more repressive the longer they remain in power. Iran. A building collapsed and killed 33. The Iranian government, incompetent and corrupt, did not send proper assistance. When citizens of the small town of Abadan (site of the collapse) protested—and accused the building's owner, in bed with the authorities, of circumventing building codes, the government sent a military contingent (a division of the Revolutionary Guards) to repress them by firing rubber bullets and tear gas point-blank. The crowd yelled, "Dictator." A citizen in the town declared, "Priority was given to repression of the protesters instead of saving lives from a disaster."[125]

Corrupt governments do what they want. They treat taxpayer money as their own, award contracts to chums. Pure degradation of the social, political, economic life of a nation.[126]

Go easy on North Korea, Iran and Russia because they have nuclear weapons? Sanction Russian oil and gas? Won't that force the West to drop its own environmental standards as it boosts coal and fossil fuel production (which wouldn't happen had we switched to nuclear 30 years ago)? That hasn't stopped India and China from purchasing Russian oil and gas. Sanction them too? The West has no choice: counter Putin with brute force. If not, he wins. He knows the U.S. and the West will not defend Ukraine, a semi-medieval, anti-Semitic, nonwestern nation, nor attack China or India. Where's the UN in all of this? Where's the U.S. in all of this? Russia and China are filling the void of our lack of leadership, our unwillingness to stand up to the new world order of authoritarian dictatorship: compare Russia, China, the Middle East, Latin America, Africa, Indonesia.[127]

---

[125] Ghazal Golshiri, "In Iran, the Collapse of a Building in abadan Arouses Anger," *Le Monde International,* May 31, 2022, https://www.lemonde.fr/international/article/2022/05/31/iran-l-effondrement-d-un-immeuble-a-abadan-suscite-la-colere_6128338_3210.html.

[126] Or, is it the other way around? Is it degraded political life that allows autocrats to rise? Before usurping complete power in Germany, Hitler was first appointed chancellor. Why?

[127] World War III now? Like Putin, should we surprise our enemies?

Most of the world hates us for our values, where the rights of the individual precede those of the state, the community: Western civilization. A win in Ukraine would be a shot in the arm. We will have done something: unite NATO. Then, let NATO replace the UN with the U.S., the only decent large nation in the world.

It's time, now, for the young to take charge, stand up for bigger things than themselves. The young know more than we think. They know, for example (which is why they don't vote), that politicians and the news media both concentrate on marginal issues: discrimination in daily life, gender fluidity, hurtful speech. In relation to the U.S.'s lack of world leadership, to the nation's lack of adherence to its Constitution (the very essence of progressivism), those issues are secondary. They're important, but they detract from preserving American democracy in a world bent on destroying it.

FRANCE

The culture of France is culture; the culture of the U.S. is business.

In a social situation, certainly at a meal, the French will never discuss business. They may discuss politics, although they never account for the fact that the underlying economy dictates all social and political relations. Marx. Since the French Revolution, the French have seen British-American individualism and commercial capitalism threatening their shared experience in equality and collective belonging.[128]

---

[128] Nowhere in France's gift to humanity, Michel de Montaigne's *Essais* (*The Essays of Michel de Montaigne*) and Marcel Proust's *A la Recherche du Temps Perdu* (*In Search of Lost Time*), is there a grasp of the underlying economy in terms of timeless economic principles. Montaigne grasps social and political relations, explaining them with timeless examples from ancient Greece and Rome, and Proust grasps social and political relations, explaining them through the eyes of psychology, but neither understood, as Marx did, that social and political relations are determined by the economy.

Americans, in a social situation, will rarely discuss culture—theatre, art, haute cuisine.[129] They, too, might discuss politics, even economics, but also without understanding that all social and political relations depend on the underlying economy—why, in both countries, political discussions go nowhere.

A generalization, yes, but the French really do think their nation's citizens should not be subject to the whims of a commercial economy. Why, to the French, controlling the economy is the very essence of civilization. French reasoning, whose roots are medieval scholasticism, plus Descartes[130] (creator of the x/y graph, who reduced everything to dualism), cannot escape their rationalism, cannot escape the most famous scholastic argument: whether a horse has four or five legs. To the French, the answer depends on the better argument. No one thinks of going outside to look at the horse.

Ridiculous? It's how the French, after World War I, decided to prevent World War II: they built a wall, the Maginot Line, at enormous expense to a war-ravaged nation, to separate France from Germany.[131] Here is the map:

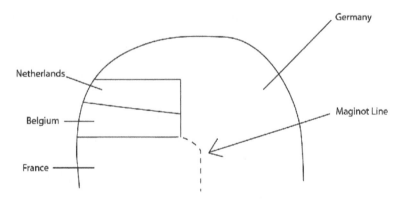

---

[129] Both countries would rather talk about movies, an absolutely commercially driven product.

[130] René Descartes' *Discourse on the Method* (1637) is one of the most famous texts in the French language.

[131] Built at a cost that possibly exceeded $9 billion in today's dollars, the 280-mile-long line included dozens of fortresses, underground bunkers, minefields and gun batteries. The Maginot Line was fortified with reinforced concrete and 55 million tons of steel embedded deep into the earth. ("Maginot Line," History, October 4, 2021, https://www.history.com/topics/world-war-ii/maginot-line.)

To build or not to build? That was the question—except no one thought to go look at a map. Germany walked around the wall, through the Netherlands and Belgium. France fell in a day.

In the 1930s, France's army was five times larger than Germany's. Should we take out Germany now? The arguments for doing nothing won. Why? Because it never occurred to the scholastic French to go see Hitler's Germany for themselves—attend a Nazi rally.

***

Do nothing? Maybe the French aren't alone. America, an enormously prosperous nation from its inception as a British colony to 1933, believed, unquestionably, in maximum individual freedom, maximum individual responsibility. Why Alexis de Tocqueville, in 1835, thought America was on its way to becoming the greatest country in the world (provided it got rid of slavery).

Until 1933, government in America acted as a neutral third party. Its purpose: protect life, liberty and property (social, political and economic freedom). In 1789, the Constitution, with its Enumerated Powers Clause, Article 1, Section 8, severely limited what government could do. To the Founding Fathers, America was *not* a democracy—it was a *constitutional* democracy. Citizens could not simply vote 90 to 10 to demand that government do whatever they wished, the New Deal, for example—why the Supreme Court vetoed it in its entirety. Unconstitutional.

All that changed in 1933: a reversal of the philosophy of America. Freedom no longer meant freedom from government; it meant freedom with government—with the ineluctable consequence: the creation of dependent citizens. Like the French, no one thought to visit the Soviet Union to see how *that* was going—before jumping into what is today European socialism.

We shouldn't have done that. It wasn't temporary. Now we can't go back; we're ruined. It is who we are today: a nation with a 50 percent tax rate (federal, state, local), whereas before 1913, there was no income tax, and then even in 1913, the federal tax rate was 7 percent for high earners, 1 percent for low earners. The New Deal, 1933, an economic Big Bang, still expanding, gave birth in 1964 to the War on Poverty, which has cost $23 trillion, three times the cost of all wars this nation ever fought. Except, that war contributed nothing. Poverty, 15 percent in 1964, is 15 percent today. On average, the needle didn't budge.[132] With increased funding for education, SAT scores dropped 25 percent (and have not come back). With Social Security and Medicare, which cost twice what they would if purchased in the market, and now paid for by borrowing, the nation is on the verge of bankruptcy.

As the French didn't check the map, America didn't check history, the fall of Rome, 476 AD. Washington, DC, you're next.[133]

Like the French, we know it's wrong, but we do nothing about it. Embracing European socialism (from which Americans fled), Americans today are afraid of democracy, of responsibility, of every man for himself. Except, that's how life works, how all species exist and survive.

F. Summary of Ideas

Summary of Ideas

1. The Founding Fathers got it right.
Maximum individual freedom. The corollary: maximum individual responsibility.

---

[132] U.S. Census Bureau, *Historical Poverty Tables: People and Families—1959–2021.*

[133] Like the Roman soldiers, will American soldiers sit on their swords while one million Chinese waltz in, post soldiers at every intersection in the country (with machine guns, not sledgehammers), then order every American to stay in place? A 100 percent lockdown easily enforced. Germany did exactly that: told the French, "Stay where you are," then walked around the Maginot Line to capture France in one day.

The purpose of government is to protect, not provide life, liberty and property.[134]

At the start of the Revolutionary War, Thomas Jefferson announced that America would be fighting for something that existed nowhere else in the world: a nation without a king or queen, a nation with *very* limited government, a nation where everyone has the vote regardless of wealth or social status, and that if you're afraid of this, you're afraid of democracy, you don't believe citizens can and do think for themselves, you don't believe that America, without as yet a military, will beat Britain, the most powerful nation in Europe. If you're afraid, leave, now! Thousands did. They fled to Canada.

2. Progressives got it wrong.

Ask not what you can do for your country. Ask what your country can do for you.[135]

In 1933, America reversed the Founding Fathers. We went from minimal government (freedom from government) to maximum government (freedom with government).[136]

We can't go back. *That* is why conservatives hate liberals: they destroyed the Founding Fathers.[137] Liberals have taken us back from

---

[134] To create the U.S. Constitution, our Founding Fathers incorporated the best political thought of 5th century Athens, 1st century Rome, 18th century Age of Enlightenment, three periods in history far superior to our day. They explained their thinking in *The Federalist Papers* and would have us understand their vision by reading "Pericles' Funeral Oration" in Thucydides' *The Peloponnesian Wars*. From such a pinnacle, a step in any direction, "progressivism" is a step downward, a return to aristocratic leadership, as in Plato's *Republic*.

[135] That's not what John F. Kennedy said.

[136] Freedom with government. Think about that. An oxymoron.

[137] In liberal coastal cities, in an act of historical cleansing, American public schools today barely mention the Founding Fathers, and then never without mentioning they were white misogynist slave owners with whom you would not want to associate. Nor do they mention that the Founding Fathers, by signing their names to the Declaration of Independence, had signed their death warrant, to be hung from the gallows should they lose the war, that maybe we should be proud of what they did.

where we fled: Europe.[138] Are we going to cancel Social Security and Medicare? No.

Extending the 1933 New Deal with the War on Poverty in 1964, America decided to spend whatever it would take to eliminate poverty. Except poverty, 15 percent in 1964, to this day has remained (on average) 15 percent. As the cost of all government wars spirals upward indefinitely, the war on drugs, Afghanistan, the War on Poverty cost the U.S. $23 trillion, three times the cost of all U.S. military wars since the American Revolution.

> The idea that government has some omnipotence or omniscience is completely absurd and counter to all the thinking that went into this country. There are many things that cannot be solved. There are many things that lie beyond or beneath government.
>
> —Jerry Brown[139]

Progressives advocate "Tax the rich." Conservatives don't even respond. Conservatives know that money, i.e., the political process, cannot solve social and economic problems, that "tax the rich" is meaningless. You can't tax the rich; they won't pay.[140] Following the advice of George Kennan in his famous white paper, "Article X" (that it wasn't necessary to counter the Soviet Union because communism, an utterly rotten system, will collapse on its own), conservatives don't protest.

Conservatives know not to listen to politicians when they run for office. Politicians want to win so badly they say whatever they think will get them elected: "Vote for me. I'll spend money in your district," or "Let's come together as a community, put the best people in charge [think FDR] and solve the nation's problems once

---

[138] In 2016, presidential candidate Bernie Sanders was asked: "Bernie, what country do you have in mind when you advocate socialism?" "Denmark," he replied. Immediately the ambassador from Denmark responded: "Don't look at us. Like Sweden, we're in the process of totally dismantling that mistake."

[139] Brown, *Thoughts,* p. 44.

[140] The rich have income-producing assets. They depreciate and borrow against those assets such that they never show income.

and for all." A conservative would respond: "Life doesn't work that way. Everything we have is because some entrepreneurial or creative person made it happen."[141]

President Biden says he'll cancel student debt. Nancy Pelosi went to Taiwan to defy China. Pure politics, liberals showing voters *they* are the creatives who get things done. No. The Democratic Party, afraid of losing both the House and Senate in the November 2022 midterm elections, is grandstanding.[142]

3. **Conservatism, classical liberalism (or classical conservatism), means "conserve."** To Edmund Burke, father of modern conservatism, it meant not tearing down in a day institutions that took hundreds of years to build and which contain more wisdom than any one person or group of planners can ever retain. Like the universe, a free economy is billions of decisions made by billions of individuals, every second—not something any individual or group can grasp; why Adam Smith explained that individuals each pursuing their self-interest to survive (by producing goods and services), without government intervention, spontaneously organize society better than anything that can ever be done by design. The opposite, the French Revolution, was Burke's warning to the British not to do that, indiscriminately kill thousands of men, women, children, priests, nuns, then tear everything down. To start over? Sounds like communism.[143]

---

[141] World War II was a successful governmental effort, but only because government drafted every person in the country (forced them to serve), then put the best in leadership positions.

[142] Because the Republican Party is picking up so many blue-collar plus Black and Latino voters (appealing to their inherent conservatism), the Democratic Party of educated coastal elites is running scared. It knows the Party is on its way out. Within 30 years it will be a minority party—with little influence.

[143] It didn't work. Napoleon came to power to save the nation from a "reign of terror"—although every male between 25 and 40 years old (as in World War I) had to die in battle—until the monarchy was finally restored. Whew! Perhaps others shouldn't criticize. The whole thing was very French. Even today, France is the sole Western nation with a viable Communist Party, the sole nation that considers participation in national strikes, barricades and street rioting as a rite of passage.

4. The U.S. Constitution is only one page.

It states how the legislature and the president will be elected; it enumerates what government can do—which is not very much, Article 1, Section 8. If you really want progressivism, an expanded constitution, move to Europe. Their constitution, the Maastricht Agreement, 254 pages, leaves everything open to discussion—because Europeans believe there is nothing to learn from history. See World War I, World War II, the war in Bosnia, the war in Ukraine. Recent history.[144]

5. Social, political and economic freedom are inherently interconnected.

The degree to which the state constrains one of those freedoms is the degree to which it constrains the other two.

The degree to which government is central to a nation is the degree to which that nation's government is open to corruption.

6. Rates of return on capital are timeless.

1–2 percent interest on bank deposits; 2–3 percent on mortgage lending; 3–5 percent on venture capital.

Any intervention in the economy causes those rates to rise, which causes small firms to be less competitive, then gobbled up by larger firms. The corporate state.

Fascist leaders want the corporate state. They want a few corporations to own everything. In exchange for their undeserved monopoly, fascist governments order those corporations to raise prices high enough for the state to take some of that profit and distribute it to citizens at large—for universal health care, education, pension, full employment, cultural access. National socialism. The abbreviation, NAZI.

---

[144] Until the beginning of the 20th century, in France, an accused was considered guilty until proven innocent. The Napoleonic Code.

7. Financial independence should be everyone's economic goal.

Save half your gross salary. Every year for ten years, with leverage, invest it in an income-producing asset. Every year, buy the house next door.

8. I am intuitive about political economy—from 150 years' professional experience in four simultaneous careers. I have the ability to correctly state the nation's problems—the key to solving them.[145]

Health care:
Problem: Price is too high.
Solution: Lower demand.

Today's high demand is artificial; it is government providing funds at a level far beyond what most consumers would ask.[146] It is government intervention in the market for health care, eliminating 300 million consumers who would normally bargain price for themselves—replacing them with a handful of government bureaucrats. Unheard of in a market economy. It caused the price of health care to quadruple. Before Medicare, the cost of health insurance was the cost of auto insurance, about $200 a month. At that price government *can* be a safety net. At $1,200 to $2,000 a month per person, it cannot. Medicare, Social Security, and the Affordable Care Act should all be provided by the market, health insurance purchasable across state lines. It's illegal (in violation of interstate commerce laws) for a citizen of New Jersey to purchase health insurance at one-third the cost in Pennsylvania (not to mention in Canada or Mexico).

---

[145] One key is never to use pronouns nor make a statement without numbers. Progressives say we should help the less fortunate—no names, no numbers.

[146] Health care can cost $500,000 for the last six months of life. When paid for by Medicare, who cares? Given a choice between depleting one's savings or leaving nothing for the children or grandchildren, most citizens would not deplete their savings. Let government decide, Medicare, who gets (or doesn't) that $500,000, in the name of social and economic justice, and no one will be deprived. There it is: artificial demand.

Poorly performing public schools:
Problem: Low test scores.
Solution: Raise education standards to the international level at which Europe and Asia compete. Barely speaking English, those students outscore Americans on the SAT, then take their place in American universities. Seventy percent of workers in Silicon Valley, the world's future, are foreign-born.[147]

Lax law enforcement:
Problem: Homeless are living on the streets.
Solution: Tell 'em to keep movin'.

Or, provide them with a place to stay—on the outskirts of town (in an abandoned factory or military base).

Problem: Illegal immigration.
Solution: Build a wall.

Or, build factories and living accommodations at the border. Then, let immigrants, stabilized by earnings, apply legally.

Problem: Crime.
Solution: Punishment.

Purposely drop a candy wrapper on the ground: prison—one hour, the first time. Everyone will get the message. It will not be necessary to build more prisons. Don't underestimate people; enforce the law.[148]

Global warming:
Problem: Too much CO2 in the atmosphere.
Solution: Remove it.

Cutting emissions by 2050 (even 2100) is not possible. Plus, it's too late; the damage has been done.

---

[147] Baron, "H-1B: Foreign Citizens."

[148] When people ask me what's the most important thing you take from teaching inner-city public schools for 40 years, I reply: "Don't underestimate people."

9. **Donald Trump won in 2016 because a national consensus had been reached—that neither political party had any intention of solving those problems *all* Americans care about:**

> The high cost of health care,
> Poorly performing public schools,
> Lax law enforcement (homelessness and immigration).

The nation thought: "Let's try something new."

It didn't work. Only a national catastrophe will reverse 1933.[149] A national budget deficit of $4 trillion, a national debt of $30 trillion (2022), unfunded liabilities (Social Security, Medicare, the nation's unfunded pensions) of $100 trillion—that has to crash. Think Rome 476. The Huns sledgehammered the city to smithereens. The Roman soldiers, strongest military in the world, didn't lift a finger to stop them. Why? They hadn't been paid. Why? All tax revenue went to pay interest on the debt. Washington, DC, you're next. That'll reverse 1933—every piece of legislation, every ruling of the Warren Court (except those that protect civil rights).

January 6 might become a national holiday.

10. We are living in the best of times.

The world has never known such a long period of peace. Except for a few World War II vets, no one alive today has experienced a world war.

Science has made enormous progress. Average lifespan in 1900, worldwide, was 46. Today, 78. Spanish Flu in 1918 killed 47 million (from a world population of 1.8 billion). COVID-19 killed 6.5 million (from a world population of 7.6 billion—with most of those deaths preventable).

Every day the media report negative news: raging fire, local crime, global warming, brutal world leaders. Stop watching or listening to the news. It's simply journalism, the reporting of events from the perspective of the moment, the reporting of what's "new"

---

[149] Trump could have been that national catastrophe had he only realized that he was.

rather than what's true. No wonder the world is anxious—everyone thinks they're living in the worst of times.[150]

11. All minorities experience discrimination.

All minorities, however, solve that problem by turning within, to their own community. If you're a Black architect and no one will hire you, work for a Black architect, work for Black clients. The market will come to you. The Brooklyn Dodgers wanted to win the pennant so badly they broke the racial barrier. Players in the Negro League were as good or better than players in the National League.

Respect is the cure for racism.

Minority test scores and low job skills are not a function of racism or a legacy of slavery. That's confusing correlation with causation. At the end of the Civil War, Frederick Douglass declared (to white do-gooders): "Don't come around with your teachers and social workers and tell us what to do. We're sick of being told what to do. We know exactly what to do. We've been living in this country for two hundred fifty years, walking your kids to school, reminding them to do their homework."[151] Twenty percent of freed slaves ran to school. For Africans worldwide, that percentage hasn't changed.[152]

Consider Henry Ford, a vicious monopolist, racist and anti-Semite. The world is better off because of him. He persisted beyond imagination (like Thomas Edison) to create an engine with all cylinders on one side. And he grasped the problems of supply chain. He produced his own—meaning he would not have been caught short as are today most manufacturers who can't get material because of COVID-19 worldwide factory lockdowns. To guarantee a supply of workers, Ford paid higher than market wages, five dollars

---

[150] Americans, be grateful you have what the whole world dreams of: a U.S. passport.

[151] Paraphrasing Frederick Douglass in Robert M.S. McDonald's "Frederick Douglass: The Self Made Man," *Cato's Letter*, Fall 2011, Cato Institute, in which Douglass also warns not to try to tie rotten apples to the tree, i.e., that some Blacks (after slavery) won't make it.

[152] Beginning in 1970, academic standards were lowered to create inclusiveness and to help most American students graduate from high school. American high school graduates today read at third- to fifth-grade level. U.S. Department of Education states (for the last 50 years) that only 36 percent of *all* Americans are proficient in reading and math, a euphemism for D+.

an hour (almost minimum wage 100 years later), then, despite his racism, went out of his way to hire Black workers because he knew they would be grateful, thus, not leave, not strike. Money counters discrimination.

America is a racist country. Period. But those discriminated against must not use that as an excuse; they must find ways to go around. The very act of countering discrimination and racism itself breeds respect.

12. Free Speech

Let a nation focus on discrimination, on equality, on empowering the aggrieved (social and economic justice), and tolerance (itself a counter to racism) will no longer be the ability to tolerate things we don't like but the ability to keep quiet, to refrain from saying what others dislike—today's tyranny of the majority.

What about satire? Offensive by definition, but its purpose is to eliminate bad ideas, not promote them. To accuse a speaker of opinionated speech of being racist or intolerant, and censor him, that's fascism. It equates words with deeds. It silences words. It imposes the norms of one group on all others—the opposite of pluralism. To say today (especially at an American university) that America is a melting pot signals that the speaker expects minorities to assimilate into the dominant culture. Why wouldn't a minority having experienced racism want to assimilate?

Free speech is integral to democracy. It provides instant information with respect to antidemocratic behavior—as a canary in a mine signals danger.

13. Inflation

During two years of COVID-19 lockdown, consumers acquired savings. Demand, therefore, is up (2022). Worldwide, with factories closed, supply is down. Price rise as a function of a rise in inelastic demand is not inflation.

The war in Ukraine removed gas and oil from the market. Price rose again. Except, after every natural catastrophe there is a price rise. A change in the economy always produces a change in price. In

2022, the U.S. economy shifted from product manufacture to product service (restaurants, travel, distribution). Now, the price of labor is rising.

It's not corporate greed. It's adjustment to a new equilibrium in the market. It's not for central banks (the Federal Reserve) to raise or lower interest rates in an evolving market. Price and interest rates, a function of supply and demand, on their own, rise or fall during any change in the economy. Interfering (unless to lower rates), the Fed risks recession—after COVID-19, risks putting people newly employed right back on unemployment.

The U.S. economy is not overheating. Worldwide market forces are driving worldwide prices. With the U.S. economy still recovering from the 2008 financial crisis, a period of enormous fraud for which the nation deserved the Great Recession, the Fed should not interfere in the economy. Deserved, since after progressive President Bill Clinton ordered Fannie Mae to purchase subprime mortgages (because "anyone in America who works hard and has good credit should be able to own a home"), banks pushed home loan applicants to lie on their applications. That disease spread throughout the financial industry as sellers of all financial instruments began lying, for example, sellers of collateralized mortgage obligations (who combine tranches of risk-free, medium-risk, and low-risk loans into one package to be sold on the secondary market, directly or as derivatives). Financial markets caught up and crashed.

America never accepted the austerity that should have followed the 2008 crisis. A nation of losers, it demanded that government, as it did for COVID-19, bail everyone out. Instead of going through a period of higher unemployment, lower profit, less production, falling asset prices, lower Social Security and Medicare payments (which would have enabled the market to self-correct in less than two years), the bailout caused the recession to last ten years, followed by ten years of low economic growth.

2008–2018, 2018–2028, we're still in those last ten years. The Fed should not be raising interest rates (2022). Trying to prove that economists know something, the Fed may very well lead us into a recession.

Inflation stems from one thing only: *an increase in a nation's money supply.* Nations that increase their money supply ease the pain of unemployment but cause inflation. If citizens paid back their COVID-19 checks (over ten or 20 years), if government retracted its increase in the money supply, inflation would subside. It's not for government to put people to work; it's for the private sector, individual entrepreneurs who know where the next technological breakthroughs are happening.

14. The Big Solution

Go back to what the Founding Fathers gave us: maximum individual freedom, maximum individual responsibility, minimum government. Reverse almost all legislation since 1933.[153]

---

[153] Except legislation that protects civil rights.

JOURNAL OF LAW AND BUSINESS

INSIDER TRADING *

I. INTRODUCTION

All economists love the following quote:

> The ideas of economists and political philosophers, both
> when they are right and when they are wrong, are more
> powerful than is commonly understood. Indeed the world
> is ruled by little else. Practical men, who believe
> themselves to be quite exempt from any intellectual
> influences, are usually the slaves of some defunct
> economist. Madmen in authority, who hear voices in the
> air, are distilling their frenzy from some academic
> scribbler of a few years back . . . There are not many who
> are influenced by new theories after they are twenty-five
> or thirty years of age, so that the ideas which civil servants
> and politicians and even agitators apply to current events
> are not likely to be the newest.[1]

Written by John Maynard Keynes, one of the world's most famous
economists, it expresses what all economists believe, namely, that
they, especially in relation to people in business, have the bigger
picture.

*Article originally appeared in *Journal of Law and Business,* 13, 2006, pp. 71–91. Reedited
December 10, 2022.

[1] John Maynard Keynes, *The General Theory of Employment, Interest, and Money* (New
York: Harcourt, Brace & World, 1936), p. 94.

Still, Keynes was an economist, not an entrepreneur. What Keynes and most economists do not fully appreciate is the extent to which the thought process of an entrepreneur (or lack of one) is so completely different from that of an economist. Even entrepreneurs who are politically to the left understand that there are always ways to get around government regulation, that the costs of regulation are always passed on to the consumer, and that the ideas of economists and philosophers are not important when it comes to operating in the dynamic. They may not admit this, but they understand it intuitively.

And what many philosophers don't know, and what many economists refuse to admit (and what many entrepreneurs may not even care about), is that in the economic affairs of man, all things are timeless. Rates of return, profit, the role of private property (three essential incentives to production)—these are timeless. Today's rate of interest on savings (2004) is what it is because it's what it's always been, 1 percent; today's rate of interest on secured lending (mortgages), 3 percent; and today's rate of return on investment capital, 5 percent (higher because of higher risk). They are what they are because it's what they have always been and will always be, the timeless rates of return on capital.[2]

Acquiring capital, however, is not a goal. The goal is to acquire assets. And the reason to acquire assets (property that holds its value over time) is to secure financial independence, the financial independence that comes from the constant income stream that assets generate.[3] The constant income stream, however, is possible only if the underlying assets continually increase in value over time

---

[2] Money, however, is not capital. Money simply represents capital (and unless it's an actual commodity like gold, it has no value). Money's main purpose is to facilitate the exchange of goods and services. This leads us to the real definition of capital, namely, surplus production. The free trade of capital is, of course, capitalism, and because capital is surplus production, it is the measure of a nation's standard of living, the measure of a nation's ability to pay for such things as health care, education and high standards in building construction. The extent, then, to which nations have capital is the extent to which nations produce.

[3] Land and art are examples of assets that do not generate an income stream directly, but when income needs to be generated, portions of the asset can be sold off, borrowed against or traded for assets that do produce income. Investors may not want all their assets to produce income.

at a rate equal to the cost of the capital plus inflation. The risk that assets may decrease in value, because the income stream may decrease, is the reason why assets must be purchased carefully, the reason, for example, why individuals (except professional investors) should never own more than one or two stocks. There's not enough time to do the research.[4]

With stocks paying little or no dividends, how, then, does one even choose a stock to invest in? One chooses a stock no differently than one chooses any asset for investment—real estate or venture capital. The investor goes to the site and observes the operation. The investor talks to everyone—to employees in the lunchroom, to tenants in the laundry room, to the CEO. The investor looks at financial statements. The investor knows full well that the statements aren't true, but because investing is for future income, investors need to have some idea of the numbers upon which a company's future is based. Investors need to have some idea as to *how* a firm plans to add value. All of this, however, is verifiable only firsthand. With stocks valued as much as forty times net income, no differently now (2004) than before the stock market crash of 2001, investors are at too great a risk that, in the future, the price of their stock will drop; that upon sale there will be no profit in the stock, and that even if the company's net income increases in the future, the price of the stock may not. This is especially so because a price-earnings ratio of 40 to 1 is not sustainable. Long run, 10 to 1, maybe 13 to 1, is. This is the timeless ratio. Considering that stocks pay low or even no dividends, the only way for investors to know how well a company is doing is to personally keep abreast of events. This is how it is for all investments.

People who purchased Enron, for example, did so without inside information and, as a consequence, lost everything. Still, information that was available should have frightened them off. Enron's financial statement for the year 2000 showed a $60 billion jump in revenue, from $40 billion in 1999 to $100 billion in 2000. In

---

[4] Those who own more than one or two stocks do so to diversify an investment portfolio, but they would do just as well to invest in the market as a whole, in the market index. Investing in the index, however, is not investing; it's capital preservation.

itself, a jump of that size should have raised antennas, but so too the enormity of the total in absolute dollars. (See Exhibit 1, page 110, *Enron Corporation and Subsidiaries Consolidated Income Statement*.) And Enron's financial statements also always disclosed off-balance-sheet items, footnotes that referred to special purpose entities, each over $1 billion, and each strapped with high debt. (See Exhibit 2, page 111, *Footnote 2, Business Acquisitions and Dispositions*.) If these things are not questioned by investors, what is?

Why didn't investors question this? Why didn't analysts from brokerage houses warn their clients? Precisely because big corporations like Enron and WorldCom tell brokerage houses not to. Brokerage houses depend upon the information they get from large corporations, and so they comply.[5]

Not only is there a questionable relationship between large corporations and their brokerage houses (and their investment banks), but in many cases, even the idea of issuing stock is questionable. The ability to raise capital from the public at large to fund large capital projects is one of the main reasons for the commercial success of the West, but the idea of not paying interest on that capital is not. (It is, in fact, one of the main reasons for the commercial failure of the Middle East.) If the public accepts the normal trade-off between no interest and high return, the public must not forget that high return exists only because of high risk.[6] Is it

----

[5]Large corporations don't tell brokerage houses directly what to do, but it's understood, because large corporations choose their brokerage houses no differently than they choose anyone else they employ. They choose people who do what they're told—attorneys to make things legal, accountants to handle audits, bankers to come up with money on demand.

[6] In the dynamic of the moment, professional investors may not think directly in terms of the relationship between risk and reward, but they structure their deals "as if" they do. They protect themselves against risk. One mark of a professional investment is the extent to which an investment is fully financed, i.e., the extent to which there is no equity to lose. Another mark is the extent to which an investment has a bailout mechanism, a way to give back or quickly sell if things don't go well. Structuring the *resale* of an investment within the purchase agreement is part of what a professional investment is. If professional investors occasionally miscalculate holding costs, or tax liabilities, this is because their leveraged acquisitions have payments that are too high or have a tax basis that is too low because of past depreciation.

possible, then, that the reason firms issue stock is that their capital projects are just too risky for banks to consider? And if the real advantage of borrowing from a bank (or of issuing corporate bonds) rather than selling stock is that profit does not have to be shared with other investors, why then would a firm ever issue stock? Buyers of stock must always keep in mind that firms issue stock either because they can't get a loan from a bank or because they don't want to pay interest.[7]

But when firms pay low or no interest, i.e., low or no dividends, what they are really saying is that the return on an investor's money must come from an increase in the price of the stock (minus brokerage fees and capital gains tax upon sale). The broader lesson, though, is that, with 5 percent, the timeless return on investment capital, there is very little for businesses to ever give away.[8]

If a firm's financial statements are verifiable only firsthand, why is it wrong then for investors to ask CEOs, or CFOs, or even brokerage houses, to keep them abreast of "recent developments"? It's not wrong! They do it all the time! In the case of Martha Stewart, the fact that her broker tipped her off was not enough for the Securities and Exchange Commission (SEC) to convict her of selling on inside information. The CEO's father and daughter, plus two of his friends, plus one of Martha Stewart's friends—all also received the same tip-off and were not indicted. Is it possible that the SEC, because of so many recent corporate scandals and because it rarely prosecutes for insider trading, decided that it had better do

---

[7] Firms will say that the issuance of stock is purely a capital structuring decision, that a firm's optimal return is a function of its weighted average cost of capital, but this is a decision in theory only. The reality of the dynamic is that firms make financial and production decisions based purely on opportunities available to them in the market at the moment.

And from the stockholder's perspective, the issuance of more stock dilutes their position, while the addition of debt may strengthen it. This is so because debt, unlike equity, can be an incentive for better performance, something that forces firms to concentrate on their business precisely because the debt must be repaid.

[8] Communist and socialist nations all know this now, but they have had to learn it the hard way. To be precise, there is no tax or redistribution of property that is not passed back to the consumer as a reduction in standard of living.

something, i.e., go after someone with a high profile? Yes. And this is why Martha Stewart was prosecuted. But when stockholders of Martha Stewart Living Omnimedia Inc., i.e., millions of Americans, are put at risk of losing their entire investment (because such a serious indictment will cause the price of any stock to tumble; plus, the issuance of any statement to counter such an indictment, if it is for the purpose of upholding the price of the stock, is securities fraud), does prosecuting for insider trading really make the nation better off? Isn't this tactic just as dishonest as the fraud committed by Enron and WorldCom?

Martha Stewart sold her stock in ImClone in early 2002. The SEC waited until June 2003 to bring charges. Why? Is it because they couldn't find anything against her and needed time, a long deposition period, to build a body of testimony, hoping that she would eventually perjure herself? According to *Reason* magazine,

> The most serious criminal charge against her is not perjury or insider trading but securities fraud, based on the fact that she denied to the press, personally and through her lawyers, that she had engaged in insider trading. This was done, the feds say, not for the purpose of clearing her name, but only to prop up the stock price of her own publicly traded company, Martha Stewart Living Omnimedia [which dropped over $400 million in value]. In other words, her crime is claiming to be innocent of a crime with which she was never charged.

> As for the SEC's civil case, it hinges on an elastic understanding of insider trading, an offense Congress has never defined. The justification for the ban on insider trading, which makes little economic or legal sense, is just as murky as the behavior covered by it. Given the difficulty of figuring out exactly what constitutes insider trading (let alone why it's illegal), it is entirely possible that Stewart and her lawyers weren't sure whether she had broken the rules. In any event, under existing case law, it's clear that she didn't.[9]

---

[9] Michael McMenamin, "St. Martha," *Reason* magazine, October 2003, p. 24.

The government says that insider trading occurs when someone buys or sells stock based on material, nonpublic information received from an insider. The government also says that insider trading is illegal because it does "economic harm" to the market. These things Martha Stewart did not do. The SEC's publicity stunt, then, is really a diversionary tactic, a tactic to divert attention away from the fact that an insider trading ban is bad economics and even worse law.

The argument, according to Michael McMenamin, the author of the *Reason* magazine article "St. Martha," as to why prosecution for insider trading is bad economics is from the classic 1966 book *Insider Trading and the Stock Market*, by Henry Manne (discussed in Part II of this essay). The argument is that insider trading makes markets more efficient in that it speeds up the accuracy and transmission of new information. The argument is also that there is no evidence that insider trading harms the market. As long as market professionals track insider buying and selling, and respond immediately, stock prices will respond immediately. It should make no difference whether buying and selling are tracked through diligence or through insider information. The important thing is that markets respond immediately, that markets be efficient.

But government intervention in the natural economic affairs of a nation, even just to ensure a level playing field, always runs the risk of creating bad law. Law that regulates the everyday affairs of millions of people has to be bad, because it is always overly broad. By economic reasoning, when laws are general rather than specific, the extent to which they help one group will be the extent to which they harm another group. But when people are harmed by a law, they do something about it: they circumvent it, and the law, like laws against drug possession, becomes impossible to enforce. Monitoring against fraud, however, is another matter. The SEC, for example, which has been monitoring and prosecuting inside traders since 1934, has never won a case before the Supreme Court unless there was a showing of fraud. In other words, no case has been won that simply showed harm to the market.[10] In practice, because they run counter to natural market behavior, laws banning insider trading laws are unenforceable. *This is bad law.* With fraud, the situation is different. Courts can apply criminal law. Law that prohibits industrial espionage and theft of trade secrets and sensitive commercial information already exists. *This is good law.* It prohibits specific actions, and it instills confidence in the market. If a stock exchange, itself a private entity, believes insider trading damages investor confidence, then the stock exchange should require that companies whose shares are traded there have rules against it.[11] This is not something governments should do.

Still, what insider trading laws are not correctly accounting for is the extent to which dishonesty in business is simply an extension of dishonesty in human nature, and thus not preventable. In this sense, Enron and WorldCom are simply a link in a long chain of corporate dishonesty, a chain that will never be broken. In the late 1980s, for example, huge corporate collapses included the Bank for Credit and Commerce (BCCI), which involved Washington insiders, and Lincoln Savings Bank, which involved members of Congress. (Lincoln Savings was part of the Savings and Loan (S&L) scandal in the 1990s that required a $500 billion government bailout [in today's dollars, closer to a trillion].) If these corporations were patrolled by the SEC, the SEC certainly wasn't looking too closely. One explanation for continuous dishonesty, over and above simple greed, is that competition in a market economy creates an incentive to act immorally. Competition for commissions on stock trades, by discount brokers, for example, pushes brokerage houses to look for analysts whose strength, instead of providing investment advice, is in bringing in investment banking.[12] Recruiters can be paid as much

---

[10] McMenamin, "St. Martha," pp. 26–27.

[11] McMenamin, "St. Martha," p. 30.

[12] Investment bankers issue new stock, IPOs. Unlike stockbrokers, they do not trade in existing stock.

as $10 million to bring in those analysts.[13] Or, transactions can become so complicated that analysts (as well as auditors and credit reporting agencies) find it easier to just trust the company rather than be skeptical. This is exactly how Enron operated.

The question, then, is, if dishonesty and greed truly are integral to human nature, whom can we trust? To whom can we delegate investment research? The answer is—no one. Investors are better off placing their money in savings accounts that earn compound interest than investing in stocks they know nothing about or turning their money over to professional advisors.[14] (See Part IV, "Discussion," for further examples of current corporate dishonesty.)

[13] Ron Scherer and David Francis, "Lessons of Enron: How Could No One Have Seen It?" *Christian Science Monitor*, January 16, 2002, https://www.csmonitor.com/2002/0116/p1s1-usec.html.

[14] Statistics show that professional advisors do not beat market indexes.

EXHIBIT 1

Enron Corp. and Subsidiaries Consolidated Income Statement

Year ended December 31,

(In millions, except per share amounts)	2000	1999	1998
Revenues			
Natural gas and other products	$50,500	$19,536	$13,276
Electricity	33,823	15,238	13,939
Metals	9,234		
Other	7,232	5,338	4,045
Total revenues	100,789	40,112	31,260
Costs and Expenses			
Cost of gas, electricity, metals and other products.	94,517	34,761	26,381
Operating expenses	3,184	3,045	2,473
Depreciation, depletion and amortization	855	870	827
Taxes, other than Income taxes	280	193	201
Impairment of long-lived assets	-	441	-
Total costs and expenses	98,836	39,310	29,882
Operating Income	1,953	802	1,378
Other Income and Deductions			
Equity in earnings of unconsolidated equity affiliates	87	309	97
Gains on sales of non-merchant assets	146	541	56
Gains on the issuance of stock by TNPC, Inc.	121	-	-
Interest income	212	162	88
Other income, net	(37)	181	(37)
Income Before Interest, Minority Interests and Income Taxes	2,482	1,995	1,582
Interest and related charges, net	838	656	550
Dividends on company-obligated preferred securities of subsidiaries	77	76	77
Minority interests	154	135	77
Income tax expense	434	104	175
Net Income before cumulative effect of accounting changes	979	1,024	703
Cumulative effect of accounting changes, net of tax	-	(131)	-
Net Income	979	893	703
Preferred stock dividends	83	66	17
Earnings on Common Stock	$ 896	$ 827	$ 686
Earnings Per Share Of Common Stock			
Basic			
Before cumulative effect of accounting changes	$ 1.22	$ 1.36	$ 1.07
Cumulative effect of accounting changes	-	(0.19)	-
Basic earnings per share	$ 1.22	$ 1.17	$ 1.07
Diluted			
Before cumulative effect of accounting changes	$ 1.12	$ 1.27	$ 1.01
Cumulative effect of accounting changes	-	(0.17)	-
Diluted earnings per share	$ 1.12	$ 1.10	$ 1.01
Average Number of Common Shares Used in Computation			
Basic	736	705	642
Diluted	814	769	695

Enron Corp. and Subsidiaries Consolidated Statement of Comprehensive Income

Year ended December 31,

(in millions)	2000	1999	1998
Net Income	$ 979	$ 893	$ 703
Other comprehensive income:			
Foreign currency translation adjustment and other	(307)	(579)	(14)
Total Comprehensive Income	$ 672	$ 314	$ 689

The accompanying notes are an integral part of these consolidated financial statements

EXHIBIT 2

BUSINESS ACQUISITIONS AND DISPOSITIONS

In 2000, Enron, through a wholly owned subsidiary, acquired all of the outstanding common shares of M&G plc, a leading independent international metals market-making business that provides financial and marketing services to the global metals industry, for $413 million in cash and assumed debt of approximately $1.6 billion.

In addition, Enron made other acquisitions including a technology-related company, a facility maintenance company and all minority shareholders' interests in Enron Energy Services, LLC and Enron Renewable Energy Corp. Enron issued 5.7 million shares of Enron common stock, contributed common stock and warrants of an unconsolidated equity affiliate and paid cash in these transactions.

On August 16, 1999, Enron exchanged approximately 62.3 million shares (approximately 75%) of the Enron Oil & Gas Company (EOG) common stock it held for all of the stock of EOGI-India, Inc., a subsidiary of EOG. Also in August 1999, Enron received net proceeds of approximately $190 million for the sale of 8.5 million shares of EOG common stock in a public offering and issued approximately $255 million of public debt that is exchangeable in July 2002 into approximately 11.5 million shares of EOG common stock. As a result of the share exchange and share sale, Enron recorded a pre-tax gain *of* $454 million ($345 million after tax, or $0.45 per diluted share) in 1999. As *of* August 16, **1999**, EOG is no longer included in Enron's consolidated financial statements. EOGI-India, Inc. is included in the consolidated financial statements within the Wholesale Services segment following the exchange and sale. Enron accounts for its oil and gas exploration and production activities under the successful efforts method of accounting.

In August 1998, Enron, through a wholly owned subsidiary, completed the acquisition of a controlling interest in Elektro Eletricidade e Servicos S.A. (Elektro) for approximately $1.3 billion. Elektro was initially accounted for using the equity method based on temporary control. In 1999, after the acquisition of additional interests, Elektro was consolidated by Enron.

Additionally, during 1999 and 1998, Enron acquired generation, natural gas distribution, renewable energy, telecommunications and energy management businesses for cash, Enron and subsidiary stock and notes.

Enron has accounted for these acquisitions using the purchase method of accounting as of the effective date of each transaction. Accordingly, the purchase price of each transaction has been allocated based upon the estimated fair value of the assets and liabilities acquired as of the acquisition date, with the excess reflected as goodwill in the Consolidated Balance Sheet. This and all other goodwill is being amortized on a straight-line basis over 5 to 40 years.

Assets acquired, liabilities assumed and consideration paid as a result of

(In millions)	2000	**1999**	**1998**[a]
Fair value of assets acquired, other than cash	$2,641	$ 376	$ 269
Goodwill	963	(71)	94
Fair value of liabilities assumed	(2,418)	6	**(259)**
Common stock of Enron Issued and equity of an unconsolidated equity affiliate contributed	(4091)	-	
Net cash paid	$777	$311	$104

businesses acquired were as follows:

(a) Excludes amounts related to the 1998 acquisition of Elektro.

On November 8, 1999, Enron announced that it had entered into an agreement to sell Enron's wholly owned electric utility subsidiary, Portland General Electric Company (PGE), to Sierra Pacific Resources for $2.1 billion. Sierra Pacific Resources will also assume approximately $1 billion in PGE debt and preferred stock. The transaction has been delayed by the effect of recent events in California and Nevada on the buyer. Enron's carrying amount of PGE as of December 31, 2000, was approximately $1.6 billion. Income before interest, minority interest and income taxes for PGE was $338 million, $298 million and $284 million for 2000, 1999 and 1998, respectively.[15]

II. INSIDER TRADING

What's generally missing from the discussion on insider trading is the extent to which insider trading is itself inherent to the stock market. That insider trading has no effect on long-term investors, that the ability to profit from insider trading is at the heart of entrepreneurial compensation, i.e., at the heart of a firm's ability to attract entrepreneurial talent, this is what the discussion should be about. The fact that people think this must not be allowed to happen and that the stock market must be a fair playing field is a denial of market reality.[16]

According to Henry Manne, in *Insider Trading and the Stock Market*,[17] the notion of unfairness, of unequal opportunity, comes from how we prosecute illegal business activity, namely, as a tort, a personal wrong. But the stock market is not something personal; it's simply a vehicle for the efficient exchange and allocation of resources, with insider trading a means for speeding up the transmission of information. This is the utilitarian argument in favor of accepting the existence of insider trading.

---

[15] Enron Annual Report 2000, https://picker.uchicago.edu/Enron/EnronAnnualReport2000.pdf.

[16] The most famous insider trading case is the 1968 case, *SEC v. Texas Gulf Sulphur Co.* Charles Fogarty, working for Texas Gulf, went ahead and purchased Ontario mineral rights before Texas Gulf could purchase them, and then sold them back to Texas Gulf. Yet, who really cared? The SEC, not Texas Gulf. Texas Gulf subsequently elevated Charles Fogarty to CEO, and after his death, another insider who traded on the same information was elevated to replace him.

[17] Henry Manne, *Insider Trading and the Stock Market* (New York: The Free Press, 1966).

There is also a moral argument. Based on the notion of prudence, the moral argument is that individuals have a duty to prevent the value of their assets from disintegrating. This argument, put forth by Tibor Machan, a cofounder of *Reason* magazine,[18] coincides with two questions put forth by Henry Manne: What empirical evidence do we have that people who are in a position to profit, even at the expense of others, offend a sense of morality? What empirical evidence do we have that this discourages investment in the stock market? According to Manne and Machan, none.

And Manne asks other questions: Do fiduciary relationships exist with respect to anonymous transactions over a stock exchange? Do insiders necessarily know more than smart outsiders? If no, it can only be that it's inherent to the stock market that shareholders assume the risk that insiders will speculate. First of all, the law allows it, and second, no one cares if speculators lose money, certainly not long-term investors. Anyone, then, who cares if their stock drops in value in the short term shouldn't be investing in the stock market.

And Martha Stewart's short-term investment in ImClone stock was probably contingent upon her being given inside information. Why? Because simple prudence dictates that investors who purchase stock whose value is dependent on a simple yes or no answer from a government regulatory body *should* be immediately notified. You can't ask savvy investors to wait around until someone at the corporation decides to make a public statement. If ImClone were a large pharmaceutical company, with hundreds of FDA approvals pending, the value of its stock would not fluctuate wildly whenever one approval is denied. How can small companies like ImClone, without offering inside information, ever sell stock?[19]

---

[18] "The Moral Case for Insider Trading," by Tibor R. Machan, a lecture at the Smith Center for Private Enterprise Studies at Hayward State University, January 24, 1996.

[19] For a company to forbid its employees to trade on inside information, or for the government to forbid its employees to trade on inside information is another issue altogether, a condition that should be set and enforced by contract.

Speculation and the obtaining of inside information are so inherent to the stock market that making it illegal serves only to destroy the market. Controlling markets always has this effect. It leads to firms trying to become so large that nothing has an effect on their stock price. It leads to the market becoming so dominated by monopolies that it is as if everything were owned by government. But this is a situation of no risk. And when there is no risk, there is no reward, and when there is no reward, there is no investment, and when there is no investment, there's no longer a market or an economy. And with only a few monopoly employers, no one, including labor, will have the luxury of taking their services elsewhere. Entrepreneurs and creative employees will no longer have the opportunity to benefit from insider information. Unlike labor, however, entrepreneurs and creative employees, even if they do not withdraw their services, can still withdraw their creativity. This is what happens in communist economies.

The importance, then, of creative producers cannot be overstated. It is *their* ideas that lead to new and better products, and even to new ways of doing business, e.g., Wal-Mart. This, in turn, leads to increased production and productivity, the very measures of an increased standard of living. With free markets, with prices free to fluctuate, resources go to the highest bidders, the most efficient producers. They pay the highest price, but, in exchange, as a consequence, they don't waste the resources. This efficiency alone is one of the most essential factors in raising a nation's standard of living.

Moreover, in a free market economy (unlike in a planned economy), resources are not wasted monitoring and controlling the actions of a nation's entire population. Resources are not wasted tracking down and prosecuting investors who, within a six-month period, went long or short in the stock market while trying to make a profit.[20] Creative producers are not constantly threatened with lawsuits, the effect of which is to discourage them from joining

---

[20] The SEC assumes that high profit in less than six months is the result of trading on inside information.

114

boards of directors, from becoming CEOs, or even from investing in the stock market.

Again, markets need creative producers. Without them, with managers content to just do their jobs, firms atrophy. According to Henry Manne, hiring entrepreneurs and encouraging entrepreneurial thinking is the essential defensive strategy for countering the outside forces of creative destruction. Firms, however, must pay for this entrepreneurial value. But how much? The exact amount cannot be known in advance, so firms let entrepreneurs create their own compensation. With the market based primarily on information, with entrepreneurs the ones who primarily provide the information, entrepreneurs simply claim the right to benefit from that information.[21] This *is* the basis for entrepreneurial compensation.

And it is the basis for another reason. Once information is made public, competition wipes out an early advantage a firm may have had, forcing its entrepreneurs to move quickly to cash in on what they know. This is still their principal incentive.[22] You cannot ask entrepreneurs to accept stock options or profit sharing as compensation. What if the value of the stock declines? Nor can corporations require that entrepreneurs be sophisticated enough to know how to short the value of their options, or that they hang around long enough to cash them in.[23] [24]

The egalitarian argument, then, that benefiting from inside information is unfair, if followed to its full ramification, according to Henry Manne, requires that entrepreneurs also be capitalists, that they actually know how to invest before they innovate. That alone is enough to discourage innovation and the pure pursuit of knowledge.

---

[21] Manne, *Insider Trading and the Stock Market*, p. 138.

[22] Manne, p. 139.

[23] The price of a short or a call option might be 10 percent of the value of the stock when the option period is short, six months, for example, but can approach 100 percent when the option period is long, five years or longer.

[24] Corporations don't want entrepreneurs to exercise their options because corporations lose the ability to yearly write off those options as an annual expense. (In response to Enron's false accounting practices, however, this tax break is being eliminated.)

Curiously, perhaps the most beneficial consequence of insider trading is that it attracts entrepreneurs to small corporations. This is so because the benefit from trading on inside information is greatest with small corporations.[25] The benefit to society, which is to say the market, is that creative business people move to small corporations and then challenge big corporations. This is exactly how the process of creative destruction starts.

To counter this, to attract these very same entrepreneurs, big corporations will pay astronomical salaries. But this doesn't work. Creative entrepreneurs are more attracted to the creative environment of a small corporation and to the potentially greater benefit from trading on the inside information of the small corporation. This market reality also explains why, in a free market, government enterprises can never compete with private corporations. They won't pay the exorbitant salaries, and, as regulated public bodies, they don't provide a creative environment (not to mention a chance to make a profit).

Notwithstanding all of the above, is it still not better for society to have laws forbidding insider trading? From a Hobbesian perspective, from the perspective of not creating the appearance of a lawless society, it might be better for a nation to at least give the impression that unfair trading will not be tolerated, although the extent to which insider trading laws are strictly enforced is the extent to which these laws create bad economic policy and the extent to which they create a police state. But as long as the Supreme Court continues to throw out all insider trading cases, except those for which there is fraud, society can just leave the law alone.

Yet, according to Manne, here are some of the issues:

---

[25] According to Manne, price movement from inside information is greatest among small corporations. "If an oil company with total assets of $50 million discovers an oil pool worth $5 million, this should cause the price of its shares to rise from $50 to $55 [10 percent]. The same discovery by a company with assets of $1 billion and 20 million shares outstanding might be so inconsequential as to have no effect whatsoever on the stock price. Theoretically, each share should rise by ¼ point, but other market forces might easily counteract that gain, whereas the certainty of realizing profit from a 5-point gain is quite high." Manne, *Insider Trading and the Stock Market*, p. 143.

Information is one of the most easily transmitted of all commodities. To prevent its rapid dissemination while it has exchange value is extremely difficult. Any attempt to regulate or police a market in information confronts two obstacles. The first is the extremely difficult one of knowing which transmissions to prevent. The second is the actual job of policing once the undesired transmissions are identified.[26]

[A]ny trade known to be made before public disclosure of information violates SEC Rule 10b-5. It is one thing, however, to detect insider trading as widely publicized as that in the *Texas Gulf* case [see Martha Stewart case today]; it is another matter to administer this rule in a nondiscriminatory fashion. The SEC has ignored these dangers by relying on the courts to develop rules for it on a case-by-case basis. Ultimately the enforcement difficulties remain, and they may be greater under this approach than they would be if the SEC faced up to the policing difficulties by promulgating detailed rules.[27]

As long as those in business know the difference between the reality of the law and the reality of the market and know how to get around the law, there is no harm in leaving the law alone.[28] The SEC, for example, has the right, at any time, to stop all trading in a stock market when it perceives insider trading. This may serve a purpose, but it's still a broad police-state action that has the potential to

---

[26] Manne, p. 159.

[27] Manne, p. 166.

[28] Even if citizens prefer honesty, politics won't allow it. It's only a matter of time before some politician wins an election on a platform that calls for an end to insider trading. See Part III, "Current Law."

However, that there is no harm in leaving the law alone is not really true. Promulgating an illusion about how markets work, that there are no transaction costs in law avoidance, no misallocation of resources, no inefficiencies (again, see Part III, "Current Law"), is harmful. If society doesn't always notice, it's because it is able to absorb the cost in the form of higher prices (for everything).

On the other hand, one can leave the law alone, because, in practice, overly broad law is unenforceable. The law doesn't even distinguish between insider buying and insider selling. Should the owner of a listed corporation, who in the middle of the night has a brilliant idea, be forbidden to buy stock in his own company simply because he hasn't yet made his ideas public? Making insider trading illegal has the potential to make all company activity and conversation illegal. Also it discourages firms not listed on the stock market exchange from ever going public. Instead of declaring insider trading illegal, why not simply increase disclosure, increase transparency? That's enforceable.

undermine the stock market, the most efficient system possible for regulating trade between buyers and sellers. In theory, it is an action inconsistent with living in a free society, a society where government does not monitor the lives of private citizens. In reality, however, on occasion, government does have to step in on behalf of citizens when citizens themselves don't step in to stop a probable catastrophe. But the best scenario is for corporations to police their own employees and for government to police its employees. If they don't, bigger government, a leviathan, will.[29]

III. CURRENT LAW

In reaction to Enron, to WorldCom, since the 1930s, in reaction to every business scandal, our nation creates new "current law." Under pressure from voters, politicians feel that they must do something. If not, new politicians will. It is exactly how politicians get elected for the first time—they use scandal to promise to do something. Legal scholars do the same. Their need to publish pushes legal scholars to draft "current" ideas about the law, to use scandal to justify their own additions to and rationale for regulation of the economy.[30]

It's as if the timeless laws of economics, of money, of human nature, can be ignored. It's as if, short of communism, something actually can be done.[31] The Glass–Steagall Act of 1934, for example,

---

[29] Corporations may want their CEOs to be able to profit from inside information as a way to attract creative talent but may not want their bookkeepers to profit. And no one wants government employees to profit from inside information, but again, this can all be controlled by contract.

[30] How often do scholars or politicians proclaim that the public should have more faith in the ability of markets to self-correct? Rarely do politicians or legal scholars declare that government interference slows down the self-correction process, that the Great Depression, about to end in 1933, was prolonged until 1942 precisely because of government interference. (Contraction of the money supply, according to Milton Friedman, was the worst thing that government could have done.)

[31] China, North Korea, Cuba, Cambodia and the Soviet Union are examples of what the Chinese philosopher, Mao Tse Tung, meant by "All political power comes out of the barrel of a gun."

in reaction to the Great Depression, in truth, in reaction to the failure of the Federal Reserve to bail out the banks, severely limited what banks could do in the future. The Act spelled out exactly what kind of loans banks could make, how much interest they could charge, and what services they could provide. Selling stock or selling insurance, for example, was forbidden. The result, of course, of adding all this complication to the market, in the competitive world market of banking, was that American banks fell from being among the top ten in the world, by the 1980s, to having no banks on the list (which is why, in part, we deregulated banks in the 1980s).

Today's "current" law, the Sarbanes–Oxley Act (SOX) of 2002, is the perfect example of politicians going through the motions. The Act is nothing more than restatement of long-standing common business practice, nothing more than a restatement of what self-correcting markets already do. Putting in writing, then, for no other purpose than to instill confidence in the market, what markets already do—analyze and audit to weed out the weak and fraudulent, is redundant. Making it illegal to tear up evidence before a court proceeding, for example, is redundant.[32]

The following summary of operative clauses shows, from a business perspective, just how nonthreatening is the Sarbanes–Oxley Act:[33]

> Section 101: The Board [the oversight board] will have five financially literate members, appointed for five-year terms. Two of the members must be or must have been certified public accountants, and the remaining three must not be and cannot have been CPAs.

---

[32] When corporations knowingly break the law, knowing that the cost of going after them is more than the benefit, knowing that this cost, a transaction cost, exists in free markets precisely because free markets are not perfect, according to Nobel economist Ronald Coase, this is a legitimate reason for some regulation of the economy, even if the countervailing cost is an amount of market inefficiency. However, there really is only one efficient regulation, and that is to impose criminal sanctions with mandatory prison terms on anyone connected with corporate fraud. Are we willing to do this?

[33] AICPA (American Institute of Certified Public Accountants) Summary of Sarbanes–Oxley Act of 2002.

In other words, if you were sick, no more than two out of five of those who treat you can be certified public physicians. Why? The financial gain in keeping you sick is too great a conflict of interest.

> Section 103: [t]he auditor [must] evaluate whether the internal control structure and procedures include records that accurately and fairly reflect the transactions of the issuer, [and] provide reasonable assurance that the transactions are recorded in a manner that will permit the preparation of financial statements in accordance with GAAP.

SOX has to say this (in leaving no stone unturned), but from the perspective of market participants, it's pathetic.

> Section 201: It shall be "unlawful" for a registered public accounting firm to provide any non-audit service to an issuer contemporaneously with the audit, including: (1) bookkeeping or other services related to the accounting records or financial statements of the audit client; (2) financial information systems design and implementation; (3) appraisal or valuation services, fairness opinions, or contribution-in-kind reports (4) actuarial services; (5) internal audit outsource services; (6) management functions or human resources; (7) broker or dealer, investment adviser, or investment banking services; (8) legal services and expert services unrelated to the audit; (9) any other service that the Board determines, by regulation, is impermissible. The Board may, on a case-by-case basis, exempt from these prohibitions any person, issuer, public accounting firm, or transaction, subject to review by the Commission.

Section 201 is very bad law because it flies in the face of how free markets actually work (including how they monitor themselves), which is precisely to ask CPAs for these services. As Glass–Steagall split the banking industry into two parts, retail banking and investment banking, SOX (Sarbanes–Oxley) will split the accounting industry into two parts—retail accounting and investment accounting. And thus, as banks were weakened, so too will accounting firms.[34] But splitting an industry leads to a loss of overall general talent, imposing transaction costs in paying more for talent. It compromises accounting firms' ability to do either job well, and forces firms to spend additional money for legal fees (and other monitoring and regulation costs) to constantly verify that they're not crossing the line (and defend themselves when they do).[35]

Solving, then, the public's perceptions of conflict of interest, of inaccurate accounting, even simply for the Hobbesian notion of creating the appearance of order and control, still create costs, at times even great costs (see Section 601). Instead of simply prosecuting for fraud, for wrongdoing and using jail time as a deterrence, politicians and government create new law, current law, law that creates structural change, law that's universal and includes everyone. The cost of compliance and monitoring, of red tape, is, of course, gladly born by the big accounting firms; they can either absorb it as a cost of doing business or pass it along to their customers. Little firms, however, are wiped out. They can't absorb the costs or pass them along. Deregulation of trucking and airlines during the 1980s, for example, was not asked for by the trucking and airline industries; it was asked for by consumers being overcharged by government enforced monopolies. And in the 1890s, with regulation of the railroads, it was the railroad industry itself, after initially opposing regulation, that ended up asking for it. With regulation, they realized they could consolidate their holdings by buying up weaker railroads and then raising prices, precisely what government regulation authorizes (and offers as an incentive for industry cooperation).

The Glass–Steagall Act of 1933, then, serves as a good predictive model for SOX. Even when changes are only cosmetic, in the long run, costs will be high. This is so because, with government regulation, there is always the added cost of avoidance of the law.

---

[34] If corporations make gross mistakes because accountants within a firm are forbidden to communicate with each other, the loss to society could be greater than is implied by the risk of collusion.

[35] Bartholomew Lee, attorney at law and late Adjunct Professor of Economics, Golden Gate University, San Francisco, CA.

Some U.S. businesses will go offshore, to Bermuda, for example, some will be replaced by foreign firms not subject to U.S. law and some U.S. firms will set themselves up in foreign countries. All of this increases operating costs.

> Section 206: The CEO, Controller, CFO, Chief Accounting Officer or person in an equivalent position cannot have been employed by the company's audit firm during the 1-year period preceding the audit.

> Section 302: The CEO and CFO of each issuer shall prepare a statement to accompany the audit report to certify the "appropriateness of the financial statements and disclosures contained in the periodic report, and that those financial statements and disclosure fairly present, in all material respects, the operations and financial condition of the issuer." A violation of this section must be knowing and intentional to give rise to liability.

> Section 303: It shall be unlawful for any officer or director of an issuer to take any action to fraudulently influence, coerce, manipulate, or mislead any auditor engaged in the performance of an audit for the purpose of rendering the financial statements materially misleading.

> Section 306: Prohibits the purchase or sale of stock by officers and directors and other insiders during blackout periods. Any profits resulting from sales in violation of this section "shall inure to and be recoverable by the issuer." If the issuer fails to bring suit or prosecute diligently, a suit to recover such profit may be instituted by "the owner of any security of the issuer."

Won't this provision encourage lawsuits, even class action lawsuits? The provision is an open invitation. And then, why do blackouts occur? Should government, the SEC, really have the right to shut down the stock market whenever it feels a crash is coming? If a crash is about to occur, there is good reason, and good reason, therefore, not to interfere. Whenever markets reach deep disequilibrium, when goods or services are severely overpriced, when credit is severely overissued, there is always potential for a crash. Does that automatically give government the right to try to prevent it, to try to prolong a condition that's unsustainable in the market? If anyone should impose a blackout, i.e., second-guess the market, it's the stock market. The stock market is itself a private entity.

As stated earlier, during a financial crisis, owners of any business have a moral duty to protect their investment, to sell off quickly if they think that is wise. Shareholders may not have the same inside information (because they are not personally monitoring the corporation), but *they don't need it*. The very act of insider trading brings stock market prices to their true value. Investors must acknowledge that insider trading is a condition of owning stock, a basic fact with respect to how any market works. In truth, such trading is the best index of future market performance.

> Section 401(a): "Each annual and quarterly financial report . . . shall disclose all material off-balance sheet transactions" and "other relationships" with "unconsolidated entities" that may have a material current or future effect on the financial condition of the issuer.

> Section 401(c): SEC shall study off-balance sheet disclosures to determine a) extent of off-balance sheet transactions (including assets, liabilities, leases, losses and the use of special purpose entities); and b) whether generally accepted accounting rules result in financial statements of issuers reflecting the economies of such off-balance sheet transactions to investors in a transparent fashion and make a report containing recommendations to the Congress.

As mentioned earlier, analysts are paid to recommend stock for purchase. This is why the big brokerage houses all recommended the purchase of Enron. The off-balance sheet transactions of Enron were always stated on Enron's financial statements (see Exhibits 1 and 2), and were all in the billions of dollars. If purchasers of stock don't verify for themselves, no one else will. Section 401(c) requires that off-balance sheet transactions be in a transparent fashion, but if the SEC really wants to protect the public, it should advocate that no stock be sold unless purchasers sign an affidavit declaring that they have read and understood the attached financial statement.

> Section 404: Requires each annual report of an issuer to contain an "internal control report", which shall: (1) state the responsibility of management for establishing and maintaining an adequate internal control structure and procedures for financial reporting; and (2) contain an assessment, as of the end of the issuer's fiscal year, of the effectiveness of the internal control structure and procedures of the issuer for financial reporting.

Section 404 may seem like the right thing to do, but, of any provision in the Sarbanes–Oxley Act, it is the most onerous. Section 404 may reduce risk, but at what price? Will a cost-benefit analysis show that the reduction in risk is worth it?

According to *The Economist*, for large companies (companies with market capitalization of over $700,000,000), implementation of SOX costs $8.5 million on average. Small companies (companies with market capitalization of $75,000,000 to $700,000,000), $1.2 million on average. And companies smaller than $75,000,000 have yet to even be asked to comply.[36] According to CRA International, the research firm that did the above study, costs are expected to fall by 40 percent, but this is nowhere near the $91,000 per company that the SEC had initially forecast. And, of course, the burden is disproportionately heavier on smaller firms.

The question is: does society as a whole benefit? Perhaps individual investors will benefit to the extent that there is less risk in investing without personally doing any research into what one purchases (referring again to the main theme of this essay), but if, because of SOX, large firms end up gobbling up smaller ones, i.e., those which can't afford Section 404 monitoring, investors as a

---

[36] *The Economist*, "The Trial of Sarbanes–Oxley," April 22, 2006, p. 59.

whole will then have less choice.[37] But, it is accounting firms that will really benefit. They have an incentive, according to *The Economist*, to be "hyper-vigilant" in implementing SOX.[38] The fact

---

[37] This is not unrelated to the mechanics of a leveraged buyout, to the mechanics of using a firm's equity as the source of the down payment for its very purchase. In other words, large firms will use the price increase as a result of SOX monitoring to create the actual revenue to pay for the elimination of competition.

And this is not unrelated to the possibility that we will be, by bundling together industries, backing into socialism via a corporate state. In the 1920s and '30s, this was at the heart of the fascist argument—controlling industry in the name of economic stability. In the 1920s, it was in response to the perceived threat of Bolshevism; today, it is in response to the perceived threat of corporate fraud.

Under fascism, the cartelization of industry is government policy. Its very purpose is to eliminate competition, to purposely create monopoly pricing (prices higher than market) such that both profitability to a nation's industries and full employment to a nation's workers is guaranteed. This is the fascist formula for economic stability. It works, however, only if the elimination of competition has no effect. It worked in the U.S. during the post World War II years, for example, with the auto industry. Union demand for high wages and benefits was accorded simply by the raising of prices on automobiles. It worked precisely because there was no competition from Japan or Germany. The elimination of competition, however, is the elimination of a market economy.

And this is not unrelated to Nobel economist George Stigler's concentration theory, which says that as an industry shrinks from lack of competition, the likelihood of collusion is directly proportional to the Herfindahl–Hirschman Index. Curiously, in the area of antitrust analysis, in which the Herfindahl–Hirschman Index is used to show how close an industry is to absolute monopoly (the accounting industry, for example, after Enron, down from the Big Five to the Big Three, would score very high on the index—a bad sign), this kind of analysis (that focuses on collusion) strays from the relevant, which is the impact of concentration on competition. The fact that profit is up or that prices are up is irrelevant.

In antitrust analysis, the 1993 U.S. Supreme Court case *Daubert v. Merrell Dow Pharmaceuticals, Inc.* is cited as a reminder that scientific evidence must be reliable, i.e., not "junk science," or else not be admitted. As per SOX Section 404, this would mean that the imposition of additional regulation of industry without reliable scientific data to prove that the cost will not exceed the benefit is inadmissible.

The 1928 U.S. Supreme Court case of *Olmstead v. United States* is also cited with reference to the dissenting opinion by Justice Louis Brandeis, in which Brandeis warns about the advancement of technology and its ability to intrude into protected areas of the constitutional right to privacy. SOX Section 404 is clearly intruding on a business's right to privacy.

And Michael Porter, professor at Harvard Business School and creator of The Institute for Strategy and Competitiveness, is cited as one of the world's leading authorities on competitive strategy and international competitiveness. Porter would remind us that standard economic models of firms and product markets actually capture little of the complexity of the dynamism of competition (and even that economic models require restrictive assumptions that are untenable).

All three, Daubert, Brandeis and Porter, remind us to be careful not to step on something we don't see. In this sense, because SOX Section 404 is stepping on competition, stepping on the very basis of a free market economy, it should not be allowed in its present form.

[38] *The Economist*, "The Trial of Sarbanes–Oxley," p. 60.

that the law, Section 404, is not clear, and the fact that accounting firms, after Enron plus WorldCom, are being audited as closely as are the firms that the accountants are auditing, creates, thus, a field day for accountants.[39]

> Section 601: SEC appropriations for 2003 are increased to $776,000,000. $98 million of the funds shall be used to hire an additional 200 employees to provide enhanced oversight of auditors and audit services required by the Federal securities laws.

First of all, what's wrong with market analysts doing this without charge? $776,000,000 a year is the price of going to war every year. Out of the $776,000,000, $98,000,000 shall be used to hire 200 additional employees. Does this mean that it costs $490,000 per employee? In any case, the cost to society of owning stock is increased by the cost of corporations complying with SOX, by the cost of lost competition; i.e., from the loss to the market of those firms that cannot absorb or pass along the costs of complying, and by the cost of $776,000,000 a year, the amount taxpayers pay out of pocket to fund this SEC appropriation.[40]

> Section 602(c): SEC is to conduct a study of "securities professionals" (public accountants, public accounting firms, investment bankers, investment advisor, brokers, dealer, attorneys) who have been found to have aided and abetted a violation of Federal securities laws.

> Title VIII: It is a felony to "knowingly" destroy or create documents to "impede, obstruct or influence" any existing or contemplated federal investigation.

---

[39] The new regulatory body for accountants is the Public Company Accounting Oversight Board (PCAOB).

[40] It's taxpayers, not corporations, who pay this tax. It's paid by citizens who do not have the personal tax write-offs to avoid it and by the population at large as a regressive consumption tax. Again, because long-term profit is never more than 5 percent, i.e., the time value of money, corporations *have* to pass this tax on to consumers in the form of higher prices, in the form of a higher cost of living to the nation.

[Reality is that a "contemplated federal investigation" is going to conflict with a Corporation's "destruction of documents" policy. Firms that have thousands of pounds of documents have policies for the destruction of documents.]

Employees of issuers and accounting firms are extended "whistleblower protection" that would prohibit the employer from taking certain actions against employees who lawfully disclose private employer information to, among others, parties in a judicial proceeding involving a fraud claim. Whistleblowers are also granted a remedy of special damages and attorney's fees.

What Section 602(c) and Title VIII have in common is that they seem reasonable, seem to be protecting "the little guy." But there is no mention of how underlying biases can distort final outcomes. An example of law set up to protect "the little guy" is rent control. Because rent control laws do not have a sunset provision, rent control ends up favoring renters at the expense of landlords and at the expense of basic property rights. A "study," then, by the SEC of how securities professionals violate securities' law will end up as an attack on these professionals. It will start off calling for more research but end up calling for more government control over the market. An unbiased study, by a university economics department or law school, for example, might lead to different conclusions.

And protecting employees from reprisal when they divulge private information to investigators has some of the negative elements of affirmative action. Corporations will find themselves defending themselves from incompetent and disgruntled employees hiding behind "whistleblower protection."[41]

Title IX: SEC given authority to seek court freeze of extraordinary payments to director, offices, partners, controlling persons, agents or employees.

---

[41] It's the reason why bad civil service employees, public school teachers, for example, are never fired.

In a free economy, do we want this? Why would this not, over time, become a right to freeze less than exorbitant payments?

> Section 1001: It is the sense of Congress that the Federal income tax return of a corporation should be signed by the chief executive officer of such corporation.

The Sarbanes–Oxley Act is typical government regulation. It's too late (like legislation that followed the savings and loan scandal in the 1990s); not necessary (because the market does it naturally); a burden on business that gets passed on to consumers in the form of higher prices; has no effect on fraud (the only real issue); and has no effect on new forms of creative financing (financing that emerges in the wake of every business scandal).[42]

Consider Lehman Brothers' new security called ECAPS, for Enhanced Capital Advantaged Preferred Securities. For the issuer, this new security eliminates risk. It calls for a long maturity, up to sixty years, interest payments as a write-off, and during hard times, the right to defer payments altogether. The IRS allows it. But how is this different than issuing stock? To credit rating agencies, it looks like equity, in which the payment of dividends can be postponed at will and for which there is no maturity, and to the IRS, it looks like debt. ECAPS, then, is the perfect example of how Wall Street, i.e., the market, responds to complicated law. It's an example of Wall Street taking any law and converting it into a business opportunity. It's precisely what it means for the market to go around. But look what's created—another opportunity for scandal. In other words, why would anyone take the risk of purchasing an ECAPS? Because the rate of return is high? That in itself is a tip-off. If a rate of return is high, risk is high. And if it's a bond that can be converted into a stock (a convertible debenture), will the holder have voting rights, or will it be preferred stock? Are these things spelled out?

---

[42] To the extent that it provides incentives to camouflage financing (to the detriment of the market's access to relevant information), SOX will drive financing underground.

Consider that regulation is like campaign financing reform.[43] It produces results that are the opposite of what is intended. For one, because regulation leads to higher costs, it leads to the elimination of smaller firms.[44] Less efficient than large firms (in that they do not have the same economies of scale that allows them to absorb the cost of regulation), small firms are forced to raise their prices, which, without some form of government subsidy, forces them out of business. Regulation, then, ends up fostering monopoly and cartel, exactly as under fascism in the 1930s in Italy, Germany and Japan—efficiency and stability at the expense of competition. Although the new regulations under Sarbanes–Oxley are mild, the Act itself still suffers from the same defect as does all government regulation—it pushes society in the wrong direction. It leads to further and faster regulation. It leads to undemocratic control over society via corporate governance, to the perpetuation of only the strongest corporations, of only the strongest politicians.[45] It leads to the perpetuation of incumbents and their contributors.[46]

Again, consider that disclosure doesn't stop investment, doesn't force investors to personally pay attention. Before the 1928 stock market crash, investors weren't personally verifying financial statements, before the 1987 stock market crash, investors weren't verifying, before the 1990s real estate crash, investors weren't verifying, and before the 2000 Enron crash, along with the dot.com bust, investors weren't verifying. And today, with stock and real estate valued at twenty to forty times earnings, investors are still not

[43] Bartholomew Lee, per personal conversation.

[44] Gerrymandering, a form of self-regulation in politics, leads to the elimination of nonincumbent and less-well-financed candidates.

[45] Technically, corporate governance has to do with how corporations are governed, i.e., with the policies of its board of directors, but in politics, it has to do with the extent to which corporations run society.

[46] Social Security, health care and education are three problems today. They are problems, however, precisely because they are regulated by government. Like banking, trucking and the airlines in the 1980s, Social Security, health care and education would benefit from deregulation. If left to the market, all three would be provided for at half their present cost. They would be provided by entrepreneurs and with twice the benefits.

verifying. You can protect against fraud, but you can't protect against irrationality.[47]

IV. Discussion

There is no end to corporate dishonesty. In a competitive market economy, the incentives to lie are simply too great. The pressure to show higher earnings, which translate to higher values, and thus higher stock prices, leads to underhanded behavior.[48] It is why Shell Oil (Royal Dutch Shell Group) refrained from disclosing in 2002 (and until they were caught two years afterward) that it had huge shortfalls in proven oil and natural gas reserves. A July 2002 executive memorandum talked of creating "an 'external storyline,' and 'investor relations script' that tried to 'highlight major projects fueling growth,' 'stress the strength' of existing resources, and to minimize the significance of reserves as a measure of growth."[49]

---

[47] In economics, there is the concept, "rational ignorance," which may have some bearing. In politics, for example, voters, as individuals, find that the benefit to them personally of verifying every proposed legislative act, every word uttered by candidates running for office, is not worth the cost. It's rational ignorance that explains why so many people don't vote (or vote simply a party line of prepackaged ideological policy). But special interest groups do vote. As individuals, they support candidates and individual pieces of legislation. The benefit to special interest groups does exceed the cost.

In business, it's the same. When all the facts in a corporation's financial statement are not disclosed, or when government regulation and taxation pervert a market, investors don't analyze the stocks they purchase. To investors, when business activity goes underground, the cost of analyzing is more than the benefit.

Another kind of ignorance, however, is pure ignorance—ignorance of how markets and an economy work. An economy has to do with the providing of goods and services (knowing that most services exist simply to make the production of goods less costly). Accountants are service providers. Asking them to be completely independent of the firms they audit, of the firms that need their advice, runs counter to how markets work. This is so because when goods or services necessary to an economy cannot be provided legally, they will be provided illegally. It means that if SOX is fully enforced, it will push more of the economy underground.

[48] If, by law, companies were required to pay dividends, then earnings would have to be real.

[49] Stephen Labaton and Jeff Gerth, "Oil Giant's Officials Knew of Gaps in Reserves in '02," *New York Times,* March 9, 2004, https://www.nytimes.com/2004/03/09/business/oil-giant-s-officials-knew-of-gaps-in-reserves-in-02.html.

Is this really important? Yes, because oil and natural gas reserves represent a central asset of an energy company. "Reserves . . . are closely followed by analysts and investors as an indicator of future profitability." It seems that 1 billion barrels of reserves "[were] no longer fully aligned" with SEC rules, and that "an additional 1.3 billion barrels were at risk, because it was no longer certain that they could be extracted during the remaining term of the licenses between Shell and three foreign countries."[50]

Again, is this really important? Maybe not. Perhaps the executives at Shell felt they would find more oil or negotiate new leases, that shortages or underestimation happen all the time, and that there is no need to scare off stockholders. Here are the exact words of part of the memorandum as displayed in the *New York Times*:

> Again, if required, note that Shell has experienced prolonged periods throughout its recent history during which organic proved RRR [reserves replacement ratio] was less than 100 percent and yet has continued to deliver world-class technical and financial performance.[51]

Those responsible for the memorandum have been fired, but were they fired because they got caught or because they lied? Perhaps executives should be more careful about putting things in writing, but the incentive for this kind of manipulation comes from the fact that Shell is a publicly traded company and will always do what it can to avoid having to publicly proclaim bad news. A private company is not under this kind of scrutiny. The only lying a private company has to do is to adjust its books for tax purposes. For publicly traded companies, George Soros once said that "artificially raising profit is what the successful business executive is hired for— there are even 'off the shelf' accounting scams (called SPEs— special purpose entities [see Enron]) for hiding aspects of the

---

[50] Labaton and Gerth, "Oil Giant's Officials Knew."

[51] Labaton and Gerth, "Oil Giant's Officials Knew."

business that make less pleasing reading for potential investors."[52] Again, this is why, before investing in the market, personal verification and inside information are necessary.

And this kind of dishonesty also applies to banks. The public thinks of banks, because they are responsible for other people's money, depositors' money, as a natural market check on risky investor behavior. But in a regulated economy, where banks are often bailed out by the government, and where moral hazard problems are created (not only by the possibility of a government bailout but also by the existence of deposit insurance), this is absolutely untrue. Banks sometimes will turn down a corporation for a loan, forcing the corporation to consider issuing stock, but if a bank sees a lot of profit in a deal, it will do the very opposite; in exchange for a percentage of that profit, it will make a loan for the entire amount of the project; it will require absolutely no equity on the part of the borrower. This is what led to the collapse of the savings and loans in the 1990s. And this is what led to the collapse of Enron in 2000. Banks weren't defrauded. They were the ones doing the defrauding. They were the ones who helped Enron design its schemes. Consider Project Nahanni, a project named after a Canadian national park known for its wolves. In this deal, Enron borrowed money from Citigroup to buy treasury bills. Within days it sold the treasury bills and paid the money back to Citigroup. According to Floyd Norris, an economics writer for the *New York Times*, why did they bother? Because Citigroup told Enron that it could report the $500 million it needed from selling the bills as operating cash flow. And Enron did just that, assuring its investors and credit rating agencies that its profits were genuine.

Citigroup wasn't "looking the other way." It was, instead, dreaming up ways to do more of this. According to Floyd Norris, it was a J.P. Morgan executive who said Enron was "enticed to pay a premium" over normal interest rates to obtain money in ways that would be, in the words of Neal Batson, Enron's court-appointed

---

[52] Martin Cohen, *101 Ethical Dilemmas* (New York: Routledge, 2003), p. 205.

trustee, "inscrutable to rating agencies, creditors and other users of Enron's financial statements."[53]

Another "inscrutable" deal involves J.P. Morgan, Deutsche Bank and Bank of America. In 2001, the three banks helped WorldCom sell $12 billion in debt, although the three banks had doubts about WorldCom's financial soundness. Because the banks papered over WorldCom's financial problems, investors lost billions of dollars.[54]

Curiously, the reverse is also a deception. Freddie Mac, in 2001, because interest rates were falling, took in way too much profit (as annual payments remained constant). It created a series of "linked swaps" of income in order to smooth over its gains, i.e., a system of income averaging. It's not clear that anyone was hurt, but because it is fraud, it confuses investment analysts.[55] They have no way to make forecasts, no way to advise investors.[56] It also creates a situation where insiders might benefit. All of this is no different than the accounting rules for pension funds that allow companies to act "as if" the stock went up as predicted, i.e., maintain lower reserves regardless of reality.

And then in 2005, American International Group (AIG) was prosecuted for false income averaging, for making it appear that, every year, no matter what was happening in the market, the public

---

[53] Floyd Norris, "Bankrupt Thinking: How the Banks Aided Enron's Deception," *New York Times*, August 1, 2003, https://www.nytimes.com/2003/08/01/business/bankrupt-thinking-how-the-banks-aided-enron-s-deception.html.

[54] Gretchen Morgenson, *New York Times*, March 15, 2004.

[55] Even if these "linked swaps" were disclosed, it's still fraud, it's still gaming GAAP, it's still declaring that income received in one year is received in another year. As common law, it's not fraud—a lie upon which one relies to one's detriment (although it may be securities fraud, a violation of Rule 10b-5, Employment of Manipulative and Deceptive Devices, of the Securities and Exchange Act of 1934), but in a moral sense, it's fraud to the extent that shareholders were deprived of information that would have changed their behavior. The value of Freddie Mac stock, when Freddie Mac was taking in substantially more money than it reported, would have been substantially higher.

[56] It means that transaction costs in acquiring information go way up, further encouraging rational ignorance.

could count on AIG's income being constant.[57] Owner and CEO Hank Greenberg was forced to remove himself, and AIG was fined $1.6 billion.

Did AIG act recklessly? Did Hank Greenberg bankrupt the company? No; he took a chance. If 10 percent of a firm's assets are not at risk, a firm is not operating creatively. By not operating creatively, not only will a firm lose creative talent, but it will lose market share to those very firms that hire away that talent. Since the $1.6 billion at risk (the fine) was less than 10 percent of AIG's $20 billion assets, the benefit of false income averaging was that AIG's shares traded at higher than market price, according to *The Economist*, at four times rather than at the insurance industry norm of two times book value.[58] And the cost, if AIG were caught, was that share price would return to market.[59] Is that really a loss?

Again, analysts interested only in producing reports that encourage buying didn't verify, and again, investors didn't verify. If stock prices rise and fall in relation to a rise and fall in net income, the only way for firms to maintain constant earnings is to manipulate the numbers. To believe, however, that firms, year in and year out, maintain constant earnings is total gullibility.

Summary: *Insider trading is inherent to the stock market. Even more, its effect is actually positive—by causing stock market prices to adjust faster than they would otherwise, it brings efficiency to the market. And it forces investors to be vigilant. It forces investors to purchase stock with the same care as they would purchase real estate or art. It forces investors not to rely on advisors nor to look to government for protection. To the contrary, it exposes government regulation, the Sarbanes–Oxley Act, for example, for its inherent weakness, namely, that it is overly broad and too expensive to implement. Regulation of the market is almost always this. It*

---

[57] AIG was prosecuted by the SEC, by the office of the New York attorney general and by other regulators.

[58] "The World's Largest Insurer Tries to Write Off Its Past," *The Economist*, February 11, 2006.

[59] In the short run, perhaps below market. AIG's share price dropped from 62 cents to 17 cents.

eliminates those who cannot afford to comply, i.e., small corporations, it eliminates competition and it creates monopoly.

Conclusion: Insider trading, then, like the market provision of any good, legal or otherwise, is inherent to the stock market. It is market reality. Government response, regulation, is always too late, is a burden on business that gets passed on to consumers in the form of higher prices, has no effect on fraud and has no effect on new forms of creative financing, the very means by which regulation is circumvented.

SOCIAL SECURITY*

I. INTRODUCTION

Social Security is insurance. The fundamental problem with Social Security is that it doesn't operate as insurance. It operates as an unfunded retirement system.[60] How did that come about? It came about at its creation, in 1935, when President Franklin D. Roosevelt forced the Social Security Act upon an opposed Congress.[61] At that moment, the only thing Congress could do to restrain the president was insist that Social Security be *totally unfunded.*[62] Congress

---

*Article originally appeared in *Journal of Law and Business* 16, 2009, pp. 19–40. Reedited December 10, 2022.

[60] Insurance is an expense for protection against future financial loss. To the buyer of insurance, the yearly premium, in relation to an unpredictable loss, is insignificant. To the provider of insurance, the yearly premium, in relation to an almost completely predictable loss (based on actuarial tables) spread out over thousands, if not millions, of policyholders, is also insignificant.

If Social Security functioned as insurance, it would function as it should, as a safety net for those who somehow lost the money or assets in their retirement account.

[61]See Part V, Law and Social Security.

[62] "These [Trust Fund] balances are available to finance future benefit payments and other trust fund expenditures—but only in a bookkeeping sense. These funds are not set up to be pension funds, like the funds of private pension plans. They do not consist of real economic assets that can be drawn down in the future to fund benefits. Instead, they are claims on the Treasury, that, when redeemed, will have to be financed by raising taxes, borrowing from the public, or reducing benefits or other expenditures. (Continued on next page)

trusted neither itself nor the president with the use of an almost unlimited and ever-increasing source of funds. What they created was the pay-as-you-go system we have today, a system dependent on continuous contribution from citizens below the age of retirement to pay for those already retired. The rate of return on citizens' contributed money was calculated as if the money were deposited in risk-free savings at the lowest possible rate, i.e., that of U.S. Treasuries.[63]

But where does government get the right to take 15 percent of everyone's wages (7½ percent employee contribution, 7½ percent employer contribution) and then hold it for them at the lowest possible rate of return? Because government has the right to tax. Social Security is a tax. It is not insurance. It is not a safety net for those who cannot take care of themselves, something that could be paid for from a small income or consumption tax. It is nothing less than government extracting a citizen's personal retirement funds (and at best, managing them by benign neglect).[64] It is an indignity and, like all personal income tax, unconstitutional.[65] It is an insult to a free people to have their income taken away only to have it given back in old age (almost without interest) for the sole reason that

---

(Continued from previous page) The existence of large trust fund balances, therefore, does not, by itself, make it easier for the government to pay benefits." (Office of Management and Budget, *Analytical Perspectives, Budget of the United States Government, Fiscal Year 2000*, p. 337 as quoted by David C. John, "Answering the Top 10 Myths about Social Security Reform," *Heritage Foundation Report*, no. 1613, Washington, DC, November 18, 2002, https://www.heritage.org/social-security/report/answering-the-top-10-myths-about-social-security-reform.)

[63] 1 percent in 2004; 0.45 percent in 2010.

[64] Today, Social Security comprises 22 percent of total federal government spending. However, all social insurance—Social Security, disability, survivor insurance, unemployment insurance and Medicare—comprises 37 percent of federal spending. Martin Feldstein, "Rethinking Social Insurance," *American Economic Review* 95, no. 1 (March 2005), https://www.aeaweb.org/articles?id=10.1257/0002828053828545.

[65] It is constitutional in that the 16th Amendment authorizes Congress to tax, but the 16th Amendment was ratified in 1913, 126 years after adoption of the Constitution, and would never have been ratified in 1789 (see footnote 90). Nevertheless, even if we allow an income tax to pay for Social Security, we should at least be aware that government's confiscation of 15 percent of citizens' wages is more than is necessary. If it is for insurance, 1 percent is sufficient. If it is for retirement and other social insurance, 4 percent, if compounded annually at 4 percent, is sufficient. (In the early 1960s, contribution to Social Security was still 6 percent, but by 2020, will probably be 20 percent.) (Continued on next page)

progressives, those who want to manage the lives of other people, believe that citizens cannot be counted on to save on their own (or that the free market cannot be depended upon to guarantee it). In a free society, and certainly in a Jeffersonian society, a society that believes that citizens can and do think for themselves, government cannot assume this.[66]

Another approach to Social Security is to excuse all citizens below the age of 30 from having to pay any Social Security tax, provided that 15 percent of their earnings are invested in solid assets,

---

(Continued from previous page)

From 6 percent, how did it get to 15 percent? According to Alan Greenspan, during the Nixon administration, Social Security was so flush with reserves that Congress took the fateful step of indexing benefits to inflation. As inflation soared through the 1970s, so, too, did cost-of-living adjustments (COLA). The inability of Congress to reduce COLA whenever inflation is out of control stems from but also reinforces Congress' propensity to create benefits without specifying the means by which they are to be funded. This has led to deficit spending in every fiscal year since 1970, with the exception of the 1998–2001 surplus from the stock market boom. (Alan Greenspan, *The Age of Turbulence* (New York: Penguin Books, 2007), p. 481.)

However, according to Greenspan, this shifting of real resources to perform such functions imparts a bias toward inflation. In the political arena, pressure for lower interest rates and for easier credit, plus fiscal measures to boost employment and avoid the unpleasantness of downward adjustments in wages, really imply that Americans tolerate inflation as an acceptable cost of the modern welfare state. In contrast, there was almost zero inflation for the previous 300 years.

It is zero inflation, however, price stability and currency stability, that allows the market to adjust quickly to booms and busts. It is zero inflation that allows suppliers not to have to factor in government intervention and regulation by resorting to needless price increases, which in turn leads to unwanted production (unsold inventory), which in turn leads to unemployment. In other words, inflation, i.e., nominal prices which exceed real prices, means, among other things, that even COLA will not completely keep up, that the value of citizens' personal savings will be reduced every year, that a nation's standard of living will be reduced every year, that the free market's self-correction process will be weakened (that the workings of the invisible hand will be weakened), that innovation and production will be discouraged (because there will be less opportunity) and, in the end, that capitalism's ability to create wealth will be weakened.

[66] In both cases, government should not assume that if it allows people to privately provide for their own retirement, government will just end up picking up the tab via an enormous safety net paid out of taxes; that without Social Security there will be riots and people dying in the streets. This is the Hobbesian argument. Acceptance of the argument, however, prevents the real solution—that government require all citizens to individually contribute to a retirement account. (The real solution is not that government *be* the retirement account.)

e.g., in a home or in the stock market.[67] For those who fear this approach, a compromise would be to have one-half of an individual retirement account (IRA) invested in risk-free government Treasuries (or if not one-half, some sliding-scale percentage in relation with age, 50 percent at age 50, for example). The whole purpose would be to encourage young people to provide for themselves, to invest for the future, to acquire assets (even to encourage inheritance to be passed to children while they are young). If by age 30 citizens had not acquired sufficient assets, then government might require a Social Security tax, and up to as much as 20 percent. We are not Europe. If Americans want more socialism, they should move to a more socialist country such as Canada or France, but not try, through progressive legislation, to foist it upon America's rare form of economic freedom.

There are good economic reasons for this. The best is that any service, when provided by the private sector (private firms or oneself), costs far less than when provided by government (a third party). This efficiency is a principal advantage of living in a free market economy, one reason the U.S. has such a high standard of living. When government provides services, Social Security or unemployment insurance, for example, costs run so high that the services eventually transform themselves. Social Security, for example, transformed from insurance to a retirement system.

It is not only that government-provided social insurance programs cost more but that they also have undesirable effects on the economy, on incentives, on economic growth. Government-provided long-term unemployment insurance raises unemployment;[68]

---

[67] Perhaps in the stock market as a whole, rather than in individual stocks. (Note: It is a myth that if the Social Security trust fund had been invested in stocks it would lose billions of dollars every time the stock market declines. This is to focus only on the short term. Long-term, since 1802, stocks have earned 7 percent on average, and since 1860, on average, 10 percent.)

[68] In the 1990s and mid-2000s, while the U.S. was at 4 percent and 5 percent unemployment, France and Germany, two quasi-socialist economies, were experiencing between 10 and 15 percent.

retirement pensions induce early retirement and depress savings;[69] and health insurance increases medical costs.[70] Again, it is because our system of social insurance is not insurance. It's a transfer back of prepaid contributions. And not only are the prepaid contributions insufficient to pay for future service, but they also include an element of reverse redistribution. Money gets transferred from poor to rich. This happens because the rich live longer and consume more health care than do the poor. Couple this with the fact that fewer people contribute to Social Security than there are retirees, and it is clear that Social Security cannot survive without government subsidy.[71]

And social insurance is expensive for another reason. It is not welfare. Welfare is at least *means-tested*. It is paid to those whose income or assets have fallen below some level—Medicaid, food stamps, subsidized housing, school lunch, for example. Social insurance, however, is paid out when some *event* occurs in an individual's life regardless of income or assets—unemployment benefits if you lose your job; Medicare if you are ill and over 65; Social Security if you are over 62; disability insurance if you are unable to work; survivor benefits to widows and children of deceased workers.[72]

---

[69] In France, a schoolteacher on the day of his or her 65th birthday must walk out of the classroom. In France, staying longer is the punishable crime of purposely depriving a young person of a job.

[70] When health insurance has no or low deductibles, its use is increased, and with increased use comes higher price. Medicaid and Medicare, for example, increase the demand for health care. People who would not demand such a high level of health care (because they can't afford it on their own or because they would not want to pay for it on their own) demand more, and push price even further.

[71] Although 15 percent of everyone's wages is contributed to Social Security (15 percent plus 2.9 percent Medicare), three times what is necessary, this is still not enough. Similarly in public education, although teachers always ask for more money, what is collected is still twice what is necessary. This is what it means to have government services. (See David Parker, *Economic Commentary on the Budget of the San Francisco Unified School District*, 2003, manuscript at Golden Gate University Library, San Francisco.)

Plus, government subsidy is paid for mostly by middle-class taxpayers, who, unlike corporations or high-income individuals, do not have the tax write-offs or the ability to pass on the tax in the form of higher prices or wages.

[72] Feldstein, *"Rethinking Social Insurance."*

Social Security also ignores permanent or lifetime income of recipients, ignores the effect of social insurance on the incentive to accumulate funds for a rainy day. Thus, Social Security benefits that replace more than 50 percent of after-tax pre-retirement income significantly reduce the incentive to save for old age. Unemployment benefits that replace more than 50 percent of after-tax wages have a similar effect on saving to finance spells of unemployment.[73]

II. Economic Consequences

Again, the problem with government provision of services is that because government is not as efficient as the private sector, government delivery of services costs more than if delivered by the private sector. In economics, this difference, which comes out of taxes, is considered a waste, a "deadweight loss" to society. And deadweight loss increases with the tendency of government to expand. Social Security is the perfect example. It transforms what should be a means-tested insurance program for specific individuals in need into a huge event-driven poverty program for everyone. The deadweight loss from this waste is shown in the following two graphs:[74] [75]

In the graph below, the shaded area *above* market price (P* = $1,000) is called consumer surplus (CS). Those consumers on the demand curve at point B, for example, for personal reasons are willing to pay $10,000 instead of $1,000 for the goods and services

---

[73] Feldstein, "*Rethinking Social Insurance.*"

[74] In economics, a deadweight loss is the loss of consumer or producer surplus that is not balanced by a gain somewhere else, yet has to be paid for. By definition, the result is a loss in standard of living.

[75] When writing for the general public, economists do not make their points well because they do not use the best tool they have, a supply-and-demand graph. They do not use the graph because they know that the eyes of the reader glaze over every time he or she sees it (even if he or she has had a year of economics in high school or college). Given the fact that economic principles are abstract (so few in number: abstract of necessity), it is understandable that economists' arguments are ignored.

they need. Consumers between points B and E can thus purchase for $1,000 what they would have paid much more for (as much as $10,000). The difference is their consumer surplus. The shaded area *below* market price is called producer surplus (PS). Those producers on the supply curve at point D, for whatever reasons—they're more efficient, for example—are willing to supply goods and services at $100 instead of $1,000. Any producer between D and E will get the market price of $1,000 for their products, although they would have accepted much less. The difference is their producer surplus.

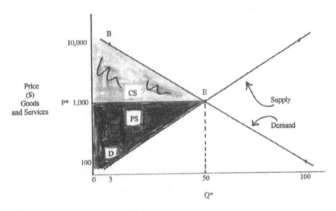

But what happens when government imposes a tax, a Social Security tax, for example? Consumers will have less money in their hands, and less money buys fewer goods and services. Consumers who were at point E (market equilibrium) move back to point F (see next graph), which means they will pay more yet receive less. Producers then will move back to point G (which means they will produce less yet receive more).[76] In other words, producers do not care—they simply raise their price from $1,000 to $2,000, the new market price, P[1]. But consumers care—they end up paying $2,000 instead of $1,000, buying 40 different goods and services instead of 50; their standard of living drops 20 percent.[77]

---

[76] At point E, total revenue was $50,000 ($1,000 x 50). At point F, total revenue is $80,000 ($2,000 x 40).

[77] But when producers produce less, even if at a higher price, they need fewer employees. A tax, therefore, not only lowers the standard of living but raises unemployment. (Note also that the area of producer surplus has increased. It now infringes on consumer surplus.)

The deadweight loss is shown in the graph below:

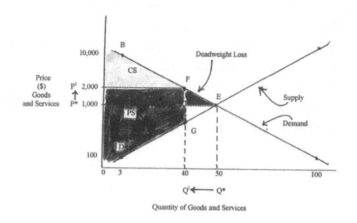

Quantity of Goods and Services

The deadweight loss to society from a government tax is no different than the deadweight loss to society from the presence of monopolies. Attempting to increase their profits, monopolies also cut back production to point G, the same production point as after the tax. Again consumers will, then, not only pay more but obtain less, while producers will produce less yet obtain more. In economics, monopolies are always given as an example of market failure, as an example of the need for government to intervene, to break them up, to encourage competition, to save the market from itself. But is there not a conflict between government breaking up monopolies to eliminate deadweight loss and, then, paying for that with a tax that creates deadweight loss?[78]

In France and Germany, deadweight loss from social insurance is so high their economies can no longer pass along the cost with higher prices. Instead, corporations lay off workers and then look for ways to increase productivity. One way they increase productivity is

---

[78] There may be value in breaking up monopolies, but, according to Bartholomew Lee, economist and attorney at law, the present value of the loss to society from taxation, because taxation tends to be temporary, is greater than the present value of the loss to society from the creation of monopolies. The former is a result of static analysis (what government and economists normally do), the latter is the result of dynamic analysis (what business normally does).

to increase capital investment—investment in plants, machinery and technology. Investment in capital rather than labor explains why France and Germany remain competitive even while their unemployment rate remains high. (The unintended consequence of unionization and high levels of social insurance is that manufacturing is made more efficient.)

Yet what socialist nations refuse to acknowledge, but Karl Marx understood, is that socialism is possible only in rich countries. A country has to be able to afford the waste, to have a market economy first in order to afford socialism. Because it is always difficult to balance the right amount of governmental and private services in deciding just how much socialism to let creep in, nations must constantly monitor benefits to see that they are worth their cost. The difficulty (one of the reasons socialism fails) is that the full extent of the cost is not evident. The loss of incentive to save for retirement, for example, (or for periods of unemployment, when you are counting on Social Security or unemployment checks), or to keep medical costs down (when you are expecting all medical bills to be paid), are major unseen costs.

And the problem is further compounded because these unseen costs, which are economic in nature, are seen by too many people as being social in nature, which leads inevitably to their solution being political in nature. Too many people believe categorically that social benefits always outweigh their costs, that, in fact, it is the very purpose of the political process to make certain that social benefits are not denied simply because a nation doesn't want to pay for them. In France, for example, a nation with an ideological majority to the left, the majority laugh at arguments asserting that the real cost to society of social insurance is the loss of individual liberty. As progressives, the French believe that they have moved on from that outdated notion. To the French, equality and brotherhood always trump liberty.[79] To the French, democracy is the will of the people, not the sanctity of written law.[80]

The U.S. suffers from the same misconceptions. It is why the underlying problem of Social Security is not addressed. Curiously, however, the fact that Social Security will be insolvent within a few years is not, according to Martin Feldstein, the underlying problem.[81] According to Feldstein, the underlying problem is that people are living longer and that there is a permanent trend toward increased longevity.

Because the underlying problem of insolvency cannot be addressed by a pay-as-you-go system, Feldstein is concerned with problems of transition from government-provided Social Security to personal retirement accounts. He is concerned that government may have to borrow to do this, that the transition may or may not have an effect on national savings and consumption; or that the extent of the problem may depend on the extent to which growth in federal debt is less than growth in the economy. These are some of the economic and financial problems associated with converting Social Security into individual social insurance accounts. But these arguments include some false issues. For one, at least in the U.S., government does not control the economy. The fact, for example, that long-term interest rates have been low for the last 15 years (1996–2010) has nothing to do with the Federal Reserve having cut short-term rates, the discount rate, but everything to do with the fact that the market supply of loanable funds exceeded their demand. And two, government does not control social conditions. The fact that

---

[79] *Sécurité, Égalité, Fraternité.*

[80] The French could never live under a constitution. They could never be happy without the ability to instantly change the law (as things come up). To the French, tyranny of the majority is a nonissue. Although Americans have a history of living under a constitution, i.e., of not changing the law every time something comes up, even if progressive ideas such as Social Security do manage to creep in, still, today, if given the opportunity to create a new Constitution, what Americans would create would look nothing like that produced by the Founding Fathers. It would look like French law, with more concern for general welfare than for principles of freedom.

[81] Harvard economist Feldstein has been writing on Social Security for over 40 years. See "Rethinking Social Insurance," *American Economic Review*, March 2005, pp. 1–24, one of his many essays on the subject.

government has money to spend does not change the fact that money is neither the problem nor the solution to social problems. The real issue with respect to social insurance is that government should not be involved in citizens' personal financial decisions.[82]

III. POLITICAL CONSEQUENCES

What is missing from all the arguments in favor of government intervention in the affairs of a nation is that the intervention comes

---

[82] A government safety net or a government guarantee of retirement funds is another issue altogether, a minor issue. However, transitioning from government provision of social insurance to a system of individual retirement accounts is a major issue (according to Alan Greenspan, $1 trillion up front). That does not mean, however, that it should not be done. It just means that nations that transfer services from government to the private sector will experience pain. The pain cannot be avoided—it is the price citizens pay for having turned over their duty to take care of themselves to the state. (See Part IV, Privatization, for an example of how one country, Chile, transitioned out of social security.)

The U.S. is like every other nation. In response to political pressure, the U.S. refuses to abandon government provision of social insurance (referred to as "The third rail of American politics," something too hot to handle). To the contrary, expenditure is increased every year. Medicare, for example, now includes prescription drugs.

Why is it, then, that conservatives or the Republican Party do not advocate against this? For one, they fear losing an election, but the main reason is that they are waiting, perhaps perversely, for the budget deficit to mushroom into a financial crisis. As President Reagan increased defense spending to a level that the Soviet Union could not afford, so, too, President George W. Bush increased domestic spending to a level that the U.S. cannot afford. Conservatives have decided that creating a crisis is the *only* way to force Congress to cut back spending, to consider for example, privatizing Social Security. This is called "starve the beast."

Still, "starve the beast" will fail. Combining horse-traded votes related to increased spending for the war in Iraq with the political reality of raising taxes, the Democratic Party will never allow an increase in revenue to be used to retire the budget deficit. In 2000, Alan Greenspan suggested that the enormous budget surplus (at the time) be saved, that it be used for debt reduction. George W. Bush said absolutely not, that it would end up being used for additional spending, that Alan Greenspan had too much faith in Congress. (See Greenspan, *The Age of Turbulence*, p. 16.) In other words, even if "starve the beast" creates a crisis, the crisis will be resolved by raising income taxes and not by cutting spending. We cannot escape the European model.

The U.S. government is not going to crash, but examples of the kind of crash conservatives are looking for do already exist in the private sector. General Motors offered its employees a buyout of their pension plan, a cash settlement at a deep discount that employees could then deposit in their personal retirement accounts. The obvious lesson is that these individuals would have been far better off had they always had their own retirement accounts.

145

with a price—a loss of freedom. Loss of freedom, however, *is* the Hobbesian trade-off, *is* the cost of living in a free society—paying off a certain percentage of the population with social programs. It is exactly what Social Security means—insurance that cannot be avoided, why, in a free society, there will always be populist politicians who run on a platform of providing ever more government services. This platform wins elections, but the fact remains that the platform is based on the underlying belief that markets cannot solve society's problems. As such, the platform is not one based on principle, on the principle of individual liberty, individual responsibility, on the Jeffersonian notion that citizens can and do think for themselves. The Left may accept this in theory but cannot rise above the theory to actually permit the idea of very limited government to become public policy. They're afraid.

The Left, the majority of the world's population, does not believe that in a civilized world, citizens should be abandoned to the unchecked forces of a market economy. The Left, proudly accepting its Hobbesian fear, makes no distinction between government provision of relief, a safety net, and government provision of full social insurance and universal health care. The Left does not believe that the inefficient use of resources that this entails leads to a lower standard of living. The Left does not believe that today, in the U.S. and in Europe, the exaggerated condition of their economic problems is a direct result of government intervention in the economy.

The Left does not believe any of this because (thanks to the Left) the world has become used to government intervention *and* has become used to the Right, at least in Europe and the U.S., not reacting very forcefully. Less affected because wealthier, the Right has less incentive; plus, resistance is politically unpopular. Unpopular, however, for a curious reason. At their inception, new government programs may be reasonable. Curious, however, because the result is always the same: the poor and middle class bear the burden. They're paying for it. Social Security, modeled in part upon Bismarck's socialism, in 1935 scheduled retirement at age 65. In the 1870s, what German workers were not told was that their life expectancy was 35; and in 1935, what U.S. workers were not told was that their life expectancy was 61. Perversely, then, at the time, the outlay for social security *was* reasonable. The poor paid in and got nothing back. Today, baby boomers expect to get a lot back, and up to the age of 90. In 2011, when boomers start retiring, with half as many workers paying into Social Security as will be receiving it, this will be an impossibility.[83] Consider that when Social Security began in 1935, during the Great Depression, when many people really did need relief, that the first check was not even cut until 1940. At its inception, then, Social Security was reasonable. At its conclusion, like almost all government programs, it has become unreasonable.

The following are some examples of what it costs today to live in a free society:

1. Individuals lose the right to provide for their retirement as they see fit. They do not completely lose the right, but when government provides Social Security, in reality only those who can afford individual retirement accounts in addition to social security retain the right. Parents paying property taxes for public schools and then paying again to send their children to private schools are in the same position. Only those parents who can afford both retain the right to provide a good education for their children. Thus, those individuals and parents lose income, lose the right to spend that income on something else (to not have to pay twice for the same service).

2. Individuals lose ownership. The 1960 Supreme Court case *Flemming v. Nestor* explicitly says that Americans have no ownership rights to the money they pay into Social Security. It is a social program of Congress with absolutely no contractual obligations. What you get back at retirement is entirely up to the 535 members of Congress. The money you paid in is not yours. You have

---

[83] Unless recipients accept lower payments, or the nation raises Social Security taxes to 20 percent.

no legal right to get it back. More than half the nation's population loses not only the freedom to create their own assets for retirement but the dignity of so doing.

The *Nestor* decision reflects the precedent in *Helvering v. Davis*. In 1937, the law ruled: "The proceeds of both [the employee and employer] [Social Security] taxes are to be paid into the Treasury like internal-revenue taxes generally, and are not earmarked in any way."[84]

Social Security may have started as supplemental income in retirement, but, for more than half the population, it has worked its way into full retirement.[85] Social Security taxes have been raised at least 40 times since 1935. Americans are clearly being denied the use of their money and the freedom to invest funds they contribute as they see fit.

If loss of ownership of one's assets is a loss of freedom, restoration of those assets, besides a restoration of freedom, is the solution to the problems of Social Security. "Of the current proposals to address income inequality, the universal 401(k) is the most likely to bring general prosperity. The core idea is simple. The federal government creates tax-free retirement accounts for lower-income Americans, supplementing private accounts where they already exist, and matching personal contributions to those accounts."[86]

---

[84] In *Flemming v. Nestor*, Bulgarian immigrant Ephraim Nestor, deported in 1956 for being a communist in the 1930s, sued, after Congress in 1954 prohibited Social Security benefits for deportees. Nestor claimed title to his FICA payments. The Supreme Court disagreed: "To engraft upon the Social Security system a concept of 'accrued property rights' would deprive it of the flexibility and boldness in adjustment to ever-changing conditions which it demands." (This is exactly like French law. See footnote 78.)

[85] "[O]nly 55 percent of Americans working full-time hold a job with a retirement savings plan; the rate is even lower for part-time workers and the poor." Tyler Cowen, Economic Scene, "Universal 401(k) Accounts Would Bring the Poor Into the Ownership Society," *New York Times*, December 28, 2006, https://www.nytimes.com/2006/12/28/business/universal-401k-accounts-would-bring-the-poor-into-the-ownership.html.

[86] Cowen, "Universal 401(k) Accounts."

Although this is a handout, this costs less than the present system, and it will save Social Security. It is more in line with Hobbesian reasoning, in which everyone (as if *they* were gods) chips in a little to take care of the poor.

3. Individuals lose choice. There is no option, no choice about paying into Social Security. Although we can choose where we live, whom we marry, where we shop, we have no choice as to where we place our retirement money nor as to how much we must contribute (not to mention that we have no right to that money once it is contributed, not even to bequeath it to our family).

This lack of choice is inconsistent with American principles and values. Compulsion is prevalent in most other cultures, but America is not Europe or Singapore. Instead of "the debate always being about insolvency, transition costs, unfunded liabilities and rates of return, the debate about Social Security should be an emotional issue about liberty and opportunity."[87]

IV. PRIVATIZATION

The entire world seems to agree that government should intervene in the affairs of its citizens to provide such forms of social insurance as Social Security, unemployment insurance and universal health care. Is there, then, not one nation with a private retirement system? Answer: Yes, Chile.

Chile took a chance, in 1981, and required that 10 percent of workers' wages be deposited in tax-free private accounts. At age 65 (60 for women), the total is then transformed into an annuity with an insurance company. Taxes are paid when the money is withdrawn

---

[87] Ed Crane, *Talking Points on Social Security #8,* Cato Institute, in The National Center for Public Policy Research, July 18, 2005.

(usually at a lower rate than when the worker was working). A worker can contribute up to 20 percent if he or she wishes a higher pension or has the ability to retire earlier, and if a worker's pension savings are not enough at the legal retirement age, the government will make up the difference from general tax revenue.[88]

In Chile, pension funds are managed by private companies who operate the equivalent of a mutual fund that invests in stock, bonds and government debt. The private companies all compete with each other and are separate from the mutual fund so that if the company goes bankrupt, the assets of the mutual fund are not affected. Government simply takes over the fund until workers assign it to a new company. Government does set some parameters for investment; it has rules for diversification and creditworthiness of investments and forbids investment in derivatives, for example.

During the transition, to encourage workers to shift to the private pension plan, the Chilean government guaranteed the safety of the funds. No one was forced to shift. Those who did received a Recognition Bond acknowledging their contributions to the old pay-as-you-go system. Upon retirement, government cashed the bond. All new workers had to go into the new system; the old (and bankrupt) system closes out when the oldest person who entered that system dies away. On that day, the government will have no pension system left. The new one thus does not complement; it is a replacement.

The real transfer cost is the money government ceases to obtain when workers move to the new system because government is still committed to paying the pensions of the people already retired and those who will retire. That transition cost, however, can be calculated. (In Chile, it was around 3 percent of Gross Domestic Debt.) How that is financed, however, is different for every country. For example, governments usually have assets they can sell. Socialist or quasi-socialist nations all have state-owned enterprises

---

[88] Details on the Chilean retirement system are from Jose Piñera, *The Success of Chile's Privatized Social Security*, Cato Institute Policy Report, July/August 1995, https://www.cato.org/policy-report/july/august-1995/success-chiles-privatized-social-security.

they can sell. The U.S. has enormous tracts of land, approximately one-third of the country, which it can sell.[89]

The main goal of pension reform is to improve the lot of workers during old age. In Chile, pensions rose 40–50 percent over the old system. A positive consequence of fully funded pensions is that it creates real personal savings, which for Chile, fueled economic growth. There was also a positive psychological consequence. Because both workers and employers saw payment to the old social security system as a tax on the use of labor, this led to reduced employment. They were encouraged, then, when they realized that depositing that money into an individual pension account led to the opposite, to increased employment. And because they lead to a higher domestic supply of capital, individual retirement accounts not only eliminate the need for foreign aid, but serve also to attract foreign investment. It is not a coincidence, then, that Chile outperforms other Latin and Central American economies. Chile raised its GDP along with its standard of living by creating economic growth. Because economic growth increases both

---

[89] Selling off valuable assets is the price nations may have to pay for having previously sold off valuable individual freedoms attempting to create socialism.

employment and wages, it is the most powerful means of eliminating poverty.[90]

V. LAW AND SOCIAL SECURITY

The real question, then, with respect to Social Security: Is there really any law? That the Social Security Act of 1935 is law is fact, but in the U.S., law created to administer social welfare is always arguably unconstitutional.[91]

---

[90] Even though trade unions (of course) advised against switching to private pension accounts, 90 percent of Chile's workers switched anyway. This is proof once again of Thomas Jefferson's belief that people can and do think for themselves. Once workers own their retirement funds, especially once those surpass the value of their homes, workers realize that they have a stake in the economy. At that point they also demand that government stay free of the economy.

And so, too, will workers in other countries once they see how well such a system works. This is the case, now, for Latvia and for Sweden, who are experimenting with this. They are phasing into a notional (or nonfinancial) defined contribution (NDC) system. According to *The Economist*, "Economic Focus: More than a Notional Improvement," February 18, 2006, p. 74 [based on an article published by the World Bank, "Pension Reform: Issues and Prospects for Non-Financial Defined Contribution (NDC) Schemes," Robert Holzmann and Edward Palmer, eds.], as with normal funded defined-contribution plans, each worker has an individual account. Workers, however, do not actually put any money into that account. The amounts in their accounts are purely "notional." Their NDCs earn interest at a rate broadly equivalent to the growth of the payroll tax base. When employees retire, their notional capital is converted into regular pension annuities in a similar way to funded plans, except that the annuities are paid out of taxes on tomorrow's workers, not their own retirement savings.

An advantage to these notional accounts is that they *set an automatic limit to the claims of tomorrow's pensioners on tomorrow's workers*. They do this by insulating public pensions from two demographic trends that weigh on traditional systems. First, the value of notional accounts responds automatically to rising longevity: the annuities pensioners receive depend on their life expectancies at retirement. Second, the accounts vary with the birth rate: a low rate will eventually feed through to the payroll tax base through stagnant or falling employment. This holds down returns on NDCs, hence on pensions. Rises in productivity growth, however, because it leads to higher wages, work in the other direction.

[91] Article 1, Section 8 of the Constitution states that "The Congress shall have Power To lay and collect Taxes, Duties, Imposts and Excises, to pay the Debts and provide for the common Defense and general Welfare of the United States." What follows are the reasons for taxation, all of which have to do with raising money for defense. In Article 1, Section 8, there's no reference to anything else, and certainly not to issues of social security. (Continued on next page)

Additionally, the Social Security Act, as administrative law, as all law created to provide social welfare, is based on expediency, *not* on principle.[92] It is why, when the Social Security and Medicare Board of Trustees declare in their annual reports that Social Security

(Continued from previous page) Although the word "welfare" is used two times in the Constitution, once in the Preamble, and once in Article 1, Section 8, Madison said later in a letter to James Robertson Jr. that he really regretted having used that word, that he knew that it would be misinterpreted. ("With respect to the words 'General welfare,' I have always regarded them as qualified by the detail of powers connected with them. To take them in a literal and unlimited sense would be a metamorphosis of the Constitution into a character, which there is a host of proofs was not contemplated by its Creators.")

And then there is the 16th Amendment to the Constitution, attached in 1913 as an afterthought. "The Congress shall have power to lay and collect taxes on incomes, from whatever source derived, without apportionment among the several States, and without regard to any census or enumeration." Had that amendment been proposed at the Constitutional Convention in 1787, there would have been a Section attached to indicate what the funds would be used for. An amendment that allows government to collect taxes in any amount for any reason is not in the spirit of the Constitution. Had the amendment stated that taxes collected would be distributed to whatever the government thought necessary, it wouldn't have been ratified. It passed in 1913 because society had "progressed." And if it hadn't passed in 1913, it certainly would have passed in 1935.

[92] In 1935, Congress couldn't believe that the "new progressives" did not understand just how reactionary Social Security and all the New Deal programs were, to what extent they were all an expedient throwback to government by an "elite" such as the philosopher kings in Plato's Republic, by either Louis XVI or the radical French directorate, Otto von Bismarck in Germany, Stalin in Russia. To Congress, the New Deal was simply an expedient attempt to take quick command of the economy. The New Deal was, in fact, a formal rejection of the self-correction process of a market economy in favor of controlling the economy via top-down management.

Yet this is precisely how Bismarck and Hitler came to power. They offered "social security" in exchange for support by the population. (The word, "Nazi," in German, is the abbreviation for National Socialism. The word "fascism," social grouping, is the abbreviation for socialism from the right.)

In contrast, however, in the 16th century, Machiavelli, in exchange for support for the right to rule, suggested the opposite—greater economic freedom. Knowing the nobility to be vain and disloyal, Machiavelli understood that reliable support would come only from those not in the nobility. Grateful for an opportunity to better their lives, Machiavelli knew that the poor and middle class would back a "prince" who gave them that opportunity. Napoleon understood this perfectly. And today, so, too, does the Communist Party in China. By offering economic freedom to the population at large, the Communist Party retains power. Recognizing that economic, social and political freedom are inherently interconnected, the regime can use its power to allow social and political freedom to blossom, thus, transition China out of communism. Or, use its power to crush those freedoms, thus, lock China into totalitarianism.

Social, political and economic freedom, Western ideas, should win out in the end. This is because those freedoms are based on natural rights, on nature itself. The most forceful are the ideas of John Locke, but John Locke read Thomas Hobbes, who studied with Francis Bacon, who studied Machiavelli. Our Lockean perspective (reflected in the Constitution and Bill of Rights) considers individual rights as natural rights founded in nature— to one's own life, liberty and property. Self-evident rights protected . . . (Continued on next page)

will not have sufficient funds within a few years and that Medicare already does not have sufficient funds, and declare also that because of this, by law, the president must propose and Congress, then, consider remedial action, nothing is done.[93] Nothing is done because expediency alone is not enough of an issue; there is no sense of urgency; no crisis is at hand; no sense that the Constitution is being compromised. Thus every year the annual reports are the same and no one pays attention to them. Social Security is seen simply for what it is, administrative law (the department is actually called Social Security Administration) for technocrats to figure out.[94] In other words, proper funding of Social Security, as well as reduction

---

(Continued from previous page) . . . by but not provided by government. From this, then, our current understanding of social security is wrong. Social security must not be provided by government, as socialism, by those in power in exchange for that power, but by individuals themselves with their own retirement accounts. Why is it that no member of Congress ever campaigns on a platform that demands the privatization of Social Security? They all know that individuals should provide for themselves, that the strength of this country is and has always been based on individual freedom and responsibility, yet they all know that if they did, they would never get elected.

Reality, then, is that, without a crisis, change is not possible. No one cares enough. The poor do not pay for Social Security or health care, and to the rich it is a minor expense. Unfortunately, the middle class doesn't care either. They do not see Social Security as a tax, as money taken away and not returned until years later at a fraction of its future value, as a subtraction, thus, from their standard of living. To the contrary, associations such as American Association of Retired Persons (AARP) see taxation as an addition to the standard of living.

[93] Social Security and Medicare Boards of Trustees, *A Summary of the 2007 Annual Reports*, http://www.ssa.gov/OACT/TRSUM/trsummary.html.

[94] How well do technocrats figure it out? The truth is that the Social Security Administration is choking on paperwork. One reason is that insurance companies, by forcing people who file disability claims to apply also to Social Security, abuse the system. Social Security usually turns them down, but insurance companies then make them appeal. In the end, even if Social Security turns them down again, and there is no fraud, there is an enormous backlog of disability claims. The average delay in getting a hearing, which requires an administrative law judge, is now more than a year and a half. (See Mary Williams Walsh, "Insurers Faulted as Overloading Social Security," *New York Times,* April 1, 2008, https://www.nytimes.com/2008/04/01/business/01disabled.html.) In other words, this wouldn't be an issue if people had their own retirement accounts.

of the U.S. budget deficit, will not even begin to happen until it must; until there is a crisis.[95]

Yet, by creating social legislation we're playing with the Constitution. We play with it, however, because we take it for granted. We do not see it (and we can hold the public school system responsible for this) as something enormously special. We do not have at all times in the back of our minds the fact that the Constitution (1787) was the culmination of two hundred years of social, political and economic thought in England, Scotland, France and America, in which the most profound underlying idea is that the success of a nation is directly correlated to the degree of freedom a nation gives its individual citizens. (Cf. Machiavelli, footnote 90.) In this sense, the 18th century Age of Enlightenment is as important as 5th century Athens and 1st century Rome, and our appreciation of the Constitution should be, as John Adams declared at the three-and-a-half-month convention that created the Constitution, "the greatest single effort of national deliberation that the world has ever seen."

We cannot, therefore, "progress" forward from the Constitution. The only progress is backward, from something superior to something inferior, from a state of individual freedom-individual responsibility to a state of expansive government and eroded freedom. From this perspective, the UN Charter, to the extent that it centers on the Universal Declaration of Human Rights, is reactionary. Its references to community and human rights are not references to individual rights. The document speaks in collective terms, in socialist terms, in terms of psychological freedom—freedom from want, for example; that has little in common with our Constitution—or with any document centered on notions of individual freedom, and nothing in common with documents centered on economic freedom. To the contrary, it is a document that advocates the redistribution of wealth. And why is it there is no

---

[95] Knowing that Medicare does not have the funds, Congress nevertheless authorized prescription drugs as an additional payout. This is the kind of spending that causes the U.S. budget deficit, not the current war in Iraq. The cost of the war in Iraq is part of the budget for national defense, 4 percent of GDP, half that of the Vietnam War (9.5 percent), and less than a third that of the Korean War (14 percent). (See Greenspan, *The Age of Turbulence*, p. 230.)

mention of psychological freedom, economic equality or economic entitlement in the U.S. Constitution? Precisely because the framers knew that the trade-off for such collective action is a cost in individual freedom.[96]

It is not by coincidence, then, that "progressive" law in socialist countries originates through force or the threat of force. In the U.S., the New Deal was imposed this way. In the 1930s, inspired by the strong-arm tactics and apparent success of National Socialism in Germany, Italy and the Soviet Union, President Roosevelt threatened to add six members to the Supreme Court to do his bidding. To get his way, to create a new and better deal for the American people, although an experiment, Roosevelt was willing to eliminate the very essence of the Constitution, its separation of

---

[96] The framers believed that charity, including broad acts of humanity in response to natural disasters, belongs in the private sector. Those who have more would most likely, but not necessarily, give more, but it is not for government to dictate that they do. *This is what it means to live by principle.* To force people to do what they should do voluntarily, because it is expedient, risks letting an overarching and coercive government worm its way into the life of the polity. Curiously, the Left has a healthy distrust of government when it comes to monitoring our personal lives yet has no qualms about letting government monitor and administer such personal matters as education, health care or retirement. Yet, according to Robert Levy and William Mellor (Robert A. Levy and William Mellor, *The Dirty Dozen: How Twelve Supreme Court Cases Radically Expanded Government and Eroded Freedom* (New York: Penguin Group, 2008), p. 218, "A living constitution interpreted to maximize political discretion can be worse than no constitution at all, because it preserves the patina of constitutional legitimacy while unleashing the political voices that a constitution is meant to restrain. In other words, if powers can be expanded with impunity, so can rights be contracted." This principle is what's missing from the philosophy of those on the Left. According to Levy and Mellor, "If the Justice Department were to enact regulations over national security and civil liberties with no more guidance than 'keep us safe from terrorists' the left is justifiably apoplectic, but when the same Congress delegates to the Environmental Protection Agency the power to enact environmental regulations with no more guidance than 'keep us safe from pollutants,' the left applauds enthusiastically." (Levy and Mellor, *Dirty Dozen*, p. 14.)

powers, its checks and balance provisions.[97] In the end, the most fundamental legal ramification of the New Deal was to turn the Welfare Clause of the Constitution from a statement on limited government into the *very source* of unlimited government.

The Social Security Act of 1935 is the most perfect example. In 1937, in the first test of its legality, *Helvering v. Davis,* the Supreme Court, literally frightened by Franklin Roosevelt, crumbled. The court held that the General Welfare Clause does uphold the constitutionality of the Social Security Act. Justice Benjamin Cardozo, in a 7–2 opinion, adopted Alexander Hamilton's view that the General Welfare Clause was a separate source of congressional authority to "lay and collect taxes," and then spend the proceeds for purposes including, but not limited to, effecting Congress's

---

[97] This has been frequently documented. Not only did Roosevelt admit that he was "deeply impressed" by what Mussolini had accomplished, but in turn, in a laudatory review of Roosevelt's 1933 book, *Looking Forward*, Mussolini wrote, "Reminiscent of Fascism is the principle that the state no longer leaves the economy to its own devices . . . Without question, the mood accompanying this sea change resembles that of Fascism." And then at the time, the chief Nazi newspaper, *Völkischer Beobachter*, repeatedly praised "Roosevelt's adoption of National Socialist strains of thought in his economic and social policies" and "the development toward an authoritarian state" based on the "demand that collective good be put before individual self-interest." With respect to the Great Depression, Roosevelt declared, "If we are to go forward, we must move as a trained and loyal army willing to sacrifice for the good of a common discipline. We are, I know, ready and willing to submit our lives and property to such discipline, because it makes possible a leadership which aims at a larger good. I assume unhesitantly the leadership of this great army . . . I shall ask the Congress for the one remaining instrument to meet the crisis—broad executive power to wage a war against the emergency, as great as the power that would be given to me if we were in fact invaded by a foreign foe." For the above quotes, see David Boaz, "Hitler, Mussolini, Roosevelt," *Reason magazine*, October 2007, https://reason.com/2007/09/28/hitler-mussolini-roosevelt/, a review of German cultural historian Wolfgang Schivelbusch's book, *Three New Deals: Reflections on Roosevelt's America, Mussolini's Italy, and Hitler's Germany, 1933–1939* (New York: Metropolitan Books, 2007).

One can say that although Roosevelt had dictatorial tendencies, still, he never intended to destroy the Constitution. So, too, in the 1930s, with Europe also in a depression, and thus experimenting with socialism, one can say that, still, not all Germans and Italians were bad people. *The lesson*, however, is that citizens of a nation must demand their government not waiver when it comes to acting on principle. Governments must not experiment with socialism at the expense of liberty. The risk is that it leads to totalitarianism.

enumerated powers.[98] The court upheld the Social Security Act as a wealth transfer program even though wealth transfer is not listed among the enumerated powers.

The Madisonian view, the opposing view, insists that the General Welfare Clause does not empower Congress to do anything beyond those particular authorizations granted in the remainder of Article 1, Section 8 of the Constitution. To Madison, a broader interpretation is a mockery of the notion of limited federal government. Congress cannot simply levy taxes for the general welfare. If in the Welfare Clause there is an implied power to tax, it is only to execute the enumerated powers.[99]

Helvering v. Davis, in 1937, was the first test of the Social Security Act, but not the first test of the New Deal interpretation of the General Welfare Clause. The first test was *United States v. Butler*, in 1933. That case struck down the Agricultural Adjustment Act (AAA) that taxed food processors and then used the proceeds to pay farmers for reducing their production. The case was struck down because it interfered with interstate commerce, although specifically it was the power reserved to the states in the Tenth Amendment that was cited. Six of the Justices agreed that "[t]he power of Congress to authorize expenditure of public moneys for public purposes is not

---

[98] The Supreme Court understood that the federal government had no right to intervene in economic or local matters, and that the Tenth Amendment—"The powers not delegated to the United States by the Constitution, nor prohibited by it to the States, are reserved to the States respectively, or to the people"—narrowly confined its legitimate activities. They knew that the New Deal should not have been validated, that they should not have bowed to the idea of changed circumstances, i.e., the Great Depression, at the expense of principle. Up until *Helvering*, 1937, the Supreme Court had, in fact, knocked down everything Roosevelt had proposed. But Roosevelt's megalomania had become so great the Supreme Court really thought he would pack the court, and so, to protect itself, succumbed.

[99] In other words, "if Congress can determine what constitutes the General Welfare and can appropriate money for its advancement, where is the limitation to carrying into execution whatever can be affected by money? How few objections are there which money cannot accomplish! . . . Can it be conceived that the great and wise men who devised our Constitution . . . should have failed so egregiously . . . as to grant a power which rendered restriction upon power practically unavailing?" South Carolina Congressman William Drayton, 4 Reg. Deb. 1632-34 (1828).

limited by the direct grants of legislative power found in the Constitution."[100]

Together, *Butler* and *Helvering* created the redistributive state that we have today. *Butler* placed limitations on spending for the general welfare by stating that if spending was quasi-regulatory, it would have to be authorized elsewhere in the Constitution, and that, in general, expenditures would have to promote the "general welfare."[101] *Helvering*, however, allowed Congress to expropriate from one group and spend it on another. *Butler* was regulatory; *Helvering* was redistributive.[102] The General Welfare Clause in *Butler* was *dictum*, an added statement to the case not binding for purposes of precedent, but *Helvering* affirmed the court would defer to Congress in determining which legislative acts served the general welfare. Thus Congress itself would be the monitor of what Congress could do.[103]

Both *Butler* and *Helvering* revolved around the Tenth Amendment, but *Helvering* specifically resolved the legality of Titles VIII and II of the Social Security Act. Title VIII states that wage-based taxes on both employers and employees shall be imposed at the same rate, and Title II states specifically that the purpose of the payments is Old Age Benefits. Justice Cardozo simply stated (as do all liberal presidents and presidential candidates) that, "needs that were narrow or parochial a century ago may be interwoven in our day with the well-being of the Nation.

---

[100] United States v. Butler, 297 U.S. at 66.

[101] Levy and Mellor, *The Dirty Dozen*, p. 25.

[102] For example, funds for Social Security are not held in a trust account; they are paid in by one group (workers) to be given to another group (retirees). In 1935, the worker group was larger than the retiree group, but today, the retiree group is larger than the worker group, and so the worker group will probably soon be taxed an additional 5 percent of their annual income. Except that what this really means is that this additional 2½ percent employer and 2½ percent employee contribution to Social Security is a 5 percent tax on business that will be passed on to society at large in the form of higher prices and reduced wages. In the long run, any price raise (prices up or wages down), creates unemployment. Why? Because less efficient firms cannot compete and will shut down.

[103] Levy and Mellor, *The Dirty Dozen*, p. 26.

What is critical or urgent changes with the times."[104] Cardozo also stated that the court would allow Congress broad latitude in deciding which legislative acts are sufficiently general to be accommodated under the clause.

According to Levy and Mellor, for all intents and purposes, the court announced that it would abandon any role in reviewing congressional enactments for compliance with a General Welfare Clause, although, according to Cardozo,

> "[t]he line must still be drawn between one welfare and another, between particular and general. Where this shall be placed cannot be known through a formula in advance of the event. There is a middle ground, or certainly a penumbra, in which discretion is at large. The discretion, however, is not confided to the courts. The discretion

---

[104] Helvering v. Davis, 301 U.S. at 641. Levy and Mellor, *The Dirty Dozen*, p. 27. It is precisely this reasoning that explains why most nations do not want a constitution—they lose the ability to make "urgent changes with the times." Even in the U.S., there are plenty of people willing to rewrite the Constitution to make it more flexible. In the U.S., that the Constitution is open to interpretation is one of the fundamental philosophic differences between liberals and conservatives.

During the 2008 presidential campaign, when asked how they would pick Supreme Court judges, the Republican candidate, John McCain, said, "I will look for accomplished men and women with a proven record of excellence in the law, and a proven commitment to judicial restraint. I will look for people in the cast of John Roberts, Samuel Alito and my friend, the late William Rehnquist—jurists of the highest caliber who know their own minds, and know the law, and know the difference. My nominees will understand that there are clear limits to the scope of judicial power, and clear limits to the scope of federal power." The Democrat, Barack Obama, said, "The Constitution can be interpreted in so many ways. And one way is a cramped and narrow way in which the Constitution and the courts essentially become the rubber stamps of the powerful in society. And then there's another vision of the courts that says that the courts are the refuge of the powerless. Because often times they may lose in the democratic back and forth. They may be locked out and prevented from fully participating in the democratic process. That's one of the reasons that I opposed Alito as well as Justice Roberts." (See *New York Times*,"On the Issues: Supreme Court," May 23, 2012, https://www.nytimes.com/elections/2008/president/issues/judges.html.) In other words, the conservative believes that defending the Constitution is what a presidential campaign is about; the liberal believes that it's about protecting the powerless. To underscore the irony of this difference, consider that the liberal candidate, Senator Barack Obama, was, for ten years, a professor of constitutional law.

belongs to Congress, unless the choice is clearly wrong, a display of arbitrary power."[105] [106]

Justice Cardozo goes on to say:

> [w]ith respect to issues of social security, that security for the elderly is a national problem that the separate states cannot tackle effectively. State and local governments are lacking in resources; they don't want to place themselves at a competitive disadvantage by imposing higher taxes than their neighbor, and they are reluctant to become a magnet for the needy and dependent who might migrate to high-benefit jurisdictions.

But then why can't these arguments be used to resolve all social problems—health care, affordable housing, low wages?

Cardozo simply says that:

> "Whether wisdom or unwisdom resides in the scheme of benefits set forth in Title II it is not for us to say. The answer to such inquiries must come from Congress, not the courts. Our concern here, as often, is with power, not with wisdom."[107]

But the courts should be concerned with legality, with ensuring legislation does not exceed the power of the federal government as carefully enumerated in the Constitution. The argument that the Constitution must be flexible, that it must adjust "to things as they come up," that the Constitution is not a suicide pact, is a false argument. The U.S. is wealthy and successful precisely because we enforce social, political and economic freedom, precisely because

---

[105] *Helvering*, 301 U.S., at 640.

[106] Would Justice Cardozo agree that because of changing demographics, times have changed again, and that retired baby boomers, because they will be exploiting the fewer-in-number younger workers, will transform Social Security into a particular rather than a general form of social welfare? As a particular, will this be constitutional? In other words, perhaps only those individuals earning less than $100,000 a year should be entitled to receive Social Security.

[107] *Helvering*, 301 U.S. at 644.

our freedom is not just economic freedom as in China or just social and political freedom as in Europe. It is why over the last 200 years, the U.S. has attracted (and continues to attract) the world's most independent and entrepreneurial people who ask only for an opportunity to succeed. Again, this kind of opportunity exists here (and nowhere else) precisely because we enforce social, political and economic freedom.[108]

Still, might Hamilton be right? Is the right to spend absolutely inherent in the right to tax? If so, then, according to Levy and Mellor, it is also inherent in Congress' right to borrow money and to dispose of property belonging to the U.S. Was it really intended by the framers that Congress could spend for the general welfare only within the enumerated powers, yet spend at will for the general welfare by borrowing or selling off property?

Yet the Hamiltonian argument, that the General Welfare Clause implies an inherent ability of Congress to tax and spend, is nowhere specified in the Constitution. It cannot possibly be part of the original intent, because the framers, themselves politicians, could not possibly have forgotten to spell it out. In Article 1, Section 8, they enumerated powers, and that Congress "could lay and collect taxes" to pay for them. The last clause of Section 8 even states that Congress could "make all Laws which shall be necessary and proper for carrying into execution the foregoing powers," but it was understood this only affirms Congress' right to tax and spend to enforce the enumerated powers.

There is no such thing as a spending clause in the Constitution, and if we are at all honest about it, no such thing as a welfare clause. The 1828 argument by William Drayton (footnote 97) makes that clear. The contemporary statement by Justice Sandra Day O'Connor also makes it clear: "If the spending power is to be limited only by Congress' notion of the general welfare, the reality, given the vast financial resources of the Federal Government, is that the Spending Clause gives power to the Congress to tear down the barriers, to

---

[108] It's not a coincidence that in 1790 the population in the U.S. was 3.9 million, yet today is 332 million. Only India and China exceed our population. (Japan and Russia have 40 percent our population, Indonesia a little more than 80 percent.)

invade the states' jurisdiction, and to become a parliament for the whole people, subject to no restrictions save such as are self-imposed. This, of course, was not the Framers' plan and it is not the meaning of the Spending Clause."[109]

VI. CONCLUSION

The premise of this essay, that citizens of a nation should have their own retirement accounts, that Social Security should not be administered by the state, is based on principle. That there are good and pragmatic arguments for going along with the social-political-economic reality of the moment, arguments that are convincing, and emotional, supported by the great majority, arguments that created Social Security in the first place, does not change the fact that the arguments are populist. Ever-changing pragmatic arguments, however, are not a basis for a constitution. Adherence to principles is a basis for a constitution.

But add to populist arguments such statements as, "None of us really understands what's going on with all these numbers," by supply-side economist David Stockman, Director of the U.S. Office of Management and Budget under President Ronald Reagan, or the following by respected research economist, Robert Hahn, cofounder and executive director of American Enterprise Institute–Brookings Joint Center for Regulatory Studies:

> Despite the magnitude of the costs and benefits of regulation [see any government program], the quality of government analyses of regulation falls far short of basic standards of economic research, and does not appear to be getting any better over time. Indeed, we do not even have answers to basic questions like whether benefit-cost analyses tend to overstate benefits, perhaps out of regulatory zeal, or whether they overstate costs, perhaps because they fail to recognize how innovation will reduce

---

[109] South Dakota v. Dole, 483 U.S. at 207–08.

the costs after regulations are imposed. Furthermore, there is little evidence that economic analysis of regulatory decisions has had a substantial positive impact. This is not to say that economists have not had an impact in important areas, such as the deregulation of airlines, but that economic analysis of run-of-the-mill billion-dollar regulations may not be having much impact.

The poor quality of analysis can help explain some of the ineffectiveness. However, regardless of how good the analysis is, politicians sometimes choose not to take basic economic ideas seriously. [110]

No surprise, then, that progressives scoff at arguments based on principle only. From the examples above, it's understandable that politicians ignore economic analysis, ignore, for example, the annual report of the Trustees of the Social Security Administration. It's all just theory.[111]

Conservatives, however, would respond that everything is theory; that in life, the only choice is between good theory and bad theory and that good theory, by definition, is based on principle. Otherwise, there's no need for a constitution. If laws are enacted based upon the apparent reality of the moment, we are back to French law, where every situation is unique and decided on its merit (or worse, as public choice theory would suggest, decided in the self-interest of those bureaucrats, lobbyists and politicians trying to keep their jobs).

Not only is the Constitution not based on the reality of the moment (being an abstraction of the best political thought from the

---

[110] Robert Hahn and Paul C. Tetlock, "Has Economic Analysis Improved Regulatory Decisions?" *Journal of Economic Perspectives*, 23, no. 1 (Winter 2008): p. 69.

[111] Still, progressives might be seduced by the thought that, beyond a constitution, a good principle would be to let common law stand as the basis for all law. Common law allows for the most individual freedom by constraining only those whose lives come in direct contact with the law.

Legislation, by contrast, can be far removed from the individual. This is so because to be inclusive, uniform and fair, legislation has to be overly broad. It cannot avoid constraining individual liberty. The Social Security Act is a good example. It includes people for whom at certain times in their life it is a great burden to contribute 15 percent of what they earn, plus another 25–30 percent in income taxes.

164

previous 200 years), it purposely avoided the reality of the moment: slavery.

Based on the reality of the moment, the best approach to Social Security other than two extremes—either state administration or self-administration—is a minimally pragmatic middle ground: the state administers security for those who cannot provide for themselves, and the rest of the population provide for their own retirement accounts.

Although government provision of nationwide Social Security is not authorized by the Constitution, we accede to it because it is law that reflects what we do anyway. What we do anyway we call custom, the fundamental reality from which law emerges, a reality in which no coercion is necessary. Law based on custom, however, is not the same as law based on what we should do or what the state says we should do. The former is natural, the latter coercive. In a free nation, government does not coerce people into doing what is in their best interest. Individuals in a community may tell each other what to do, but government does not have the right to demand that everyone, on an annual basis, turn over 15 percent of their income for the sole purpose of preventing them from spending it. In a free nation, government does not force citizens to turn over their retirement money because it thinks that citizens will just squander it, and that government will have to pay for it in the end. To latch desperately on to the Welfare Clause, claiming that it is not counter to the spirit or intent of the Constitution to tax citizens to provide for their welfare is nothing other than an act of expediency. This betrayal shows a lack of understanding of how markets work, and it demonstrates genuine disbelief in the ability of markets to prevent such things as poverty and unrest.[112]

---

112 Why is it that the destiny of individual freedom is defended more by economists than lawyers or political scientists? Is it because lawyers and political scientists do not make the connection that social and political freedom are interconnected with economic freedom? Wrapped in the details of their profession, lawyers and political scientists tend not to develop a profound understanding of how markets work, tend not to understand that there are economic consequences for making people do things for their own good.

In America, a nation where great personal freedom has led to great national wealth, where both charitable organizations and individuals (baby boomers especially) are today loaded with money (with no idea how to spend it), why should government not get out of the charity business? Instead of paying for Medicare, Medicaid, housing, food stamps and aid to dependent people, if the state just gave citizens back their money, why would individuals, each with $20,000 or $40,000 or $100,000 in tax refunds, not give generously to privately run social services?

This is the Jeffersonian approach, the independent approach, the approach that created American democracy, that created citizens who think for themselves, responsible citizens who can be counted on to do "the right thing." This is the approach that created those citizens who voluntarily risked their lives to fight at Concord rather than to fly to Canada. They weren't asking for social security.

VII. EPILOGUE

A letter from the Social Security Administration, "Your Social Security Statement—Prepared especially for David G. Parker," arrived June 30, 2008. It confirms everything in this essay. Here, in Social Security's words, is its text:

- Social Security is the largest source of income for most elderly Americans today, but Social Security was never intended to be your only source of income when you retire.

- Social Security system is facing serious financial problems, and action is needed soon to make sure the system will be sound when today's younger workers are ready for retirement.

- In 2017 we will begin paying more in benefits than we collect in taxes. Without changes, by 2041 the Social Security Trust Fund will be exhausted and there will be enough money to pay only about 78 cents for each dollar of scheduled benefits. We need to resolve these issues soon to make sure Social Security continues to provide a foundation of protection for future generations.

- You may decide to continue working beyond your full retirement age without choosing to receive benefits. If so, your benefit will be increased by a certain percentage for each month you don't receive benefits between your full retirement age and age 70. This table shows the rate your benefits increase if you delay retiring.

Year of Birth	Yearly Increase Rate
1937–1938	6.5%
1939–1940	7.0%
1941–1942	7.5%
1943 or later	8.0%

Therefore, Social Security will increase my benefits by 8 percent a year, i.e., four times the rate of return of U.S. Treasuries or bank certificates of deposit. If Social Security is capable of producing that kind of return, why is there a problem? Or is it that Social Security is just saying anything that obfuscates the pending shortage, that Social Security has no intention of paying that return? Plus, how does Social Security plan to get an 8 percent return? By investing in derivatives or subprime mortgages?

3

LETTERS TO THE EDITOR

Appeared in *Financial Times*/January 5, 2023

Three ways Big Tech got it wrong

Brooke Masters' "Three ways Big Tech got it wrong" (Dec. 29) is the *Financial Times*' article of the year. Missing only is a direct (rather than implied) statement that the laws of business, money and economics are timeless, back to Babylon, and that because they broke those laws, of the top 100 corporations listed on the DJIA in 1961, only three are there today.

Big Tech's strategic model of "innovate rapidly and splash out to woo customers" (short-term growth versus long-term profit from having produced an excellent product) has no historic basis. No surprise the price of Google, Amazon and Facebook stock is down 40 to 60 percent.

Then, turn the page. Readers will find that LEX., "China property: structurally unsound," is another example. China's government should not have loaned so much for real estate development simply because units were presold. Those loans did not factor in a rise in interest rates or a rise in construction costs. Gambling in defiance of timeless rates of return: 1–2 percent savings; 2–3 percent mortgage lending;

3–5 percent venture capital, those loans are in default. Competition guarantees those timeless rates.

Savvy investors, of course, have been waiting for this day— for the value of mortgages to be more than the value of the properties that secure them. They purchase those mortgages 50 cents on the dollar (or assume them as a leveraged buyout).

David Parker
Political Economist
San Francisco, CA

Appeared in *Financial Times/* **April 24, 2022**

In the clash of civilizations, all claim to have a theory

Janan Ganesh writes that "no grand theory can explain the Ukraine crisis" (Opinion, April 13). Oh yes it can! Bashar al-Assad in Syria, leaders in the Middle East, the great Singaporean statesman Lee Kuan Yew, Lenin, Stalin, Che Guevara. All claim that "the end justifies the means".

In a clash of civilizations all sides will claim the theory— although the world would do better to forget teleology and remember Adam Smith, who said society, without planning, without government, with individuals simply pursuing their self-interest to survive (by producing goods and services), as if led by an invisible hand, will organize itself better than anything that can be done by design. That, too, is elegant theory. To paraphrase Immanuel Kant: man is the goal of betterment, not the means.

David Parker,
San Francisco, CA

Appeared in *Financial Times/* June 26, 2018

Trump's policies embody citizen rage

Janan Ganesh is correct: we are headed toward a campaign against immigration of the perfectly legal kind ("Do not mistake Trump's motives on immigration," June 21). But so, too, is President Donald Trump correct. His election and immigration policy embody citizen rage that western civilization is being undermined by multiculturalism, the idea that there are many ways to live life and organize society, for example, that the community is as important as the individual [a notion absolutely contrary to western civilization]: rage, then, that the U.S. Constitution, rather than rule of law, has been turned into rule of thumb.

David Parker,
San Francisco, CA

Appeared in *Financial Times/*March 25, 2018

Business cycles must run their course

Sir,

From the perspective of someone in business, nothing that Martin Wolf says in "Economics failed us before the global crisis" (March 21) rings true—even when it is true.

Mr. Wolf advises us not to believe in the efficient market hypothesis and in rational expectations—except that anyone in business knows that rates of return are timeless:1–2 percent on savings, 2–3 percent on mortgage lending, 3–5 percent on venture capital, and that in a competitive market, that is an efficient market, investors expect profit to be pushed to 0.

He advises that economies would be more resilient if they were less leveraged. No. Companies not leveraged will be eliminated by those that are. A 5 percent return on 100 percent cash cannot compete with a 5 percent return on 100 percent debt. A 5 percent return on $1 million cash, $50,000, does not compare to a 5 percent return on $10m financed, $500,000. The return on leveraged investment is so high that owners of leveraged companies will lower the price of their products until their competitors are driven out of business.

Mr. Wolf believes in a strong fiscal and monetary response to a recession. No. Business cycles must run their course. Except to prevent a financial crisis, intervention in an economy only prolongs a recession. You don't offer a seven-course meal to someone who just threw up from overeating.

David Parker,
San Francisco, CA

Appeared in *Financial Times*/December 23, 2017

Teach by the Socratic method—keep asking

Sir,

Lucy Kellaway, in "End of Term Diary" (December 23), absolutely said the right thing: that teaching is not taking children on a "journey," teaching is showing children the beauty of a theorem.

It's the teacher's job to facilitate and motivate. Show students the beauty of things. And, teach by the Socratic method. Ask a question. If the student doesn't understand, ask another question. Keep asking. When they understand, they've learned.

David Parker,
San Francisco, CA

Appeared in *Financial Times/*November 6, 2016

Chinese have a single end in view with investment

Sir,

In "Chinese investors take a tumble on the global stage" (October 31), James Kynge observes that Chinese investors make as many mistakes, enter into as many stupid ventures as do westerners—and then gives several very good examples. With his foxlike thinking, Mr. Kynge is insinuating that we in the west can take comfort: "See, they're no smarter than us."

Wrong! The Chinese are hedgehogs. They know one big thing: pursue relentlessly western assets in order to one day own enough to control the world's economy. No other nation has such a goal.

David Parker,
San Francisco, CA

Appeared in *Financial Times/*May 30, 2016

Demagogues the answer to what's on our minds

Sir,

Martin Wolf, in "How to defeat right wing populism" (May 25), makes the statement that demagogues do not give answers. They don't have to. They are the answer to what is on the public's mind: unpunished crime, failing public schools, unemployment—and no political party doing anything about it.

Mr. Wolf then makes a comment that a first glance sounds very intelligent—that populist candidates are unaware of the institutions upon which society is based, and the extension to which those institutions are responsible for today's prosperity. That intelligent statement is not what it seems. It's really fear of democracy, of letting the masses vote for whomever they choose. (It's Plato's *Republic*.)

David Parker,
San Francisco, CA

Appeared in *Financial Times*/October 10, 2015

Reverse the downturn by letting the cycle run its course

Sir,

Kenneth Rogoff's rational analysis of the current economic forces at play ("This slowdown is a hangover not a coma," October 10) is not what it appears. Rather, it's a plea for what everyone wants, Keynesian government intervention. "President Barack Obama once proposed creating an infrastructure bank which would employ technocrats to provide objective analysis. It was a very good idea." But that's been done: it's called the New Deal, which turned a recession into a 12-year depression.

There is an alternative: Austrian economics, in which economic cycles are allowed to run their course—the only way to reverse a downturn. In the 1980s Federal Reserve chairman Paul Volcker knocked out inflation by imposing high interest rates; today, knocking out the hangover from the financial crisis requires imposing low economic growth—the only way.

David Parker,
San Francisco, CA

While driving to Sonoma, Christiane at the wheel, me in the passenger seat reading *The Economist*, I stumbled upon a Letter to the Editor. My first reaction: "That's something I would have said. Wow, I'm not alone in the world." When I finished the letter and looked to see who wrote it, imagine the shock: David Parker, San Francisco. Dashing off letters to the editor at four in the morning—one forgets. Here's the letter: Appeared in *The Economist* (Buttonwood)/ December 4, 2010

Why is the Austrian explanation so little discussed?

The reason why the Austrian explanation is so little discussed is because the Austrian response to the crisis (2008) is simply to wait it out. There is nothing to discuss. The Austrian school agrees with Jean-Baptiste Say, a French economist in the early 19th century, that all recessions are the result of overexpansion of credit. The implication will follow.

Then in the mid-19th century, in *Lombard Street*, Walter Bagehot wrote that if that contraction turns into a crisis, forget about economic theory, just bail out the banks. There is nothing to discuss.

—David Parker, Political Economist,
San Francisco, CA

These two "Letters to the Editor" were printed alongside mine:

Buttonwood asked, "Why is the Austrian explanation of the crisis [2008] so little discussed?" ("Taking von Mises to pieces," November 20).

The short answer is that the "Austrian school of economic ideas has not been taught for a long time in any university department: hence the response of the economic establishment that the current crisis could not have been foreseen. Outside this establishment there are some exceptions, and one whom Buttonwood did not mention is the estimable Bernard Connolly, who has described the unfolding crisis for over a decade with more accuracy than any other economist on the planet.

—Derek Scott, Economic Advisor to the British
Prime Minister 1997–2003, London

And Buttonwood might find the answer to his question in the quote he cited from Friedrich Hayek: "The curious task of economics is to demonstrate to men how little they really know about what they imagine they can design."

I can't imagine economists admitting how little they actually know. If they admit to themselves it will hurt their ego: if they admit to others, it will hurt their job prospects.

—Josef Mattes, Austrian
Economist, Vienna

Unpublished Letters to the Editor

July 4, 2003
Editor, New York Times
229 West 43rd Street
New York, NY 10036

To the Editor:

Why does *The New York Times* need to upset the American public on the 4th of July? Two front page headlines, "US Jobless Rate Increase to 6.4%, Highest in 9 years—Blacks Fare Worst," and "Israelis Sense They've Won," do exactly that.

Why not "US Jobless Rate of 6.4%, Lowest of All Industrial Nations."

Why not "Blacks No Longer Afraid to Report That They're Looking for Work." The article even says that is the reason for the higher rate.

"Israelis Sense They've Won" is not something Israel would say.

Why left-wing anti-American yellow journalism on the 4th of July? We are not living in the 1930s, when unions and newspapers were a Soviet mouthpiece. Why is The *New York Times* wrecking its reputation by printing "All the News that's Unfit to Print"?

December 12, 2016
James McBride
New York, NY 10108

Dear Mr. McBride:

I'm a jazz musician, political economist, inner-city public-school teacher and professional real estate investor. All four, equally.

I read, enjoyed and understood *Kill 'Em and Leave*. Well done.

May I pass to you a few thoughts? You and I know how great James Brown was, but your readers might not. You could have said at the outset, perhaps with examples, that unless you, the reader, are a musician, you cannot fully appreciate just how great an artist James Brown was. Consider the sports journalist who remarked when Tiger Woods first came on the scene: "Unless you're a professional golfer, you can't know just how great a golfer Tiger Woods is."

You paint a truthful and vivid picture of the Jim Crow South —a reminder for everyone. Yet, you didn't say that James Brown wouldn't have wanted anyone to use that as an excuse for not making it.

Finally, your last paragraph brought tears to my eyes, implying that all along, James Brown knew what he was doing; as a great artist, knew that if *anyone* listened carefully to his music, that they would not only know who James Brown is, but who *they* are. Speaking about his fellow bandmates, The *New York Times'* obituary last paragraph said it best: "I taught them everything they know. I didn't teach them everything I know."

December 8, 2016
J.D. Vance

Dear Mr. Vance:

As the presidential election [2016] showed, the timing of *Hillbilly Elegy* was perfect. It reminded the nation that working-class communities are a big part of the country. As the beautiful new film *Manchester by the Sea* illustrates, do not underestimate the intelligence and humanity of the working class.

I agree with your message: government cannot solve cultural problems—except for those on the margin, kids, for example, that have some support, somewhere.

I'm glad I heard your book—a first for me, in that I accidentally ordered the CD instead of the book. You put a lot of thought into it. May I make one comment? It's not possible to put the triangle right side up. A middle-class school or neighborhood can accept a few low-income students or residents, those on the margin who would benefit, but not too many because if there is more than one rough student per classroom, more than one rough family per neighborhood, everyone leaves. Cost-benefit analysis.

In California, according to the California Commission on Teacher Credentialing [in the 1980s], although less true today, 50 percent of all new teachers quit in three years, 75 percent in five. Young, motivated, eager to help the less fortunate, with degrees from Stanford and Berkeley, they can't take it. Neither can most students, why their parents pull them out. I know. I taught and continue to teach in Bay Area inner-city public schools.

Working-class students who can't make the grade should be given a voucher to attend private schools. Then, private school parents spending $30,000 a year [today $40,000 or more] per child, could send their children back to the public schools—provided those schools maintained high academic and behavioral standards. The same for cities. With high standards in law enforcement, middle-class families would move back. That would put the triangle back on its base— although it would not necessarily integrate neighborhoods.

Again, thank you for a very well-written book.

4

FOUR ESSAYS

9/11 AND THE ALEXANDRIAN LIBRARY

The 20th century gave us socialism, mankind's greatest error, ever. Every nation tried it (to some degree). Counter to natural social and economic behavior, socialists, via the political process (or communists via revolution), ordered the state to eliminate certain business contracts between individuals, then forcefully purchase (or confiscate) private property. Today, no one denies what ensued: economic collapse. Cuba, North Korea, East Germany, the Soviet Union—all saw a return to the Middle Ages.[1]

Freedom also has a downside. Applying free market economics, nations may become wealthy, but they risk becoming arrogant, risk having everything they created torn down in a day. Outrage, jealousy, the French Revolution, the Alexandrian Library.

So, to not sow the seeds of their own destruction, wealthy nations must not throw their weight around (what the Roman Empire knew). Powerful, developed wealthy nations still must live with their neighbors. As the world discovered on September 11, 2001, any nation can be attacked. The best philosophic and cultural ideas may

---

[1] To turn over ownership of the means of production to the workers (the state) is to replace members of the orchestra with the stagehands. Not possible; they're two separate skills. With their immoral slogan, "the end justify the means," Marxists (in their hearts creating mankind's future) murdered 30 million in the Soviet Union, 30 million in China, two million in Cambodia, four to five million in North Korea—and what *you*, reader, might relate to, imprisoned millions for life for having protested, for example, in Cuba, where Che Guevara felt it his duty to personally shoot in the temple hundreds of land and factory owners who refused to turn over their life's work: their property.

181

win in the end, but not the nations that produced them. With nations in possession of nuclear weapons, survival of the human species depends upon mutual acknowledgment, tolerance and awareness of the moment. A perfect historical example of lack of acknowledgment, lack of awareness of the dynamic of the moment, was the relationship of the Alexandrian Library to the city of Alexandria, Egypt. More than anything, it was arrogance that led to its complete destruction in 391 AD.

At first,

> [I]ts population [Alexandria] was marvelously diverse. Macedonian and later Roman soldiers, Egyptian priests, Greek aristocrats, Phoenician sailors, Jewish merchants, visitors from India and sub-Saharan Africa—everyone, except the vast slave population—lived together in harmony and mutual respect for most of the period of Alexandria's greatness.
>
> The city was founded by Alexander the Great and constructed by his former bodyguard [Ptolemy I Soter]. Alexander encouraged respect for alien cultures and the open-minded pursuit of knowledge. According to tradition —and it does not much matter whether it really happened —he descended beneath the Red Sea in the world's first diving bell. He encouraged his generals and soldiers to marry Persian and Indian women. He respected the gods of other nations. He collected exotic life forms, including an elephant for Aristotle, his teacher. His city was constructed on a lavish scale . . . graced with broad avenues thirty meters wide, elegant architecture and statuary, Alexander's monumental tomb, and an enormous lighthouse, the Pharos, one of the seven wonders of the ancient world.
>
> But the greatest marvel of Alexandria was the library and its associated museum (literally, an institution devoted to the specialties of the Nine Muses). Of that legendary library, the most that survives today is a dank and forgotten cellar of the Serapeum, the library annex, once a temple and later reconsecrated to knowledge. A few moldering shelves may be its only physical remains. Yet this place was once the brain and glory of the greatest city on the planet, the first true research institute in the history of the world. The scholars of the library studied the entire

Cosmos. *Cosmos* is a Greek word for the order of the universe. It is, in a way, the opposite of *Chaos*. It implies the deep interconnectedness of all things. It conveys awe for the intricate and subtle way in which the universe is put together. Here was a community of scholars, exploring physics, literature, medicine, astronomy, geography, philosophy, mathematics, biology, and engineering. Science and scholarship had come of age. Genius flourished there. The Alexandrian Library is where we humans first collected, seriously and systematically, the knowledge of the world.

In addition to Eratosthenes [who predicted the circumference of the world] there was the astronomer Hipparchus, who mapped the constellations and estimated the brightness of the stars; Euclid, who brilliantly systematized geometry and told his king, struggling over a difficult mathematical problem, "There is no royal road to geometry"; Dionysius of Thrace, the man who defined the parts of speech and did for the study of language what Euclid did for geometry; Herophilus, the physiologist who firmly established that the brain rather than the heart is the seat of intelligence; Heron of Alexandria, inventor of gear trains and steam engines and the author of *Automata*, the first book of robots; Apollonius of Perga, the mathematician who demonstrated the forms of the conic sections [later used by Johannes Kepler to understand the movements of the planets]—ellipse, parabola, and hyperbola—the curves, as we now know, followed in their orbits by the planets, the comets and the stars; Archimedes, the greatest mechanical genius until Leonardo da Vinci; and the astronomer and geographer Ptolemy, who compiled much of what is today the pseudoscience of astrology; his Earth-centered universe held sway for 1,500 years, a reminder that intellectual capacity is no guarantee against being dead wrong. And among those great men was a great woman, Hypatia, mathematician and astronomer, the last light of the library, whose martyrdom was bound up with the destruction of the library seven centuries after its founding.

The heart of the library was its collection of books. The organizers combed all the cultures and languages of the world. They sent agents abroad to buy up libraries. Commercial ships docking in Alexandria were searched by the police—not for contraband, but for books. The scrolls were borrowed, copied and then returned to their owners.

Accurate numbers are difficult to estimate, but it seems probable that the library contained half a million volumes, each a handwritten papyrus scroll. What happened to all those books? The classical civilization that created them disintegrated, and the library itself was deliberately destroyed. Only a small fraction of its works survived, along with a few pathetic scattered fragments. And how tantalizing those bits and pieces are! We know, for example, that there was on the library shelves a book by the astronomer Aristarchus of Samos, who argued that the Earth is one of the planets, which like them orbits the Sun, and that the stars are enormously far away. Each of these conclusions is entirely correct, but we had to wait nearly two thousand years for their rediscovery. If we multiply by a hundred thousand our sense of loss for this work of Aristarchus, we begin to appreciate the grandeur of the achievement of classical civilization and the tragedy of its destruction [work with dissection of the atoms, work with aeronautical flight, work with ancient history, history dealing with Creation to the Flood, a period understood to be about 432,000 years previous, one hundred times longer than the Old Testament chronology].[2]

But why was it destroyed, and what were the real consequences of that destruction?

The library was destroyed because it ignored the social, political and economic reality on the ground. The library had become an elitist center completely removed from the lives of those who actually lived in Alexandria. The library was a *royal* library, sponsored and controlled by the Ptolemies, the ruling dynasty of Egypt. The Ptolemies liked the idea of a Greek city—beautiful architecture, free flow of ideas—but not the idea of a Greek city-state, with self-government and direct democracy. And so, to prevent people from taking direct action, the Egyptians, as would any centrally controlled society, created an enormous bureaucracy (that exists today!). Individual ideas may have freely flourished, but individual action ground to a halt. Unlike in Greece, individuals were deprived of owning property and were deprived of the

[2] Carl Sagan, *Cosmos* (New York: Random House, 1980), pp. 18–20.

opportunity to participate politically. The only way citizens could make themselves heard was by rioting.[3] In any society, when citizens have no political or economic opportunity, either they turn within or they riot. Rioting, however, is not an everyday occurrence— precisely why Europe, the Middle East and Asia are culturally so highly developed: deprived of political and economic opportunity (historically), they turned to the arts, to philosophy, to food and fashion.

Still, to turn within is to turn your back on freedom and opportunity. That cannot last. Citizens of a nation continually deprived of freedom and opportunity either leave or the nation ends up destroying itself. As late as the 20th century, that is what happened in Russia, China, Japan and Germany: socialism.[4] In the case of Alexandria, because rulers and scholars were so indifferent to the needs of the citizens, citizens burned down the library.[5]

And what was the consequence of burning down the Alexandrian Library? The Dark Ages. From the perspective of Carl Sagan, a 1,000-year postponement of space exploration.

And what will be the consequence of the September 11 bombing of the World Trade Center? A retreat to the Dark Ages, to

---

[3] John Arthur Garraty, ed., *The Columbia History of the World*, 1972, 10th ed. (New York: Harper & Row), pp. 185–189.

[4] Communism is socialism from the Left; fascism is socialism from the Right.

[5] This is an oversimplification (and may not even be true), but stated this way, it dramatically makes the essential Jeffersonian point that arrogance and power must be broken wherever they occur. Whenever societies do not create the social, political and economic institutions that allow and encourage nature's self-correcting social, political and economic forces to work on their own, they will see those natural forces operate on their own anyway: violently. No one knows how the museum and library were destroyed. The *Encyclopedia Britannica 11th Edition* (1911) simply states that the library was destroyed in the civil war that occurred under Aurelian (an extremely barbaric Roman emperor) in 3rd century AD, and that the "daughter library" was destroyed by fanatic Christians attempting to erase all pagan knowledge in 391 AD. Other ideas of how the library was destroyed, and no less arrogant, are that Caliph Umar of Damascus, in the 7th century AD, ordered it burnt. His thought was that if the contents of the library were in disagreement with the Koran, they were heresy, and if the contents were in agreement with the Koran, they were superfluous. In both cases, the library should be burned. There is also the idea that part of the library was destroyed around 48 AD when Julius Caesar, as a diversionary tactic to flee Alexandria, burned all of his ships in the harbor, at which time the library, adjacent to the harbor, accidentally caught fire.

technologically reinforced barbarism? A return to non-Western philosophy and culture, with societies organized and dictated to on the basis of spiritual, aesthetic and communal values?

Or, was the bombing of the World Trade Center simply an act of revenge for perceived grievances? There are plenty of reasons for the Arab world to want revenge, but this was more than revenge; this was hatred. To the Arab world, and not just the extremists, the presence of the Western world in the Middle East is no different than the presence of the scholars of the Alexandrian Library in the midst of a Roman and Christian Alexandria. The Arab world sees the U.S. and the West not only as a threat to their way of thinking but as indifferent and arrogant. They see the U.S. and the West as barbarians reenacting the Crusades against Islam. They see the U.S. indiscriminately aiding *any* side in a political or military conflict: the Shah of Iran, a man hated by his own people, because at the time he protected our oil interests; Saddam Hussein, because at the time, when Khomeini threw us out of Iran, he attacked Iran; Pakistan, because at the time, it aided the Taliban in fighting the Russians; the Saudis, because both then and now, they still have oil; and, then, *not* aiding those who did help us, the Kurds, for example, in northern Iraq because *at the time,* there was no direct U.S. security interest involved.

To destabilize the world, to destabilize regimes in the Middle East, to destroy Israel, all of these are acts of revenge. But the hatred is in response to something more: British, American and Israeli arrogance. The hatred responds to the arrogance of Israeli settlers and the Israeli military, both of whom taunt the Palestinians, including children, as they move on to their land, building settlements on what most of the world community believes will be Palestine in a two-state solution. The fact that the Palestinians have always behaved badly to the Israelis, that they continue to commit acts of terrorism, has nothing to do with it. The fact that Israel, a Western democracy, was plunked down in the middle of an autonomous non-Western region—*that* is the problem. The creation of Israel, a state for Jewish people, may have been legitimate (beginning with migration at the end of the 19th century, no

186

differently than migrations that have created every nation, internationally recognized via the Balfour Declaration in 1917, a pledge of British support for Jewish people to have a homeland in Palestine, and legalized by the UN in 1948), but the creation of Israel to satisfy U.S. interests in the region was not. It's not just that the U.S. wants a democratic nation in the Middle East; it's also that the U.S., during and after World War II, did not want (and did not let) Jews fleeing Europe come settle here. Anti-Semitism in the U.S. was as strong as it was in Europe. In this sense, Israel exists as the result of U.S. immigration policy. Unwavering support in the U.S. for Israel today is partially in atonement for this.

Truman's very narrow presidential victory in 1948 (the year that Israel became a nation) is due partially to securing the Jewish vote in New York, Pennsylvania and Illinois, three high electoral states. Truman could continue Roosevelt's policy of not letting in Jewish refugees by endorsing Zionism, the creation of a Jewish homeland, which is what he did. After the Soviet Union (also to detract world attention from the fact that Jews were neither welcome nor well treated there), the U.S. was the second nation to recognize Israel. And, the U.S. supplied Israel with arms for its War of Independence.

Bad acts, however, are committed by all nations:

1. The Arab nations commit bad acts all the time. Hafez Hassad of Syria [1982] eliminated Sunni fundamentalists in his country simply by leveling the entire commercial center of Hama, killing 20,000 people and dispersing the rest as refugees.[6]

2. At its birth in 1948, not only did the Arab world, 50 million against two million, try to knock out the new state of Israel, but they attacked Jews in all Arab countries,

---

[6] Robert Bartley, "Thinking Things Over," *Wall Street Journal*, October 15, 2001.

causing 500,000 to flee to Israel.[7] The Palestinians in Israel also fled, but that was only because they *assumed* the Israelis would do the same to them. Yet, unlike Israel, which accepted the fleeing Jews, the Arab states did not accept the fleeing Palestinians. They have purposely been kept in refugee camps, in conditions of hopelessness, in order that they would one day rise up, with world opinion on their side. That strategy is working. For 50 years, generations of Palestinian children have grown up in a barren environment. Deprived of any opportunity for a meaningful future, left with a self-destructive attitude that leaves them vulnerable to the glories of martyrdom, a martyrdom constantly displayed to them on television and in civic parades, those young seeds have blossomed into today's terrorists.

3. Before its birth, Israeli terrorists acted badly toward the British. The Irgun, under the leadership of Menachem Begin, blew up the King David Hotel (which served as the British military headquarters), killing over 90 people; the Stern Gang assassinated the British Minister of State

---

[7] Forcing Jews to flee their homes was mean. Jews practically created the Middle East. They were among the 8th century mathematicians (disguised as Muslims), and the writers of the Old Testament, New Testament and Koran. (Alexander the Great planted a colony of Jews in Alexandria. Their numbers grew until, at the beginning of the Christian era, they occupied two-fifths of the city and held some of the highest offices. *Encyclopedia Britannica 11th Edition*, p. 575.) However, when their importance gets beyond their numbers, Jews tend to become arrogant—why Germany eliminated them from Europe, why Arab nations dream of doing the same in the Middle East, why they were thrown out of Spain by the Inquisition (which the Jewish scholar Benzion Netanyahu declared, like the pogroms of Eastern Europe and 20th century Nazi Germany, had nothing to do with Christians hating Jews, but everything to do with racism, the true basis of anti-Semitism).

Like the scholars at the Alexandrian Library, Jews in 20th century Europe didn't see it coming. They do now! (This time, if they are forced to leave Israel, unlike their flight from Egypt under Moses, the UN may require that Jews first put things back the way they found them: mosquito-infested swamps, desert, a few olive groves, nomads. [Putting back the olive groves is easy: cut an olive tree into 50 branches; stick them in the ground; they'll grow. No skill required; olive is the world's most easily transplantable tree.] Removing an advanced industrialized civilization, *that* will be hard—and unfair to the Arabs. They'll be completely unemployed.)

in Cairo; and together, both gangs indiscriminately assassinated and publicly hung British soldiers.[8]

4. The bombing of the World Trade Center was also an act of arrogance—another example of fundamentalist Muslims wishing to extend their own 8th century crusades, using the sword to convert infidels to their way of thinking.

But committing bad acts has repercussions. It's not enough to say that a nation's bad acts are minimal compared to the good things they do. (Compared to what other nations do, often to their own people, the bad acts of the U.S. are negligible. Compared to its acts of generosity, no nation in the world is as generous. Plenty of Arabs in Bosnia and Kosovo are thankful that the U.S. stepped in to protect them from massacre.[9]) But one bad act is all it takes. What Israel is doing to the Palestinians today will have far-reaching consequences. Committing bad acts against a people who have no means of expressing themselves other than through violence can only produce hatred and hatred acts of revenge out of proportion to the original misdeeds. This is at the heart of Arab terrorism. This is what they think is their reality. The bombing of our embassies, our battleships, the World Trade Center, the Pentagon, the attempt on the White House, all of this may be only a beginning (2001).

Israel and America represent highly developed civilizations, but the reality is that plenty of people in the world don't agree. If Israel and America think that they can arrogantly impose their values, Western values of individual freedom, of democratic self-

---

[8] Ritchie Ovendale, *The Origins of the Arab-Israeli Wars, 2nd Edition* (London: Longman Group UK Limited, 1992).

[9] No differently than watching the rise of Hitler and Nazism in the 1930s, again in their own neighborhood, Europeans didn't lift a finger to stop the Serbs in Bosnia and Kosovo.

government, they risk having those values destroyed—no differently than the values integral to the great Alexandrian Library.[10]

The nature of American arrogance is profound in the sense that Americans are unaware of the effect of American culture on the rest of the world. Even when abroad, Americans are unaware that when they walk with an air of lightness, with heads held high, as a free people, this is offensive to people whose history and memories are those of war, starvation, pillage and rape: the histories of Europe, Asia, Native America, Latin America, Africa. It is this unawareness that explains why Americans know so little about the rest of the

SUNDAY, SEPTEMBER 23, 2001

MIKE LUCKOVICH / Atlanta Constitution

[10] The Alexandrian Library is a heuristic example (in that no one really knows why it burned) because it makes the point that the existence of the library in the middle of a region of religious fanatics (see the death of Hypatia) is no different than the existence of Israel in the middle of religious fanatics. Jews, Christians, the Alexandrian Library—all contradict the essence of Islam. When rulers are the absolute descendants of Mohammed, and civil law, *sharia*, is the absolute word of God, there is no need for democracy; there is nothing to vote for.

world, why so many Americans thought the attack on September 11 was unprovoked.

If the U.S. is to better understand the Arab world, not to mention the rest of the world, does this mean the U.S. should withdraw from those areas and let the vacuum that's created be filled by others? If the Arab world hates us more for who we are rather than what we do (considering that they behave worse than we do), what should we do? Are we hated because we corrupt pure Islam, or because pure Islam needs a scapegoat for its absolute inability to provide for its people in a material way? How is it possible to invest money in Islamic nations when paying interest on money is a sin? (It's also a Christian sin, but at least Christians pretend it isn't.) And then how is it possible in the 21st century to exclude women from public life? Why is it better to see the West as an infidel oppressor and a capitalist exploiter rather than as a partner with whom a fruitful friendship is possible? Are the differences truly irreconcilable?

Is there an analogy between the British, who ruled the waves in the 19th century, creating *Pax Britannica*, and the U.S., which now rules the waves (and the air), creating *Pax Americana*? Because it cost the British everything, will it cost the U.S. everything? Do we need to own or control the resources of the rest of the world, the oil in the Middle East, for example? Why can't we just trade for it? If the only valuable resource in the world is human imagination, then we certainly don't need to control other nations. As long as we are free (or, freer than other nations), we will continue to attract, as we have throughout our history, the best minds of the world. Unlike any other country, we have a self-selected immigrant population. It's our strength. At the beginning of the 19th century, the U.S. had the smallest population in the world, less than five million, but two hundred years later, at the beginning of the 21st century, after China and India, the U.S. has the *third* largest population in the world: 332 million (2022).[11]

---

[11] *Worldpopulationreview.com/states*. Indonesia has 276 million, Russia 145 million, Japan 124 million. (In 2002, when this essay was first written, the population of the U.S. was 287 million, Indonesia 242 million, Russia 142 million, Japan 126 million. Twenty years later, people are still immigrating to the U.S., not to Russia or Japan.)

In other words, owning or controlling other countries (colonialism) has dire economic consequences. It ruins a nation. It costs too much financially and costs too much politically and socially. The loss to Great Britain of the American colonies is the perfect example. Before the loss, here is what Adam Smith said in his concluding paragraph of the *Wealth of Nations*.[12]

> The rulers of Great Britain have, for more than a century past, amused the people with the imagination that they possessed a great empire on the west side of the Atlantic. This empire, however, has hitherto existed in imagination only. It has hitherto been, not an empire, but the project of an empire; not a gold mine, but the project of a gold mine; a project which has cost, which continues to cost, and which, if pursued in the same way as it has been hitherto, is likely to cost, immense expense, without being likely to bring profit; for the effects of the monopoly of the colony trade, it has been shown, are to the great body of the people, mere loss instead of profit. It is surely now time that our rulers should either realize this golden dream, in which they have been indulging themselves, perhaps, as well as the people; or, that they should awake from it themselves, and endeavor to awaken the people. If the project cannot be completed, it ought to be given up. If any of the provinces of the British empire cannot be made to contribute towards the support of the whole empire, it is surely time that Great Britain should free herself from the expense of defending those provinces in time of war, and of supporting any part of their civil or military establishments in time of peace, and endeavor to accommodate her future views and designs to the real mediocrity of her circumstances.
>
> The U.S. today maintains its overseas presence through a coalition of nations. The U.S. has learned the world does not like it when we act unilaterally or act arrogantly. This approach is necessary to avoid acts of terrorism, but only to the extent that it does avoid them. If acts of terrorism are and have always been a part of human history, then a fine line has to be drawn between the extremes of not doing anything, showing restraint and

---

[12] Adam Smith, *Wealth of Nations* (Indianapolis, Indiana: reprinted by Liberty Classics, an authorized reprint by the Oxford University Press, 1976).

192

taking unilateral action using military force. In response to September 11, going into Afghanistan, even if unilaterally, to wipe out Al-Qaeda and Osama bin Laden, was the correct thing. It had the possibility of success. If the Chinese had bombed the World Trade Center, would we have gone into China? Would we profile all American Chinese as potential suspects? Possibly the worst consequence of September 11 is that by declaring acts of terrorism equivalent to acts of war, we justify a reduction in our own civil liberties. Perhaps the proper perspective is to view 9/11 not as an isolated incident but as an act for which there is precedent, for which there is a future.[13]

In other words, the world will have to adjust to sporadic acts of terror that cause approximately ten thousand deaths per year. This type of warfare will characterize the 21st century (unless nuclear war or bioterrorism)—the kind of terror Israel experiences every day, to which it has adjusted. (Occasional Israeli overreaction is understandable.) Ten thousand deaths per year equal one million per century. If the 21st century experiences one million deaths from terrorist attacks, this will compare favorably with 140 million deaths from warfare and genocide in the 20th century.[14]

We do not know (2002) if there will be a long-term economic consequences from the September 11 attack, but there will be an economic consequence if the prosperous nations in the West do not deal with the failing nondemocratic nations of the rest of the world. Even if the developed world cannot solve its problems, it must appear to be trying, not appear to be indifferent. We do not live in isolation; the price of freedom is responsibility. The developed world must distribute some of its wealth. It's an insurance premium— although economic reality is that wealth redistribution breaks classical laws of business and economics, thus, useless. All that

---

[13] Why has the Search for Extraterrestrial Intelligence (SETI), since 1984, not revealed radio signals anywhere in the universe? Because all civilizations that reach our level of development self-destruct.

[14] The figure of 140 million was mentioned in his speech to the Commonwealth Club in San Francisco, November 2001, by Robert McNamara, Secretary of Defense under Presidents Kennedy and Johnson; McNamara said that in the future, we could get the numbers down by not killing so many civilians.

matters is that lesser-developed nations think we're trying to help. The world does not need another socialist revolution.

Economic reality is that large-scale wealth distribution makes rich nations poorer, less able to purchase what goods and services lesser-developed nations manage to produce. Nor does it solve their main economic problem, namely, that those nations don't produce.[15] For the developed world to raise the standard of living of the lesser-developed world, it must, then, drop its trade barriers, allow lesser-developed world exports to enter duty-free, or, which is the same thing, allow their own low-skilled manufacturing jobs to go abroad. Give the lesser-developed world a chance! Multinational corporations and private foreign investors (globalization) will build the factories, but it is the working class in developed nations who will make the biggest contribution—as they switch to the manufacture of products in which their nations have the comparative advantage, jobs and products that require science, technology, engineering and mathematics (STEM). Were he alive, Marx would be proclaiming, "Workers of the industrialized world, stop making labor-intensive products!"

The September 11 attack affected some industries, especially airlines and tourism, but in a globalized economy, those industries always recover. Governments may want to prevent bankruptcies in particular industries when bankruptcies are caused by natural catastrophes or acts of war, but should never offer stimulus packages

---

[15] Norway is about to experience some economic decline (2022) as it discards its creative entrepreneurs (à la Soviet Union) in favor of enforcing a 1.1 percent wealth tax on income over $172,000 (to redistribute wealth to its own people).* Result: Norway's 30 richest families moved to Switzerland. They took their wealth, $3 billion, and their annual tax payment of $61 million. (In Norway, the only way to avoid paying is to move.) That 1.1 percent tax on wealth, no matter the profitability of the firm, *forces* those families to borrow against their assets, or dilute the value of the stock by selling more shares, not to mention lose the incentive to create new products (when all you're thinking about is how you're going to pay that tax, or how you're going to get your money out of the country—today, 2023, how you are going to conform to citizen demand for environmental, social, and governmental (GSE) accountability). See Robert Milne, "Rich Norwegians Flee to Low-Tax Switzerland as Wealth Levy Bites," *Financial Times*, December 17, 2022, https://www.ft.com/content/ca33dc93-78c0-4d7a-a647-cde18ab6a1fd.

*Creative art and creative business are two sides of the same coin. Throw out your creative industrialists (those who purchase art because they need and want it), and you throw away your artists.

to an economy in recession. Stimulus packages provide temporary relief, but they prolong recovery. They deaden initiative.[16]

This is why the 2002 recession must be allowed to run its course—because it was a market correction to an overpriced stock market, as opposed to the previous 1990 recession, which was a market correction to an overpriced real estate market, or the 2008 financial crisis, which was a market correction to government-ordered subprime lending (which opened the floodgate to unprecedented fraud throughout the entire financial system). Because the market recognizes stimulus packages for what they are: a onetime thing which never makes the hoped-for adjustment. If a government wants to stop a recession, it must throw trillions of dollars over a period of years.[17]

Why? Because government intervention in an economy cannot change timeless laws of money and human behavior. People are cautious during a recession. The Keynesian multiplier (government stimulus to the economy) has no effect. Consumers hoard their handouts in preparation for the recession worsening: the Ricardian equivalence. At the end of a recession, when producers and consumers are again confident, stimulus may have an effect—but it's no longer necessary.

If terrorism makes the public afraid to fly, nothing can be done to reverse a downturn in the tourist industry. Revival of the tourist industry will happen on its own as free markets self-correct. They see economic stimulus—injection of cash or a tax reduction—as

---

16 Japan Inc., before the government started its spending spree on public works for the purpose of pulling the country out of recession, had a budget surplus of $500 billion. It now has a budget deficit of $500 billion and no change in the recession. (As in Europe, where public spending includes unemployment insurance, this is true in 2022.) The recession continues because the Japanese refuse to deal with the underlying problem: their bankrupt banks. Bad loans are still on the books (to save face) because interest rates were lowered to zero and payments on principal suspended. Japanese loans are, thus, never in default.

Yet, when the U.S. experienced a similar recession in the early 1990s, also because of an overextension of credit by banks, the U.S. eliminated its bad loans. Private investors bought them up at a discount, and bankrupt banks were permanently closed (mostly savings and loans). The U.S. did the right thing. It solved the underlying problem.

17 Those trillions of dollars, $3 trillion a year, are almost the entire federal budget—except they're not coming out of the budget; they're paid for by borrowing.

unnatural, why government borrowing to provide stimulus only stimulates high interest rates, which pushes the economy back to recession.[18] Why should airlines, which made enormous profits in the 1990s, with lax airport security up until September 11, an industry figuring, as Ford Motors did with its Pinto in the 1970s, that the cost of tighter security, or in Ford's the cost of correcting a deadly defect, was more than the cost of paying claims, be reimbursed for lost travel business?

There are no quick solutions. The way the West developed via increased commercial production is how lesser-developed nations must develop (if they want the things money will buy: modern health care, education, safety standards in building construction, protection of the environment). Globalized markets are important for lesser-developed nations because they provide a market for their products. Globalization (which does not mean unsustainable exploitation of resources) provides an international market for creative entrepreneurs whose domestic market is too small. The lesser-developed world should accept foreign aid and government intervention in the economy only to the extent that promotes small-scale, independently owned production, *not grand infrastructure schemes*. The International Monetary Fund burdening those nations with debt, telling them how to run their economies—*that* is pure arrogance.

---

[18] Government borrowing to cure the 2008 financial crisis did not cause interest rates to rise (they were in fact lowered to zero) but caused another distortion: the price of assets to rise. Another bubble.

GREECE AND THE EURO CRISIS

October 2012

There is no euro crisis. Since 2009, during the entire turmoil surrounding the threat of a Greek default on its government bonds, the euro has not dropped in value (at the time of this writing, for three years).[19] This explains why European leaders, over the last several years, unlike those in financial markets who panic at every nanosecond change in unfounded bits of information, have kept cool heads. It is why European leaders, heads of state, politicians and bankers all go through the motions (2012) of staging "last chance" summits when, in fact, they are really stalling, waiting for the Greeks and the rest of southern Europe to become serious and acknowledge the reality of their situation.[20]

European leaders all know how the so-called euro crisis will be resolved: by a European banking union (complete with European-wide deposit insurance), recapitalization of ailing banks with funds from the new European Stability Mechanism, and the conversion of national debts into Eurobonds.

---

[19] The euro dropped in value from a high in 2008 of $1.60 to what it should be, approximately $1.25 in 2012, considering that the dollar is low. Otherwise, the euro would be about $1.10 to the dollar, the rate projected at the euro's outset, although, then, in 1999, because the dollar was high, it was around $0.90.

[20] At the creation of the euro, January 1, 1999, European leaders did not properly account for crises such as the current one (2008) because, then and now, Europeans cannot step out of their egalitarian mindset that leads them to deny that there are two Europes: Teutonic and Latin.

In Europe, there are different economies and different democracies that reflect diverse histories, values and cultures. "If you jam diverse economic cultures into a single currency, you are bound to get an explosion." See David Brooks, "The Technocratic Nightmare," *New York Times*, November 18, 2011, https://www.nytimes.com/2011/11/18/opinion/brooks-the-technocratic-nightmare.html.

Europe is unifying legally and economically, although there really is no common language or common conversation. Leaders may embrace "federalism," but the word means one thing in Britain and another in Germany. Plus, European elitism. "Off the record, European technocrats would say the most blatantly condescending things: that Europe's peoples were not to be trusted and government should be run from the top by people like themselves." Brooks, "Technocratic Nightmare."

Alan Greenspan, former chairman of the U.S. Federal Reserve, also makes this clear: Europe is confronted not just with differences … (Continued on next page)

(Continued from previous page) ... in labor costs and prices, but with differences in culture.* "Euro-north has historically been characterized by high saving rates and low inflation, the metrics of a culture that emphasizes longer-term investments rather than immediate consumption. In contrast, negative saving rates—excess consumption—have been a common feature of Greece and Portugal since 2003."

*Alan Greenspan, "Europe's Crisis Is All about the North-South Split," *Financial Times*, October 7, 2011. https://www.ft.com/content/678b163a-ef68-11e0-bc88-00144feab49a.

To Greenspan, the proof is that sovereign bond credit risk spreads relative to the German Bund (October 2011) ranged from 370 basis points (Italy) to 1,960 basis points (Greece) [19.60 percent]. Northern eurozone countries have tight spreads against Germany —40 to 80 basis points for the Netherlands [0.4 to 0.8 percent] (Greenspan, "Split"). "The ranking of credit risk spreads by size across the eurozone in 2010 was almost identical to the ranking of the level of unit labor costs (relative to that of Germany), suggesting that the higher labor costs and prices have rendered 'euro-south' less competitive and so more subject to credit risk." (Greenspan, "Split"). In other words, according to Greenspan, the competitively priced exports of the northern eurozone have been subsidizing southern consumption since the onset of the euro. Worse, even before January 1, 1999, in anticipation of the euro, southern eurozone sovereign bond rates dropped significantly, 450 basis points relative to German Bund rates (allowing enormous expansion of state welfare rather than enormous reduction in state debt).

Edmund Phelps, recipient of the Nobel Prize in economics, reminds us how Germany became so competitive: Gerhard Schröder forged an agreement with the unions for restraint in return for jobs. Phelps reminds us that Italy and France could have preserved their competitiveness by doing the same, but that Germany simply showed better vision and leadership. See Edmund Phelps, "Germany Is Right to Ask For Austerity Before Any More Union," *Financial Times*, July 20, 2012, p. 7. Thus, according to Phelps, the difficulties of so many European countries [no differently than in the Middle East, Indonesia, Russia] derive from their corporatism: state projects serving cronies [under the guise of "infrastructure"] and vast social protection programs run by progressive elites. These surged in the 1970s and 1980s. The prospect of a lifetime of such benefits—sweet contracts, soft loans, early pensions—created something new ["brave new," the offering of which is how populist politicians come to power]: social wealth. Phelps, "Germany is Right."

How was this paid for (in the U.S. also)? By deficit spending. By Basel I (a worldwide central bank agreement), in 1990, which "lowered to zero banks' capital requirement on sovereign debt—no matter how risky." Phelps, "Germany is Right." With no real check on government spending, benefits continually outpaced taxes. The Keynesian thought was that debt and wealth would increase consumer demand. But wealth led to higher wages. In the southern eurozone, these so exceeded productivity that the unit cost of labor rose to a level at which those nations could no longer compete. Now, they can no longer pay their debt: thus, default.

Keynes also said that a boom, not a slump, is the right time for austerity—that austerity during a recession only deepens the recession. That's true, except that for the last 50 years, a period of great economic prosperity, Western nations systematically increased rather than reduced their budget deficits. *Now, that spending option is closed.* Nations no longer have a choice: they must cut back expenditures and lower their labor costs. That decision is at the center of the 2012 American presidential election, and should be (but isn't) the focus of most European elections.

Greece will either be bailed out or its debt will be forgiven (or some combination of the two).[21]

---

[21] Capitalism has invented two ways (both essentially the same) of overcoming insurmountable debt: default or bankruptcy. These are the only ways an economic system can purge itself of its excesses. If not, those excesses remain embedded and prevent a solution.

Since the birth of capitalism (the Renaissance), there have been nearly 100 sovereign defaults in Europe, usually followed by a restructuring, but each followed by devaluations of the currency. (In truth, sovereign default is as ancient as sovereign debt itself—as in 4th century BC, when 10 out of 13 Greek municipalities in the Attic Maritime Association defaulted on loans from the Delos Temple.)

If Greece's government cannot pay its debts, and the institutions that insured those debts cannot cover them, Greece should default. It was default by such insuring institutions, American International Group (AIG), for example, that triggered the 2008 financial crisis: those companies could not cover their credit default swaps. There is precedent for bankruptcy. (Bankruptcy does not mean going out of business; it means eliminating your loans.)

Default is not the only solution. The IMF has been pressuring the European Central Bank (ECB) to take a hit below face value as part of a program to prevent the collapse of Greek debt markets. It has also been accepting Greek bonds as collateral for cheap loans to teetering Greek banks. The bonds, however, with estimated yields in excess of 7 percent, will provide a *big* return if Greece does not default and they are held to maturity.

The IMF has been pressuring the ECB to take the hit because the ECB is the correct vehicle to prop up markets, by buying bonds in the secondary market. The IMF itself is forbidden from financing countries directly, by EU treaties and its own statutes, yet through the ECB, the IMF can circumvent those rules. (All financial regulations—Sarbanes-Oxley Act (SOX), Dodd–Frank, Basel III—are nothing other than foundations upon which new means of circumvention are built.)

There is some legal basis for such a plan: European Council regulation 3603/93 exempts central bank loans to the IMF from the prohibitions on government financing. Article 23 in the central bank's own statutes allows it to conduct transactions with international organizations. See Neil Unmack and Wei Gu, "A Way to Finance Europe's Rescue," *New York Times*, November 22, 2011, https://www.nytimes.com/2011/11/22/business/a-way-to-finance-europes-rescue.html.

Such loopholes aren't legally watertight; neither clause was ever intended to fast-track large bailouts. Unmack, "Rescue." (Similarly, the U.S. Constitution was never intended to authorize such enormous general services such as Social Security or universal health care, but by converting the right to tax for national defense into the right to tax for anything, for general welfare, by the 1930s, that non-intention was permanently circumvented.) One way to get around such a bailout would be to place it under strict conditionality: relieve the central bank from having to make a decision, i.e., to automatically loan whenever there is a problem, and inadvertently create a moral hazard problem. Then, use a gentlemen's agreement that the IMF will get its money back before other creditors. Unmack, "Rescue." (Security for repayment to both the IMF and ECB is already superior to existing investors.)

In other words, the obstacle to an IMF/CB program is political, not legal. Eurozone nations will not like giving up control of their destiny, and IMF member states will not like underwriting big eurozone risks; that is why reducing risk requires passing losses back through the central bank. Financing the IMF through the central bank may be unorthodox, but hardly less than the current policy of secondary market purchases. Unmack, "Rescue."

In Europe, the U.S., anywhere, in the end, taxpayers will pick up the tab.[22]

Bailout is the only solution to a major financial crisis. The reasoning is in *Lombard Street*, by Walter Bagehot. First published in 1873 and still in print, it remains the best guide for handling a financial crisis. Bagehot stated quite simply that when a nation's

---

[22] As a result of tax-code exploitation, reality is that it is always the middle class that picks up the tab: rich and poor don't pay taxes.

There will be taxpayer resistance then to the requisite Eurobonds, but those bonds have already actually been issued—they are called euros. EU countries are already pledged to make up any capital loss of the ECB, and this must eventually come from tax revenues. Converting debt to Eurobonds transfers risk, which may then be transferred further in credit default swap markets. But risk does not evaporate. With a default, the ECB will step in and pay on behalf of the taxpayers. See John H. Cochrane, "Last Chance to Save the Euro," *The Wall Street Journal*, September 29, 2011, https://www.wsj.com/articles/SB10001424052970204422404576594971418554358.

The morality of this is another issue. Paying off debt with more debt will lower bond yields, but it will also raise pension fund liabilities in relation to their underlying assets. Calculated originally at a return of 8 percent, those assets today at best return only 4 percent, which, of course, is how they always should have been calculated. U.S. state and local government pension deficits have risen from $3.1 trillion to $4.4 trillion for this reason. See Buttonwood, "A Trillion Here, $500 Billion There," *The Economist*, October 15, 2011, and Hal Weitzman and Nicole Bullock, "Courts Dash US States' Plans on Public Pension Reform," *Financial Times*, April 9, 2012. In other words, according to Daniel Hannan, a British Member of Parliament, paying off debt with more debt, reflating the bubble to prevent another recession, is like avoiding a hangover by remaining drunk. (See speech to The Heritage Foundation, San Francisco, October 25, 2011.)

But, is the world making too big a deal of this? The EU can handle a default by a tiny country, Greece, with a GDP of $320 billion, the same as Maryland's, its population of 11 million equal to Los Angeles. What needs to be accounted for is that the window period of 1945 to 1975 is over—when unions were able to push up wages and benefits beyond market, with factories passing that cost on as higher prices at a time of no competition from Japan and Germany (destroyed during World War II). That party is over! The world's unfunded health insurance, Social Security, public and private pensions, like today's loans, are now all due. Everyone was reckless; now, everyone must take a hit. Reflating the economy is hit avoidance.

Why must everyone take a hit? Because society is like a construction site: first the site is secured (from theft and vandalism), *then* construction takes place. Rome fell in 476 AD precisely because it could no longer secure its construction site, the Roman Empire: there was no money for defense—all of it went to pay interest on the budget deficit. (Sound familiar?) Unopposed, in that the military, which hadn't been paid, didn't lift a finger, Huns simply walked in and destroyed the construction site (except for the Vatican, because Attila the Hun, a spiritual person, was convinced by the pope, a spiritual person, not to—see Verdi, *Attila the Hun*.)

financial system is at risk of total collapse, that nation must abandon whatever economic theories they hold and just bail out their banks.[23]

But not just any bank. According to Bagehot, bailout must go only to those banks capable of someday repaying the loan, that still have assets, that are willing to offer ownership warrants as security. Those banks, when they return to profit and pay back the bailout, will buy themselves back. (In a free society, government does not compete with the private sector.)

Although, with complete economic collapse, really, the correct solution is bankruptcy. Those nations or individuals who loaned money to Greece deserve to lose: they were gambling. They were making subprime loans to a nation without the means to repay, and for no other reason than to obtain an above-market rate of return. Bankruptcy rightfully wipes all of that out. It wipes out the borrower's debt; it makes the borrower once again a good credit risk.

If Greece, Spain, Portugal and Italy were to leave the euro, their currency (and the potential euro crisis) would self-correct. Restored to their old currencies, which would immediately be devalued by the market, citizens there would experience austerity. At first, indirectly, because nominal wages and pensions would remain the same, but later, directly, as inflation increases, the price of foreign goods and services for personal consumption, intermediate manufacturing, and eventually all goods and services. Yet, with their devalued currency, those nations would then export their own goods and services at prices below market and grow their economies. This may be true, however, only for Italy. Greece, Spain and Portugal, inefficient and uncompetitive in world markets, may be forced back

---

[23] Walter Bagehot, *Lombard Street, A Description of the Money Market* (New York: John Wiley & Sons, 1999). Walter Bagehot was both founder and long-time editor of *The Economist* magazine.

into low-wage, labor-intensive, low-skill industry—where their comparative advantage probably lies.[24]

None of this is going to happen! The cost to the Teutonic countries of the Latin countries abandoning the euro is more than the benefit (see this essay, Part III). European nations will come together, as did the American states in 1787 when they abandoned their loose Articles of Confederation in favor of a strong Constitution. European nations will join a fiscal union to their monetary union and then centrally control all national budgets.[25]

---

[24] Currency devaluation happens naturally in the market as a function of world demand for a particular nation's currency. If there is no demand, that currency can be sold only by devaluing it, offering two for one, for example.

Who sells currencies? Exporting nations that receive foreign currency at the point of sale of their products. When BMW sells a car in Athens and is paid in drachmas, it has to sell those drachmas (greatly devalued) to repatriate income to pay its employees in Germany.

[25] Helmut Kohl, in his 1970s dream of a European Union, understood that a monetary union would be the precursor to a fiscal union, that the two together were the *sine qua nons* of a United States of Europe. Kohl understood that without political union, a common currency, the euro, would be nothing other than a prenuptial joint bank account, inherently unstable, as the weaker party (or parties) cannot help but abuse it; cannot help but let their friends and relatives tap in. Anything less than complete political union, then, makes the euro simply a gold standard, not a common currency; it makes the euro simply a loose confederation of trading partners. Anything less than complete political union leaves the EU unstable and vulnerable to exploitation by speculators. See Kenneth Rogoff, "A Euro Parable: The Couple with a Joint Account," *Financial Times*, April 24, 2012, https://www.ft.com/content/bb16c228-8d2d-11e1-8b49-00144feab49a.

The above statement may not be entirely true; it may simply be conventional wisdom. Monetary policy unrelated to worldwide fiscal policy is certainly possible. The gold standard was such a policy, and so too, use of the dollar as a standard—between the U.S. and several countries, including China, which pegs its exchange rate to the dollar. According to John Kay, columnist for the *Financial Times*, if France and Germany had created a monetary union between just the two of them, or perhaps with a few other northern eurozone countries, that could have been the experiment, the springboard for expansion. "The eurozone's difficulties have been created by member states, not markets. Giving members more resources to fight markets makes things worse, not better." See John Kay, "Europe's Elite is Fighting Reality and Will Lose," *Financial Times*, October 26, 2011, https://www.ft.com/content/d5215992-fe6e-11e0-bac4-00144feabdc0. (Brexit 2016).

Democracies get away with this all the time. Because creditors know that they will be paid back, there is no limit to how much they will lend. Democracies, then, postpone the crunch point rather than eliminate it. The more stable the democracy, the higher its debt can be (in relation to GDP). The harsh truth, however (felt today), is that no matter how often they vote, democracies cannot make foreign nations extend them credit. See Buttonwood, "Democracies and Debt," *The Economist*, September 1, 2012, https://www.economist.com/finance-and-economics/2012/09/01/democracies-and-debt.

Like the U.S., Europeans will establish a European Treasury, European debt, and a European central bank.[26] The central bank already exists, but has not acted robustly enough to stop the euro from disintegrating. It's not enough, for example, to stop depositors in Spain from withdrawing their money and sending it to Germany (in preparation for a return to a highly devalued peseta).

More time is required for Latin Europe to swallow its pride and accept the fact that Teutonic Europe is going to control their national budgets. Teutonic Europe will recapitalize their banks and convert their debt to Eurobonds, but Latin Europe will be forced to reform itself. Will Latin Europe swallow its national pride? Will Latin Europe accept Germany as a colonial master?

The recent case of Latvia was similar to Greece, but Latvia had its own currency, devalued it, and with self-imposed austerity, solved its economic problems.[27] Latvia is a good example of doing this. Its economy grew. Latvia recovered, but Latvia paid a price.

The price: Latvia's GDP plummeted, its unemployment rose and entrepreneurial talent was lost to emigration. Wages dropped and prices dropped, yet together, all these elements, including gross inequality, allowed its economy to grow.[28]

---

[26] If Europeans had a treasury secretary (such as Henry Paulson, *circa* 2008), which they don't, they might have created a TARP-like program to buy up bad loans. The head of the ECB could buy up bonds from troubled nations, but first would have to secure the money (or permission to secure the money) from European presidents, especially in France and Germany, who are reluctant to give to a eurozone rescue fund. That really was part of the original Maastricht Treaty agreement, along with such requirements as limiting national budget deficits to not more than 3 percent, and debt-to-GDP to not more than 60 percent—all of which have been flouted.

In truth, Germany can save Europe simply by guaranteeing all debt—national debt and bank debt. That would calm markets: prudent Germans rescue spendthrift Greeks and Italians. The pig that made his house of bricks saves his brothers—the pigs that made their houses of straw and sticks. The brick pig does not turn down his brothers: "Sure," he says, "come on in, but sign here. Here are the terms!"

[27] Greece, to the contrary, was happy to join the euro—more valuable than the drachma, it allowed Greece to expand its welfare state.

[28] The process of internal devaluation can be compared to the painting of one's house. According to Nemat Shafik of the International Monetary Fund, "If you have an exchange rate, you can move your brush back and forth; if you don't, you must move the whole house." Attached to the euro, Greece must move its whole house.

Latvia's internal devaluation was better than currency devaluation. The currency peg still gave the nation credibility, i.e., it did not drive away lenders. It eliminated inflation *and* the burden of paying back euro-denominated loans in a devalued currency. Deep front-loaded austerity (cutting social services) wins back market confidence.[29]

With a Greek default, here are some considerations:

1. Countries at risk of default will see the rate on their government bonds rise. The cost of government borrowing will rise so high that repayment will be impossible. To borrow $10 billion due in one year yet receive $9 billion, for no other reason than to pay for unfunded social services, is completely self-defeating.

2. Countries that receive bailouts will see the cost of their government bonds rise. Why? Because bailout money is senior in security to those bonds, causing them— government bonds—to no longer be risk-free. That is why European banks do not want to be bailed out by the European Central Bank (ECB).

3. Countries at risk of default or bailout will see an erosion of confidence, the most fundamental underlying phenomenon with respect to markets. When suppliers fear a government default, they stop producing. Then, unemployment rises, as both foreign and domestic

---

[29] In tough financial times, progressive politicians have nothing to offer. Their concern for inequality and government intervention in the economy only makes things worse. In the 1930s, it was the U.S. government's retraction of the money supply that caused the Great Depression (plus all the social programs to reverse unemployment, such as the Works Progress Administration, which had absolutely no effect). Contrast this with the fact that although depressions usually last two to three years, government intervention in the 1930s caused a normal depression, about to end in 1933, to become the Great Depression and continue an additional eight years.

investors take their money out of the country. If only to restore confidence, some debt will have to be forgiven. As in business, so too for nations: bankruptcy is sometimes the only solution.

With the three scenarios above, credit markets already have a message: you European officials—politicians and bankers wrangling with investors to cut Greece's debt—will get a deal, but not the one you want.[30]

Currency trading (2012) in Greek bonds and credit default swaps (CDS) already reveal that credit markets believe an agreement will be reached. Still, there are bondholders who would like to

---

[30] As mentioned, European officials—bankers and politicians—know how they will resolve the euro crisis (which is why it is not a crisis). They also know that if they do nothing, credit markets will do it for them: devalue the euro in its entirety. That, however, will lead to a lost decade—ten years for the market to purge itself of bad debt.

Devaluing the euro will benefit any nation that exports, Germany included, but will also create inflation, and not just in peripheral countries, but in Germany. That is something Germans do not want: they do not want it on principle, and they do not want it because it will cause the price of all financial goods and services to rise—lowering Germany's standard of living as punishment for building their houses of brick.

The point is that those who don't care about inflation, or who suggest getting out of the euro, don't remember the recent past. Germans do. They remember inflation in the 1920s (the misery and the war that that brought), and they remember how it was before the euro. From the perspective of the vast swath of small and medium-sized companies, known as the *Mittelstand*, which account for 60 percent of German jobs, there is no nostalgia for the days when they and their customers had to keep an eye on the value of a dozen European currencies, a time when the deutsche mark sometimes became so strong that it threatened to price them out of foreign markets. See Jack Ewing, "A Risk-Averse Strategy Helps German Business Weather the Troubles of the Euro Zone," *New York Times*, August 14, 2012, p. B1. The *Mittelstand* has benefited a great deal from the euro, which has made it easier for small companies to behave like multinationals (to sell all around Europe and in China). People may think of BMW and Siemens when they think of German business, but the *Mittelstand* is arguably the soul of the German economy. It reflects the values Germany is known for— stability more than growth, no debt, and prudence more than profit. Ewing, p. B1.

Yet, according to Martin Feldstein, and to his surprise, all eurozone experts he consulted agreed that a lower value of the euro is necessary for the survival of the single currency. See Feldstein, footnote 20. (Although Boris Johnson, mayor of London (2012), is quoted as saying: in saving the euro, there is a danger of "saving the cancer, not the patient." *Financial Times*, December 8, 2011, p. A4.)

In other words, there are always economic trade-offs: quantitative easing, pumping money into Greece, Spain, Portugal, Ireland and Italy, literally printing money, will cause their stock markets to rise—short-term, a sugar high. The low interest rate that will make their stock markets rise, in that the quantitative easing raises the supply and thus lowers the value of money and, as a consequence, creates lower yields in the bond market. (Continued on next page)

declare a default. European politicians and bankers may be trying to structure a deal in which investors agree voluntarily to a reduction, which would prevent bondholders from making a credit default claim, an event that would trigger a CDS payment. But the CDS market is not standing still. Expectation of a default can be seen in the rising cost of Greek CDSs. The cost of issuing $10 million of Greek bonds for five years (the cost of a credit default swap) has risen to $7 million from $6 million.[31] Traders say the higher cost of insuring against Greek default reflects the growing belief that some bondholders, mainly hedge funds, will not voluntarily agree to a deal. Some hedge funds are, in fact, specializing in the purchase of short-term Greek debt, hoping to profit from delays in structuring an agreement because, in theory, any delay triggers a CDS payment.[32]

Should hedge funds not sign on to a restructuring, Greece may be obliged to force them into a deal. That, too, would trigger payments on a CDS. Force means that Greece would literally rewrite national law to impose restructuring on all bondholders, most of whom are banks or asset managers, not sovereign countries, and not hedge funds (which are perhaps 10 percent of the market, a market that currently has pretty well dried up).[33] Doing so would codify what is already reality, namely, that Greek bonds trade between 21 percent to 24 percent of face value.[34]

(Continued from previous page) However, a high-priced stock market means high-risk investment with ever higher demand for global firms whose profit is diversified, which also means that the commodities market will rise—with low interest rates, the opportunity cost of holding non-yielding assets is down (with commodities also a protection against possible inflation from quantitative easing). A counterargument is that as German exports rise, Germany, with a low unemployment rate, will demand more workers—from Greece and Turkey—with the consequence that German salaries will rise, in effect countering the inflation. Germans may not like this counterargument.

[31] Tom Lauricella, Matt Wirz, and Alkman Granitsas, "Markets Bet on Greek Debt Deal," *Wall Street Journal*, January 13, 2012, https://www.wsj.com/articles/ SB10001424052970203721704577157061371440278.

[32] Lauricella, "Markets Bet."

[33] Lauricella, "Markets Bet."

[34] Lauricella, "Markets Bet." See Markit, a loan pricing service.

Still, some hedge funds are snapping up debt as it comes due, betting that if they hold out, Greece may end up repaying in full. Those bonds are trading at 40 percent of face value.[35]

The price of Greek bonds is calculated as follows: investors are already willing to accept 50 percent of face value in exchange for cash; accounting for the fact that these bonds will be rewritten with long maturity and low coupons, they calculate the real loss is close to 70 percent; they then add another 5 percent for the risk that restructuring will not take place, that Greece will default, or that down the road there will be a second restructuring. This 75 percent reduction translates to bonds that trade at 25 percent of face value.[36]

Historically, nations have dealt with their deficits by devaluing their currency. Were Greece not straddled with the euro, it would do the same. The value of the new Greek drachma would drop because there would be no demand for it, yet with a low exchange rate, Greek exports would rise, the economy would grow and the deficit would be paid off.[37] As mentioned, pensions and wages would not be reduced. Greeks would pay a high price for foreign products and, in general, experience inflation. But with a devalued currency, austerity is easier to take psychologically, and civil unrest might be prevented.[38]

---

[35] Lauricella, "Markets Bet." That is an example of professional investment (or speculation): taking an outright position. Hedging, stock options—these are insurance policies for the risk-averse or for those with actual positions: a farmer with a harvest on the line, an oil company with a contract on the line. It is not possible via an insurance strategy to achieve an above market return. Except in down markets, no one beats the market by thinking in terms of capital preservation.

[36] Lauricella, "Markets Bet."

[37] The fact that Greece may have nothing to export is another issue. Greece does, however, have a genuine tourist industry with related products and construction.

[38] Austerity, like beauty, is in the eye of the beholder. Greece may have to cut civil servant and government-provided pensions by 30 percent. (The U.S. should do the same.*) For someone counting on that income for the final 25 years of their life, that's pretty austere. But when the specific pension in question is, for example, the monthly €1,800 ($2,300) paid to a retired assistant garbage truck driver in the Peloponnese (according to the source, Alexander Singer, in "Letters" to *The Economist*, May 26, 2012, who adds, "I kid you not"), perhaps some term other than austerity would be more appropriate.

*The Bureau of Labor Statistics says that the cost of benefits for state and local government workers in the U.S. has risen 50 percent more than those for private sector employees since 2001. (Continued on next page)

II

If Greece defaults, there are other considerations:

1. Does Greece have the means to grow its economy? The International Monetary Fund (IMF) bailed out Mexico, Argentina and Indonesia. Why can't it bail out Greece? Because Greece has no means to grow its economy. There is no way to apply Brady bonds. Brady bonds, at full value, unlike the proposed Eurobonds for Greece, were a restructuring, not a forgiveness of debt. Interest was reduced to zero, but repayment was guaranteed, collateralized with U.S. Treasury, 30-year, zero-coupon bonds paid by the debtor nation using a combination of IMF, World Bank and the country's own foreign currency reserves. Brady bonds converted foreign loans into tradable

---

(Continued from previous page) [Note: it should be the other way around. Civil servants historically work for less than those in the private sector in exchange for job security and for a less demanding work environment.] See Bureau of Labor Statistics *at "Employment Cost Index Historical Listing March 2001 to March 2012,"* http://www.bls.gov/ect/#tables.

Again, whoa! If conversion to the drachma is ever seriously considered, panic would overtake Greece. There would be a nationwide bank run, as everyone tried to pull their money out, which, if converted to drachmas, would overnight be worth only a fraction of the euro. Suitcases of money would start flying out of the country. (Suitcases of money, the new drachma, would start flying in. In 2003, to replace the Saddam Hussein-era currency in Iraq, Thomas de la Rue, a British specialty printer with a squadron of 27 Boeing 747s and 500 armed Fijian guards, flew in the new Iraqi currency.) Then, computers, vending machines and payment machines (freeway toll booths) would have to be converted. Not impossible. It was done not that long ago to convert to the euro. It might be better than austerity.

Of course, another solution would be to just devalue the entire euro, which would benefit both Greece and Germany. According to Harvard economist Martin Feldstein, that might rescue the eurozone, " . . . although the eurozone would still face the problem inherent in the single currency, an inappropriate monetary policy in different countries at different times." Yet, according to Feldstein, "other problems of the euro may not continue. The bond markets will prevent excess borrowing by governments and private individuals . . . and peripheral countries are beginning to take the necessary reform steps that could reduce differences in productivity and unit labor costs." See Martin Feldstein, "A Rapid Fall in the Euro Can Save Spain from Collapse," *Financial Times*, July 25, 2012, https://www.ft.com/content/63848d68-d578-11e1-af40-00144feabdc0.

bonds, which allowed those lenders to get that debt off their balance sheets. This was possible because Mexico, Argentina and Indonesia could regrow their economies. If willing to wait, lenders would get paid back in full.[39]

2. Is Greece capable of maintaining a currency? A country that finds it difficult to run its financial affairs cannot possibly manage a national currency. According to Ernst Weber, an Australian economist, the restored drachma would stay in circulation only if the Greeks were denied

---

[39] A zero-coupon bond paid back years later is a loss in that the lender earns no interest and, after years of inflation, receives back principal worth less than when it was lent.

In 2001, Argentina ended its "permanent" link to the dollar. The peso quickly floated down by two-thirds, and the dollar-denominated foreign debt automatically tripled in pesos, from 60 percent to 180 percent of gross domestic product, which was unsustainable, i.e., it was not possible to collect enough taxes to pay the interest. Argentina then defaulted across the board, including on its IMF loans. See Ernest Preeg, a trade and finance advisor, "Greek Exit Need Not Be a Disaster," "Letters," *Financial Times*, April 10, 2012. But because Argentina was capable of growing its economy, lenders were eventually paid back.

Greece, however, starts with a 150 percent debt-to-GDP ratio and with a huge current account deficit.* A resurrected drachma would thus float down by at least 50 percent, raising the debt ratio above 300 percent, even more unsustainable. Moreover, Greece has already defaulted on most of its private sector debt in the second bailout, so this time, the default would center on eurozone and IMF debt. Preeg, "Letters."

According to Preeg, the effect of such default on the IMF would be seismic. Since 1978, the IMF system of market-based exchange rates, not to mention manipulated currencies, has led to a sharp decline in IMF loans to members with exchange rates, while the recent very large bailouts to eurozone members without exchange rates have resulted in the eurozone accounting for 80 percent of total IMF loans, which would rise to 90 percent with a bailout of Spain. The IMF, in effect, is being transformed from an IMF to an EMF, or Eurozone Monetary Fund, unrelated to exchange rates. Preeg, "Letters."

The IMF board would thus face a dilemma from a Greek default: other eurozone defaults. Further eurozone bailouts, including Spain, might then be opposed, and the IMF would have to beg the eurozone to honor Greek IMF loans, i.e., beg Germany. Preeg, "Letters."

(The IMF could be criticized for having a managing director who was a French finance minister and one of the strongest supporters of maintaining the euro no matter what the cost, largely for foreign policy reasons.) "Prudent banking practice would have been recusal as lead IMF negotiator for loans to the eurozone." Preeg, "Letters."

*A current account deficit means that a nation's central bank does not have enough foreign currency to pay importers when they ask to convert that nation's currency to their own. This forces the nation's central bank to borrow from China or the IMF, then, place that money in the bank's capital account to balance the negative current account. Thus, the expression: balance of payments (BOP). (A current account is negative when, for example, U.S. exporters put into the central bank less foreign currency from sales abroad than foreign importers put in U.S. dollars from their sales in the U.S.—the case when imports exceed exports.)

access to foreign exchange, preventing the informal use of the euro. That, according to Weber, would require draconian exchange controls of the type put in place by Germany after World War I, which ensured the circulation of the depreciating deutsche mark during a period of hyperinflation.[40] In this sense, Europe can give Greece a sound currency, but it cannot give Greece a sound fiscal system.

3. If Greece is bailed out, would there not be an unsolved moral hazard problem? According to Germany's chancellor, Angela Merkel, any comingling of eurozone debt would remove incentives for southern economies to adopt structural reforms.[41]

To Germans, the calls for burden-sharing (from the IMF, the Organization for Economic Co-operation and Development (OECD), and François Hollande, France's new president, who strongly backs common eurozone bonds), besides creating a moral hazard problem, i.e., removing the incentive for Greeks to reform, has the potential to raise German borrowing costs by diluting its creditworthiness across the currency union. Germans, thus, are not interested in bailing out Greece.[42]

---

[40] Ernst Juerg Weber, "Greece on the Precipice," "Letters," *The Economist*, May 26, 2012.

[41] Germans are gradually and more intensely losing respect for Greeks for their allergy to work and their nonchalance towards budgeting. In *Le Monde Diplomatique*, Thilo Sarrazin, past board member of Deutsche Bank and well-known author, declared that to assure peace among peoples, nations must respect how others wish to live. For example, that Greeks prefer siesta to work, or are accustomed to three-hour office breaks to spend quality time with their mistresses, is no one else's business, provided they [the Greeks] do not ask us [the Germans] to pay the bill. See *"L'Effroi du retraité allemande face à l'épouvantail grec* (The Horror of the German Pensioner Facing the Greek Scarecrow), *Le Monde Diplomatique*, July 2012, pp. 1, 8 and 9.

[42] Joshua Chaffin et al., "Germany Refuses to Share Debt Burden," *Financial Times*, May 23, 2012.

Are economists indifferent to Germany's plight? The Institute for New Economic Thinking, financed by George Soros, wrote, "Europe is sleepwalking ... (Continued on next page)

III

If Greece exits the euro, what effect will this have on Germany? At a minimum, Germany will no longer be able to sell its products in Greece: the Greeks won't be able to afford them, and Germany won't want the Greek drachma. (Nobody will want the Greek drachma.)

If Greece exits the euro, and that starts a chain reaction, the euro may dissolve. *That* is what Germany fears—that European nations will return to their original currencies, and that Germany will have a deutsche mark at such a high rate of exchange in relation to other currencies that no one will purchase German products. Germany benefits from a low-valued euro precisely because most European nations can't compete with Germany—which explains why 40 percent of German exports stay in Europe.[43] This is the heart of the euro crisis: countries running current account deficits.

But then, why should Germany do anything that would affect its competitive position relative to the U.S. and China? According to Floyd Norris, a financial writer for the *New York Times*, this would happen if inflation were allowed to rise in Germany.[44] Yet, according to Norris, Germany's rigid belief that others must suffer to preserve the system may yet compel another country's decision to take the risk of ending what has become a very bad marriage.[45]

(Continued from previous page) ... toward a disaster of incalculable proportions." In that report, the Institute urged countries with strong economies, like Germany, to accept greater short-term "burden-sharing" for the long-term good of all. "Absent this collective constructive response, the euro will disintegrate." Jack Ewing and Paul Geitner, "Spanish Debt Auction Reflects Brittle Position," *New York Times*, July 25, 2012, https://www.nytimes.com/2012/07/25/business/global/daily-euro-zone-watch.html.

[43] Rana Foroohar, "The End of Europe," *Time*, August 22, 2011.

[44] Floyd Norris, "In Europe, A Marriage Shows Signs of Fraying," *New York Times*, April 27, 2012, Section B, page 1.

[45] Norris, "Fraying," Section B, page 1.

Again, that's not going to happen! Angela Merkel will force everyone to deal seriously and in detail.[46] That's her strength. Yes, Germany will take a hit, but so too will everyone else—private bondholders, speculators, sovereign states. Merkel will not allow private bondholders who lent recklessly to get off the hook (at

---

[46] Seriously and in detail. Here's what that means:
- Eurobonds would be limited to 60 percent of GDP, the maximum ratio of debt-to-GDP, first intended for the monetary union (see Maastricht Treaty). For debt above that 60 percent, Bruegel, a European think-tank, proposes a liquidity premium. Unfortunately, as demand for the safe Eurobonds rises (those limited to the first 60 percent of GDP), the liquidity premium will rise. (Demand will rise because the new Eurobond market will be much larger than the previous national sovereign-debt market.)
- Bruegel calls the debt above the 60 percent threshold "red" Eurobonds (as opposed to the government-guaranteed "blue" Eurobonds). As a caution to would-be lenders, those red bonds, with their high liquidity premiums, will have high borrowing costs associated with them. Those red bonds will quickly become "red-hot," and vulnerable nations will not be able to borrow at all. (Euro nations that couldn't maintain the 60 focus—an unpalatable percent limit before the crisis—will not be able to maintain it afterward.) See "An Unpalatable Solution," *The Economist*, 8/20/11, https://www.economist.com/finance-and-economics/2011/08/20/an-unpalatable-solution.
- Eurobonds would be guaranteed by countries that themselves are vulnerable if their over-indebted neighbors should have problems. Differences in culture will not have been reconciled. It's not obvious that southern eurozone nations will reform themselves long run and that the crisis won't renew.
- Since governments feel a need to encourage economic growth, yet do not want to spend their own tax money, they will borrow. As borrowers, they will be rated, but because they do not want low ratings, which translate to high borrowing costs, governments, as do corporations, will manipulate the rating agencies—who are paid directly by those they rate.
- (We are touching on an enormous underlying problem: modern governments play an enormous, often defining role in modern economies. As public choice theory explains, this makes political leaders a huge source of patronage in the form of business contracts, social benefits, jobs and tax breaks. These are valuable to the recipients, their very constituents, whereas the cost to the average voter of any single perk is small. Perversely, beneficiaries, therefore, have every incentive to lobby for the retention of their perks, while taxpayers have little reason to campaign against them. Over time, the economy, like a barnacle-encrusted ship, is weighed down by these costs. The Greek economy is a textbook example. See Buttonwood, "Democracies and Debt," *The Economist*, September 1, 2012, https://www.economist.com/finance-and-economics/2012/09/01/democracies-and-debt.
- Reform of sclerotic labor markets and financial sectors, less well-run and less well-capitalized than American banks, may not be possible. Austerity measures (lower salaries, lower pensions), plus coping with the possibility of riots, will lead populist politicians and economists to stoke xenophobia such as anti-Semitism and anti-immigration resentment. See Rana Foroohar, *Time*, August 22, 2011. (Continued on next page)

German taxpayer expense). Nor will she allow mismanaged governments to get off the hook to evade serious reform. A total solution, thus, is a job for politicians, not economists.[47]

Economists predicted neither the 2008 financial crisis—in part because none had ever seen, let alone used, a derivative—nor the 2009 euro crisis.[48] That is why Angela Merkel said, "We must re-establish the primacy of politics over the markets."[49] Europeans created the euro to prevent crises caused by currency speculators except that, now, they are being pushed around by bond investors. If nations don't want to be pushed around by markets, they shouldn't borrow from them: Norway and Saudi Arabia, for example, are net creditor nations.

The problem Angela Merkel faces is that those European nations in financial trouble are entrenched in their ways. Thus, Germany is unwilling to pay their debts or to monetize the euro. Germany's problem is not simply that Germany would never be

---

(Continued from previous page)
- Acknowledging that dropping Greece from the euro is not the least costly solution. Adding up all the loans to Greece might come to €320 billion, with Germany's share at €110 billion—which may seem like a bargain, especially since it would save German taxpayers from an open-ended commitment to Greece—but it isn't. The simple act of showing that the euro is reversible will throw markets into a panic. Ireland, Portugal, Cyprus and Spain will consider dropping out: those nations are holding on only because they believe that the euro will not break up. Let the euro break up, and those nations will experience an immediate run on their banks. That will put the entire eurozone in peril. With a risk of depression, Angela Merkel will be under huge pressure to pay whatever it takes to save the rest of Europe. She will then have, according to The Economist, no time to negotiate the Pan-European federal discipline that she has always demanded as the price for German aid. A rescue would simply be a blank check. Rather than €100 billion, think €500 billion. See "Tempted, Angela?" The Economist, August 11, 2012, https://www.economist.com/leaders/2012/08/11/tempted-angela.

[47] The euro is not primarily an economic creation; it is a political creation to bind Europe.

[48] Jagdish Bhagwati, a Columbia University economist, at a Bank of International Settlements conference in 2008, asked if any of the economists there had ever seen a derivative. All replied no. (In his July 31, 2012 e-mail to me confirming the above, Bhagwati stated that most of the prominent commercial and central bankers at the conference "did not understand the new financial instruments which had precipitated the crisis.")

[49] Buttonwood, "Voters Versus Creditors," The Economist, November 19, 2011, https://www.economist.com/finance-and-economics/2011/11/19/voters-versus-creditors.

repaid but that Germany will be called on again, perhaps several times, to bail out Latin Europe. Those nations are so uncompetitive they are doomed to experience years of recession. Even with debt forgiveness, they will have years of austerity ahead of them, an austerity which, if it reduces the bloated public sector, will also reduce tax revenues. Of course, this will do nothing to address the regulatory burden overhanging almost all European countries—a burden that chases away not only investors, foreign and domestic, but their own entrepreneurial talent. As with Latvia, austerity might return those nations to prosperity but not without high unemployment and low welfare payments, the very condition that allowed Hitler and Mussolini, even Franklin D. Roosevelt in the U.S., to come to power in the 1930s.

Why not simply repay those loans? Why can't Greece and the other Latin-European nations do what any family does when it can't pay its debts: sell assets—the car, the family silver, luxury items? Why can't Greece sell or pledge hard assets, its islands, for example? That would eliminate the need for austerity.

Greek pride will prevent this, as does, were Germans the bidders, the memory of how they were treated by Germany during World War II—thousands lined up and massacred, hundreds of villages eliminated. Before lending to Greece, Germany should have thought of that.

Still, there is no crisis, and Greece is not going to leave the euro. A Greek exit would not relieve the remaining euro members of the burden of supporting Athens. According to one expert, in addition to protecting their own banks from the shockwaves, they will have to prop up Greece for at least a decade: "The notion that the rest of the European Union would sit by and let Greek citizens scavenge for food in rubbish heaps—I don't think European citizens would stand for this. It's often lost in the currency crisis, but the founding principle of the European Union is one of solidarity."[50]

---

[50] Thomas Krause, European Council on Foreign Relations and author of a book on the creation of the euro, in "A Hazard Puzzle to Solve: As Europe's Leaders Speculate Openly About a Possible Greek Return to the Drachma," *Financial Times*, November 11, 2011.

I

The key to understanding any problem, let alone solving it, is to state the *underlying* issue. To understand the 2008 financial crisis, then, it's not enough simply to say that banks made reckless loans. The underlying issue is that banks didn't function as banks, as institutions that lend money entrusted to them by their depositors; they functioned as finance companies, companies that lend money borrowed from others. It is what led banks, since 2001, to facilitate $62 trillion worth of lending and investment, an amount completely beyond their capacity and, in fact, beyond anyone's comprehension.[51]

How did this come about? President Bill Clinton. He ordered Fannie Mae, a government agency, to buy up the nation's subprime mortgages.[52] That started the ball rolling, a ball that ricocheted throughout the economy. Encouraged to provide "any" working

---

[51] $900 billion in 2001, $62 trillion in 2007. "A Deregulator Looks Back, Unswayed," an interview with Phil Gramm, Eric Lipton and Stephen Labaton, *New York Times*, October 17, 2008, https://www.nytimes.com/2008/11/17/business/worldbusiness/17iht-17gramm.17881800.html, and Buttonwood, "Swap Shop," *The Economist*, April 26, 2008, https://www.economist.com/finance-and-economics/2008/04/24/swap-shop.

Since the 1980s, the trend had been for banks to act as finance companies: first, to borrow in the secondary market and lend those funds to their customers (then sell those loans back to the secondary market to obtain yet again more funds); second, to take their profits in the form of loan fees and finance charges—from ATMs, credit card debt and account overdraft protection.

[In 2022, Silicon Valley Bank and First Republic Bank failed because they bet all their depositors' money (something a finance company would do) on long-term government bonds, whose value, when interest rates rose, dropped to zero.]

[52] "In a move that could help increase home ownership rates among minorities and low-income consumers, the Fannie Mae Corporation is easing the credit requirements on loans that it will purchase from banks and other lenders.

"The action, which will begin as a pilot program involving 24 banks in 15 markets—including the New York metropolitan region—will encourage those banks to extend home mortgages to individuals whose credit is generally not good enough to qualify for conventional loans. Fannie Mae officials say they hope to make it a nationwide program by next spring.

"Fannie Mae, the nation's biggest underwriter of home mortgages, has been under increasing pressure from the Clinton Administration to expand mortgage loans among low and moderate income people and felt pressure from stockholders to maintain its phenomenal growth in profits. (Continued on next page)

person with a mortgage, banks, their coffers replenished with unlimited funds, made loans based simply on borrowers' "stated" rather than "verified" income. Hedge funds and investment bankers followed suit. They, too, provided fraudulent loans and fraudulent products—investments that personally they would never have made.

All of this was and is possible because banks, even if indirectly, have access to the nation's savings. There is no limit to how much they can loan.[53] As every financial crisis has proven, when institutions do not use their own money, they do not care what happens to it. Historically, banks have been a natural check on reckless borrowing precisely because they are responsible for their depositors' funds. But since 2001, they have walked away from that responsibility. *They* are the ones (again, thanks to Bill Clinton) who

---

(Continued from previous page) "In addition, banks, thrift institutions and mortgage companies have been pressing Fannie Mae to help them make more loans to so-called subprime borrowers. These borrowers whose incomes, credit ratings and savings are not good enough to qualify for conventional loans, can only get loans from finance companies that charge much higher interest rates—anywhere from three to four percentage points higher than conventional loans." Steven A. Holmes, in "Fannie Mae Eases Credit to Aid Mortgage Lending," *New York Times*, September 30, 1999, https://www.nytimes.com/1999/09/30/business/fannie-mae-eases-credit-to-aid-mortgage-lending.html.

In the U.S. we separate church and state. We don't want clergy making social decisions on behalf of the nation. And we separate economy and state (we used to). We do not want politicians making business decisions on behalf of the nation—funding private companies (Solyndra), funding health care (Affordable Care Act), funding banks (subprime loans). Politicians cannot do what markets do.

[53] Unlike stocks and bonds, investment banks (often owned by commercial banks and thus part of the definition of a bank) have no fixed supply of raw material, i.e., mortgage-backed securities and collateralized debt obligations, plus derivatives based upon these, such as credit default swaps. Yet because these instruments are opaque—not stated on company balance sheets, often bought and sold without cash exchanging hands, without any credit check—there is no way to know, monitor or limit how much is lent.

Yet, when bank income is derived mostly from fees rather than from careful lending, they have an incentive to make more loans: they earn more fees and have no liability for depositors' funds—they're not using them. There is, then, no self-regulation. And because there is no use of depositors' funds, there is no government regulation. Depositors' funds are not at risk.

caused the 2008 financial crisis.[54] As agents for Fannie Mae, *they* fueled an overexpansion of credit, which fueled a rise in demand, pushing up prices, that pushed up property values beyond what income levels could support—a house of cards that ended in a crash.

Acting as finance companies, as free agents (yet insured by the government), banks transferred one group of investors' funds to another (then transferred them again a few more times). There was little risk to the transferee, i.e., the purchaser of the underlying securities (packaged, for example, as very large pools of mortgages or credit card debt). Investors assured themselves of a particular return by buying a tranche (a specific portion or slice of the total security priced to reflect a specific level of risk) and then insured

---

[54] They are the ones who caused the savings and loan scandal in 1990. With deposits insured by the government, banks walked away from their responsibility to protect those funds. They loaned without regard to the value of the underlying security.

One could conclude from this that if a nation truly wants its banks to be a natural protection against reckless spending (and reckless lending), as opposed to government being that protection, it must not, in effect, indemnify those banks. As examples, a nation might pass a law stating that banks may loan only their own money, i.e., not borrow from investors or from the government; a law stating that deposit insurance cannot exceed $10,000. Neither is necessarily a good idea, but if government is the lender of last resort, the moral hazard problem increases. Expand the lender or banker of last resort, and you expand the moral hazard problem.* Knowing that government will back them up, banks will not (perhaps cannot) be careful. But government should not back them up. Depositors should know they're taking a chance when they entrust their money to banks. Even a bank with a AAA rating is not as safe as the U.S. Treasury. (In 2008, Wells Fargo was the only bank in the nation with a AAA rating.)

What about the credit rating agencies? Are they being paid to give high ratings? Yes.** And who is rating moral hazard problems? No one, yet moral hazard exists precisely because risk is not being priced correctly, i.e., rated correctly. If banks knew the price of a bailout would be government stepping in to nationalize them (which is the right price), they wouldn't lend so recklessly. In a financial crisis, when asset values drop and the equity of a bank is reduced to zero, it may be in the short-run interest of the nation to take over that bank (obtain the right to acquire shares via stock warrants), and when the economy is again robust, sell them back to the public at a profit. *That should scare a few banks into prudence.*

*The mistake Lehman Brothers made (in running itself into the ground) was not being reckless enough. Had it made more bad debts in the derivatives market, government would have feared financial chaos and nationalized it. The mistake government may have made was miscalculating the extent of Lehman Brothers' debt. By not bailing them out, government contributed to the financial crisis by scaring investors into pulling their money from similar funds—a run on Wall Street.

**"The securities issuers pay [credit] agencies to issue ratings, and the agencies' interests can eclipse those of investors." Jerome S. Fons, managing director for credit policy at Moody's until 2007, as told to the House Committee on Oversight and Government Reform. Gretchen Morgenson, "House Panel Scrutinizes Rating Firms," *New York Times*, October 23, 2008, https://www.nytimes.com/2008/10/23/business/economy/23rating.html.

that tranche with a derivative called a credit default swap. It was an insurance game in which no one could lose.[55]

So why did everyone lose? Why did the system fail? Because there are no games in which no one loses. The 2008 financial crisis was a game in which too many people were playing, and playing from "naked positions"—shorting assets they didn't own, actually betting that the system would fail. Like the house in a casino, where losers pay for those who win, the market is like zero on the roulette wheel, where the house takes a cut—at those times everyone loses.[56]

In the commodity futures market, for example, as in roulette, everyone *can* bet wrong. A wheat farmer can bet that prices will rise (or not drop) and that, therefore, he should plant for future sale. Still, the wheat farmer will hedge that bet with an opposite bet, a short position in the wheat market. He may lose with his own wheat, but will gain with his hedge. It's a wash, exactly what is intended— someone with an actual position, a farmer with wheat trying to cover that position, simultaneously wins and loses. The cost of the cover,

---

[55] No one could lose because debt was packaged in such large pools there seemed to be no risk; the whole pool was not likely to default. (No one could lose? That should have raised antennas.)

Yet most of the $62 trillion was credit default swaps, not collateralized debt obligations. At first, the two products were closely intertwined, but soon demand for corporate bonds and other debt was so strong that "synthetic" collateralized debt obligations were created, in which one party agreed to insure the other in the event of default (in return for a fee, the insurance premium). Buttonwood, "Swap Shop."

[56] The opposite also exists, where the house loses, and a few people win so big it's as if everyone won. But when the house can't pay, the casino is bankrupt. With credit default swaps, when the counterparty, i.e., the real insurer, for example, American International Group (AIG), international finance and insurance in 80 countries, employing 49,000 people in 2019 (which is why they were bailed out in 2008), can't pay, the financial system is bankrupt. Worldwide, then, it's all just an insurance game, but unlike normal insurance, fire insurance or life insurance, where risk is clearly calculated, there were no actuarial tables for derivative insurance. Now there are.

According to one San Francisco insurance broker, Peter Brown, in a letter to this author dated January 26, 2009, "I think that AIG's parent holding company got into big trouble by moving from insurance to gambling. They not only lacked understanding of the risks they undertook, they seemed to do little to keep track of their overall exposure. During the last few years, a number of people raised the alarm about the enormous, mostly unchecked growth of Fannie and Freddie. No matter how obscure, there is almost always some actuarial data to assist underwriters in measuring not only the probability of loss but potential severity as well. When you drift away from this basic, you drift away from insurance."

the commission and capital gains tax, is the insurance premium, an expense factored into the cost of production of the wheat.[57]

But what if wheat prices rise unexpectedly? As soon as he can, the wheat farmer will get out of his short position by purchasing wheat. It will, however, be at a loss, because the price will be higher than he originally agreed to sell at, but he will simply take possession of the wheat and hope its price keeps rising. He will clearly be able to sell his own wheat at a profit. Yet, what if just before selling his own wheat, plus the wheat he picked up as a result of getting out of his hedge, prices rebound the other way, and the price of wheat unexpectedly falls (perhaps there is an unexpected worldwide bumper crop)? The wheat farmer now no longer has his hedge, and if he can't hold the wheat for a year or more (assuming that prices will again rise in the future, and provided the wheat doesn't rot), he is ruined. Now, add to this millions of speculators in wheat, none of whom are actually wheat farmers, all of whom are holding naked positions, and it's possible the market can't handle it.

II

With respect to the 2008 financial crisis, which no one predicted but which economists did talk about in theory but then dismissed as unlikely to happen, systemic risk would become reality. Economists did not account for nor did they send out an alarm because they, as well as most financial advisors, did not (or could not) understand the complexity of the derivatives that were being created. In 2002, with Enron, because they did not understand the complexities of Enron's false off-balance sheet items, economists and financial advisors

---

[57] With a short, you agree to sell wheat now at a certain high price to a buyer who agrees to take possession of it in the future. The buyer is willing to do this because he thinks that price will be even higher when he eventually takes possession of the wheat. However, the wheat that the farmer gives the buyer is not yet in the farmer's possession! He's waiting for the price to drop before he buys it. If wheat prices do drop, the farmer's wheat sitting in a silo will be sold at a loss, but that loss will be countered with the gain on the hedge. (If wheat prices rise, the farmer will lose on his short position, but will gain on the sale of his own wheat.)

simply turned their heads. They all assumed that because Enron was so successful, it must know what it was doing. In fact, this was their basis for recommending the stock. Yet they never asked the commonsense question: How did Enron's income rise over three straight years from $20 billion to $60 billion to $100 billion? They never asked if perhaps Enron was boldly committing fraud.[58]

This accusation was also thrown at Alan Greenspan. But he, as well as others who advocated for unregulated hedge funds, such as Phil Gramm, chair of the Senate Finance Committee, did understand what they were: insurance. They were a means for banks to reduce their exposure, not something that government would want to eliminate. What they didn't see, or believe, was that taking and actually creating an asset class out of credit had the potential for systemic risk.

The risk had two parts: first, structured finance is not the same as corporate bonds. With structured finance, a modest imprecision in measuring or estimating parameters of acceptable variation can lead

---

[58] For a more complete discussion of the pitfalls of investing in assets about which one knows nothing, and to view an Enron financial statement, see Insider Trading in Chapter 2.

Similarly, why did no one ask in early 2008 why the five-year CDS (credit default swap) spread had more than doubled to 740 basis points? At a cost of $740,000 to insure $10 million of debt, why did no one ask the commonsense question: Why was the spread so high? The only possible answer is that everyone was betting the system would fail. Since the spread was so high, which meant that return was low, which meant that risk was low, i.e., that the bet was a sure thing, knowledgeable investors must have known that the system would fail.

One underlying reason financial systems fail, which is why at other times they expand wildly, is confidence: overconfidence leading to an overexpansion of credit, and lack of confidence leading to an overcontraction of credit. Human beings are either too trusting in those whom they do not know (sending agents on errands with your money is not a formula for success—neither is making investments in assets you know nothing about) or, after a crash, are too distrusting (irrationally overreacting—consumers stop spending money, banks pull in their capital, deleveraging, refusing to lend—the very reason for the $700 billion bailout in 2008, to create liquidity in financial markets because government will buy up bad debt. In both cases the underlying issue is trust. Why? Because it's unavoidable human nature to trust; it's encoded in our genes; it's survival of the species. Like sheep when lost, human beings will follow a leader off a cliff.* Why appealing to confidence is the rube by which all confidence men work. They approach people and tell them precisely that they need to have more confidence in their fellow man, that the world cannot function otherwise. Herman Melville, *The Confidence Man*. Bernard L. Madoff, December 2008, where $50 billion was entrusted to a messenger, a confidence man.

*Read latest discoveries in behavioral economics that prove instinct plays a greater part in economic decision-making than rational choice.

to a wild swing in the probability of default. With a comparably rated corporate bond, no. (This problem is further compounded by the fact that credit ratings do not properly account for systemic risk. To have extrapolated from the last ten or 20 years of economic expansion as a basis for future earnings was naïve.) With structured finance, tranches, for example, risk is so low on senior claims that junior claims end up overcompensating, offering too high a return which leads, just as importantly, to an explosive demand for senior claims, fueling a financial bubble—with no breaks put on by investment bankers because they are still collecting their fees.[59] And the supply of structured finance grew not only because of demand but because of change in minimum capital requirements for banks. (Set forth in Basel I and II, in that banks holding AAA-rated securities were required to hold only one-half as much capital. This led to a yield advantage which in turn increased supply.[60])

The second part of this risk is that money managers—pension funds, insurance companies and hedge funds—were speculating. They didn't see that when everyone is insured against everything, no one is insured.[61] With credit default swaps, everyone is insuring themselves, betting that the value of their insurance contract will rise if default becomes more likely. Unfortunately, betting in this manner guarantees that it will happen. By the time insurance reached $62 trillion (with AIG holding most of the bag), the only able counterparty left was government. In the end, it is counterparty risk that creates systemic risk; risk that, in the worst-case scenario, counterparties will not be able to pay. The financial crisis of 2008

---

[59] Joshua Coval, Jakub Jurek, and Erik Stafford, "The Economics of Structured Finance," *Journal of Economic Perspectives*, 23, no. 1 (Winter 2009): p. 20.

[60] Coval, "Structured Finance," p. 22.

[61] It's pure Tragedy of the Commons. When no one owns a resource (in this case, credit as an asset), except to the extent one has an option to purchase a slice of it, there is no incentive to prevent overuse.

was a worst-case scenario. Financial collapse did not happen because government acted to prevent it; it bailed out the counterparties.[62]

Why wasn't this predicted? Because the only people capable of predicting such a thing are the players themselves, those with substantial capital at risk. It's just not possible to know these things *a posteriori*. One has to feel it. If economists can't feel it, that's understandable; they don't generally have skin in the game. Their profession is concerned with comparative statics, with analyzing data before and after an event. Economists are not financial advisors. They usually don't have investment and finance experience. Too often neither do financial advisors. Although they do deal with events as they unfold, when they advise consumers to purchase stock in companies such as Enron, or to purchase derivatives designed by companies such as Lehman Brothers, they are paid to do so. Unlike rating agencies, however, who are paid directly by the companies they rate, financial advisors are paid indirectly. They are given inside information that otherwise would be withheld, information that enables them to make more knowledgeable recommendations to the public than their competition. For their fraudulent advice to the public, those financial advisors and investment bankers involved in the 2008 financial crisis should all be prosecuted, found guilty, fined and imprisoned.[63]

Should consumers, those who lost their life savings or their pension funds, be compensated? Probably not. Why? Because certain things in life must never be delegated. If citizens cannot delegate their obligation to be on the lookout for threats to democracy, then neither can they delegate their obligation to pay

---

[62] Alan Greenspan admitted that he had put too much faith in the self-correcting power of free markets (which is to say that he forgot that free markets do not necessarily self-correct in the short run, that they have to overexpand first and then crash, and that after they crash, the shock to the economy might be more than it can handle). And he had failed to anticipate the self-destructive power of wanton mortgage lending. "Those of us who have looked to the self-interest of lending institutions to protect shareholders' equity, myself included, are in a state of shocked disbelief," he told the House Committee on Oversight and Government Reform, "Greenspan Concedes Flaws in the Deregulating Approach," *New York Times*, October 24, 2008, https://www.nytimes.com/2008/10/24/business/economy/24panel.html.

[63] Tarred and feathered?

attention to where they put their money. We have public schools in the U.S. precisely because Thomas Jefferson was so afraid that an uninformed citizenry would let democracy slip away. In other words, at the expense of individual freedom, would let government increase in size. If alive today, Jefferson would advocate that public schools, now, besides teaching reading, mathematics and history, the three essentials for preserving democracy, also teach economics.

If the 1990, 2000 and 2008 financial scandals mean anything, it is that you can't delegate your obligation to be financially aware, to choose your investments, to study carefully what you're buying. Being preoccupied with your career is not an excuse. When you're young and have time to learn your multiplication tables, you also have the time to learn basic economics—principles of money and investment. That learned knowledge cannot be delegated to professionals. Why? Because professional financial advice doesn't exist.[64] *People who know about money don't make a living advising others.*[65]

The key, then, is to understand that if a final party of such magnitude is allowed to fail, U.S. financial markets will fail. Similarly, U.S. financial markets, with their estimated bailout at $700 billion (in 2008, which may rise to $1 trillion), could not be allowed to fail; it would have taken down the rest of the world.[66]

Still, for the system to fail, something has to trigger it. As overexpansion of credit triggers economic expansion, *contraction of credit* triggers financial failure, withdrawal of credit at the moment when capital is needed. Lehman Brothers failed because it couldn't

---

[64] Neither does professional protection, such as government oversight (see footnote 22). In other words, the very purpose of a recession is to uncover what the auditors missed.

[65] Tevye in *Fiddler on the Roof* says, "If I were a rich man . . . I'd have time to give music lessons on the side and make a little extra money."

[66] Thus, the $1 trillion is an insurance premium. Cheaper than going to war, it's the Hobbesian premium to ensure world peace. Still, might it have been easier to have gone to war? Government found out that it was almost impossible to help homeowners with their subprime mortgages. Those mortgages had all been sold on the secondary market as securities so tranched (cut up), no one could determine their owners. The owners, the holders, could be as far away as a communal farm in China. Or might it have been better to have just left the market alone ... (Continued on next page)

hold on; it couldn't raise capital to support its bad subprime mortgage investments, although its asset management division— mutual funds and financial instruments geared to high-net-worth individuals—was very profitable. Valued at $6 billion, investors were offering as much as $4 billion for that division. But not in time.[67]

Is there ever a way to prevent overexpansion of credit? No, because there is no way to prevent overconfidence. Is there a way to prevent booms and busts in business cycles? No, because there is no way to prevent human nature from being the cause of economic cycles. There is no way to prevent human beings from latching onto and then misusing economic and financial models. With respect to financial models, experienced investors know that "[t]o confuse the model with the world is to embrace a future disaster driven by the belief that humans obey mathematical rules."[68] There is no way to prevent human beings from latching onto and misusing false or dangerous economic incentives such as government-inspired subprime mortgage debt. No way to prevent human beings from acting overly reliant on government regulation (including government bailouts of the economy) and not personally monitoring what it is they are investing in. And no way to prevent businesses from doing whatever they can to try to earn higher returns—life

---

(Continued from previous page) ... and the problem be solved by the market's own self-correction process? In other words, why wouldn't it have been more efficient just to let bankrupt companies fail and better firms buy them up? Isn't that the most efficient use of resources? This is what is meant by "creative destruction." This is what it means to live in a free society, i.e., a society tied to the market—the dilemma of no protection, the dilemma of living with risk. In other words, some activities are inherently risky—freedom, for example. So, too, with financial markets, for which there is no insurance except, for Hobbesian purposes, a government bailout. Just think, the very notion of financial engineering to turn risky loans into risk-free securities (which everyone bought so that too much capital went there) is only one example of the inherent risk in investing. And the next crisis will reveal something completely different.

[67] Tom Abate, "Hellman-Friedman Ponder Lehman Brothers Unit," *San Francisco Chronicle*, September 19, 2008, https://www.sfgate.com/business/article/Hellman-Friedman-ponder-Lehman-Bros-unit-3194587.php.

[68] Emanuel Derman, physicist and managing director at Goldman Sachs, from "Modeling Risk—Financial Engineers Failed to Account for Human Factor," *New York Times*, November 5, 2008.

insurance companies, for example, seeing people living longer, therefore demanding rates be lower—recalculating actuarial tables, then "churning" clients' investments (or anything else they can think of) to increase fees and boost the company's overall return.

III

We live today in an economy where government is involved in its regulation (or deregulation—it makes no difference) yet also provides a huge backstop of security. This is not how free markets work. It's how mixed markets work. But with mixed markets, there is automatically a moral hazard problem, a situation where no one cares what they do with their money because government is expected to bail them out. The price of a mixed market, then, is the potential for a financial crisis of more than average seriousness. In free markets, yes, there are always recessions, natural corrections from previous excesses in human behavior such as reckless expansion of credit, but those corrections do come to an end. In free markets there are greed and envy, yet, to the extent society tries to eliminate greed and envy, by forcing everyone to share things, there is a proportional drop in the standard of living. Greed, envy and competition are prime motivators for high levels of production, a high standard of living, in any economic system.[69]

With acts of regulation or deregulation, with government offers of employment or welfare, with any intervention in the economy, the underlying reasons for a recession or depression are covered over, thus, never resolved. Covering over, itself an outside element, prolongs a recession. The four-year depression of 1929 to 1932 had run its course, but Franklin Roosevelt's New Deal intervention in the economy, from 1933 on, was completely unnecessary. It turned that four-year depression into the Great Depression, which lasted until

---

[69] This is the basis of Bernard Mandeville's *Fable of the Bees*, first published in 1723 (and still in print), which contributed to Adam Smith's notion in *The Wealth of Nations* (first published in 1776, and still in print), that society will be far better organized if individuals pursue their own rather than someone else's interests. The idea is not new. "He who hates vice hates mankind" is attributed to Pliny the Younger, as mentioned by Thrasea, a stoic Roman senator.

1941, and even then ended only because the nation undertook enormous debt and expenditure to fight World War II. Without the war, the U.S. economy was headed toward the corporate state 1930s model for Germany, Italy and Japan: national socialism.[70]

As government intervention in the economy in 1933 prolonged the depression, in 1990, such intervention caused the 2008 financial crisis. Trying to do the impossible, regulate a market economy, government ineluctably made mistakes. In the 1980s, for example, deregulating the savings and loan industry, government made the unbelievable mistake of simultaneously insuring their deposits. Deposits insured to $100,000 allowed individual depositors to deposit millions of dollars in multiple $100,000 accounts across the nation without ever asking or caring who owned those S & Ls, whether they were sound, what their lending policies were. That moral hazard problem created the 1990 savings and loan scandal. Then, as explained earlier, for the ten years preceding the 2008 financial crisis, government encouraged banks to make subprime mortgage loans to individuals who didn't qualify, because government would *guarantee those mortgagees*. Huge mistake.

---

[70] Franklin D. Roosevelt was deeply impressed by what Mussolini had accomplished, and in return, in a laudatory review of Roosevelt's 1933 book, *Looking Forward*, Mussolini wrote, "Reminiscent of Fascism is the principle that the state no longer leaves the economy to its own devices . . . Without question, the mood accompanying this sea change resembles that of Fascism." At the time, the chief Nazi newspaper, *Völkischer Beobachter*, repeatedly praised "Roosevelt's adoption of National Socialist strains of thought in his economic and social policies" and "the development toward an authoritarian state" based on the "demand that collective good be put before individual self-interest." With respect to the Great Depression, Roosevelt declared, "If we are to go forward, we must move as a trained and loyal army willing to sacrifice for the good of a common discipline. We are, I know, ready and willing to submit our lives and property to such discipline, because it makes possible a leadership which aims at a larger good. I assume unhesitantly the leadership of this great army . . . I shall ask the Congress for the one remaining instrument to meet the crisis— broad executive power to wage a war against the emergency, as great as the power that would be given to me if we were in fact invaded by a foreign foe." For the above quotes, see David Boaz, "Hitler, Mussolini, Roosevelt," *Reason* magazine, October 2007, a review of German cultural historian Wolfgang Schivelbusch's book, *Three New Deals: Reflections on Roosevelt's America, Mussolini's Italy, and Hitler's Germany, 1933-1939* (New York: Henry Holt and Company, 2007).

"Fannie Mae Corporation is easing the credit requirements on loans that it will purchase from banks and other lenders...The nation's biggest underwriter of home mortgages has been under increasing pressure from the Clinton Administration to expand mortgage loans among low and moderate income people."

– New York Times, September 30, 1999

Again, the 1990 and 2008 financial scandals happened because government encouraged banks to make loans they otherwise would never have made, in total disregard of normal precautions—laws of business and economics, consumer credit criteria, valuation of underlying assets. Government simultaneously regulated *and* deregulated banks—which encouraged banks to create financial instruments they never would have made. Financial innovation is the response to an incentive. Derivatives, credit default swaps, mortgage-backed securities, off-balance-sheet accounting—all a response to financial regulation; all vehicles to circumvent government intervention. Thus, in response to Sarbanes–Oxley, credit default swaps enabled banks and investment houses to convert risky assets into ones that appeared safe.

In the end, all populist arguments for government regulation of financial markets are rooted in the argument expounded by the 20th century American economist Hyman Minsky, who stated that economic stability only encourages greater leverage and ambitious debt, arguing that stable finance is an illusion. By that reasoning, of course, is the commercial success of the West, success based entirely upon the free exchange of capital and ideas, an illusion?[71]

Those on the Left believe this to be so. Why the Left relishes the 2008 financial crisis; it is their opportunity again to advocate for

---

[71] "In recent decades, as planned economies collapsed under their own contradictions [what Minsky seems to have ignored], this utopian experiment [communism] has proved to be a systemic failure. Citizens who had endured long years of economic, moral, and political disaster were eager to get rid of them. Of course, the market economy is not a perfect system. But the market's flaws stem from the additions and motivations of its human participants rather than from its design. (Continued on next page)

expanded government and heavy regulation, to advocate for a New Deal, their chance to blame the financial crisis on the market economy. This is because the Left *never* makes the connection that economic regulation is always at the expense of individual freedom, that social, political and economic freedom are inherently interconnected, and that regulation is always at the expense of a nation's standard of living.

It's not that the Left is wrong to blame financial crises on the market economy, it's that their conclusion, *more* regulation, is meaningless. In other words, if you don't want financial crises, if you value security more than economic freedom, then install socialism. However, with government regulation of the economy, all financial crises in the 20th century and so far in the 21st century have been caused equally by government and the private sector. What the private sector did to cause the 2008 crisis is unpardonable, lying to investors about the safety of their money, but so too, what government did was unpardonable, creating incentives for banks to loan recklessly. The Left will always believe that an economy can be regulated, but the very existence of Wall Street is proof that it cannot.[72]

(Continued from previous page) Experience has taught us that a free market is closely associated with a free society. And in free societies, people are better able to act in concert to improve their lives. Free societies afford people the opportunity to make their own political and social systems more just. In general, these activities support rather than corrode morality." Qinglian He [an economist in the People's Republic of China], John Templeton Foundation report, "Does the Free Market Corrode Moral Character?" *https://integrityseminar.org/wp-content/uploads/2018/03/Templeton-Foundation-Free-Market.pdf*

[72] There is a timeless and therefore legitimate difference of opinion about the extent to which the conduct of a nation's citizens should be circumscribed by law and government. There is, however, the reality of actually enforcing law. One underlying reality is that, in general, government employees are less qualified than those in the private sector, precisely because they are paid less and work in a less creative environment. How, then, is it possible for government to control the activities of citizens whose very careers and salaries are directly dependent upon their ability to circumvent that control? It can't. Why government could not find lawyers equal to those hired by O.J. Simpson. The SEC apologized for not having stopped Bernard Madoff or companies such as Enron and WorldCom—the SEC said they just didn't understand what those companies were doing.

(Continued on next page)

The following is a list of what created the 2008 Financial Crisis:

1. Wall Street's listed firms were totally fixated on short-term quarterly results. This caused unethical behavior to meet expectations, to produce ever higher returns, and by the time of the crash, even higher than market returns. In contrast, privately held firms, i.e., firms not listed in the stock market, did not experience the same level of irresponsible behavior.

2. Wall Street "engineered" products that were incomprehensible. Plus, there was no clearinghouse to create transparency, to provide disclosure, to do credit checks.

(Continued from previous page)

This is true worldwide. In Europe, especially Eastern Europe with all its regulation, there was no one to stop the use of real estate mortgages denominated in currencies other than that of the home country. Interest rates were lower in Swiss francs, for example, which meant lower payments, but later those payments became astronomical as home country exchange rates plummeted (from the delayed but natural market self-correction in exchange rates).

In Europe and the U.S., ineptitude shaped the Basel Accords, international accounting agreements that allow firms to use internal rather than objective ratings for measuring credit risk. What this did, in 2004, was encourage Henry M. Paulson, then head of Goldman Sachs, along with other top investment bankers, to go to Washington to lobby for relaxing the net capital rule, which regulated large trading firms' reserves held against investments. That rule limited leverage, hence profit. Paulson's lobbying succeeded, and the SEC revoked the net capital rule (in exchange for it having more access to oversight, which allowed regulators to look more closely at company books but which, as in the case of Enron, because the books were purposely opaque, was meaningless). As a result, the door opened to further increases in the market for mortgage-backed securities (MBS), collateralized debt obligations (CDOs), and credit default swaps (CDS) that funneled even more money into housing.*

*James A. Dorn, "Creating Financial Harmony: Lessons for China," *Cato Journal* 28, no. 3 (Fall 2008): p. 537.

3. The Federal Reserve was asleep at the wheel. At the height of the bubble, interest rates remained at 1 percent.[73] [74]

4. Government encouraged home ownership by persuading bankers to make subprime mortgages.

5. Very large institutions gambled they would be deemed too large to fail, that government would bail them out.

Because of the 2008 financial crisis, government will again create new regulation.

If that regulation creates more transparency, no one will object. If that regulation allows maximum flexibility and innovation in the economy, no one will object. But if the regulation is for the purpose of crushing unfettered capitalism, the nation will pay a price—as the railroads did in 1890 (see Part IV)—only the giant corporations will survive, monopoly will be the norm, and a price will be paid in the

---

[73] Is Alan Greenspan to blame? What he did, keeping interest rates at 1 percent, was wrong (in hindsight), but it was he who invented the term "irrational exuberance." He may have had the power to pull the plug, to deflate the bubble, but his thought was that it was not for one person to do; that if experienced financial advisors, bankers, and real estate investors were going along with things as they were, perhaps the bubble was not yet ready to burst. Perhaps the bubble would increase two or three times. Perhaps the bubble wasn't really a bubble after all, but a fundamental change in the world economy, a functional change in long-term economic forces relating to the potentially overwhelming economies of China and India. A reasonable posture. Greenspan hesitated. It was a judgment call. In 1980, at the height of another financial bubble, Chairman Paul Volcker did not hesitate to pull the plug —also a judgment call. In other words, that central bankers are responsible for financial bubbles because they rely on the "efficient market hypothesis" (the idea that markets are always and everywhere correct) is not the reason that Alan Greenspan did nothing to deflate the bubble. (See George Cooper, *The Origin of Financial Crises*, and Part VI of this essay.) He did nothing because he wasn't certain what to do. On the other hand, Keynesian central planners would love to have that kind of power. Fortunately, the world has learned its lesson and some countries have seen them off.

[74] From a monetarist perspective, however, the 1 percent interest rate had the effect of devaluing the dollar. The result was worldwide inflation in commodity prices, oil and copper, for example, because they are sold in dollars. With the devalued dollar, U.S. exports rose, yet the rise in U.S. expenditure on imported commodities, as a result of their increased price, rose much further. According to Steve Forbes, in a speech to the Commonwealth Club of California, August 7, 2008, the U.S. now spends $700 billion overseas, whereas it spent just $200 billion a few years before.

loss of individual freedom and opportunity, and a drop in standard of living. One cannot improve a regulatory system by adding thousands of new regulations and layers of red tape. Not a solution. [Dodd–Frank passed in 2010.]

IV

There are no solutions to a financial crisis. Financial crises have to work themselves out. Regulation is not a solution because markets always go around;[75] and bailouts are not a solution because there is no guarantee that banks will not just hoard the money.

Not only does regulation serve no purpose (except psychologically to instill confidence), but perversely, to the contrary, it is actually desired by large corporations. They alone benefit. In the 1890s, the railroads fought regulation tooth and nail until they realized (a great capitalist epiphany) that only *they* could afford the regulations. Since the smaller railroads could not, the larger roads gobbled them up, acquiring them with money generated from the new high rates, the monopoly pricing guaranteed by government in exchange for the railroads allowing themselves to be regulated. There it is, classic: government facilitating anticompetitive leveraged buyouts.

It did not take long for 20th-century airline and trucking industries to figure this out, then beg for regulation, although it did take a long time for the nation to figure it out, to elect a president, Ronald Reagan, who deregulated those industries. As a result of President Reagan's deregulation, airline and trucking prices dropped in half. Unfortunately, with the financial scandal typified by Enron in 2002, Congress again enacted regulatory legislation, the Sarbanes–Oxley Act (SOX), with the very same windfall for large corporations. New New Deal regulations following the 2008 financial crisis will do the same. [Dodd–Frank]

---

[75] Again, this is why Wall Street exists—to go around government regulation and taxation. But not only Wall Street. Why offshore tax havens, the internet and cryptocurrency thrive—to circumvent federal jurisdiction.

This applies to bailouts as well. They, too, serve no purpose (other than psychological), although big suppliers of money are very happy: those bailouts pad their deposits yet do nothing to compel them to lend. A fundamental lesson in economics is to understand that lenders, suppliers of money, are no different than suppliers of any good or service, *producers,* the very people who stop and start an economy. Why? *They alone are at risk.* Suppliers will never start production simply because they or consumers have money in their hands from government stimulus. An increase in the money supply (monetary policy that makes cash or credit available), or a lowering of taxes (fiscal policy that makes cash available), is artificial. Suppliers will not start production unless consumers are spending their own money. Demand must be real.[76]

From a Hobbesian perspective (citizen desire for an overarching governmental framework and safety net), during a recession, government must appear to be doing something— regulation, bailouts, large infrastructure works—even if it knows they serve no purpose.

Government intervention cannot stimulate an economy (outside of spending for war). It doesn't need to if citizens believe in Keynes' precepts—the idea that government can revive an economy by putting people to work building infrastructure. As Japan believed: to ease recession in the 1990s, Japan converted $500 billion of government surplus into $500 billion of debt to build roads to nowhere. But recession there is still ongoing (2023), and Japan's national debt is now $9.2 trillion.

---

[76] The only way banks will open up credit is if government hands out two to three times what banks really need, $1.5 to $2.0 trillion. In times of crisis, banks want a large cushion. (Alan Greenspan, in a rare signed article in *The Economist*, December 20, 2008, said as much.) Money, however, is not the problem; it is not in short supply. Venture capital, private savings, sovereign wealth funds are all available—they're just not sitting in institutions government can influence. Thus, with respect to the 2008 financial crisis, the only thing government could do was print trillions of dollars, loan them to banks and hope they repaid.

The disciplined approach would have been to let insolvent banks fail—the quickest way to end a recession. In theory. In 2008, it would not have solved the problem if *all* banks had been insolvent—why Walter Bagehot, one of the wisest theorists on financial crises, during a severe financial crisis advocated abandoning theory: loan money to any bank that will probably repay. (The U.S. Treasury did not bail out Lehman Brothers because it looked as if they would be unable to repay.) (See Part V.)

At the outset of the Great Depression, 1933, Franklin Roosevelt did likewise. He put people to work building infrastructure. Unemployment not only rose every year, but there were periods when it jumped from 15 to 25 percent (until World War II). Those projects brought hope, prevented riots, prevented the overthrow of capitalism, so, yes, because the free world will *always* be fighting some form of socialism (tribalism is rooted in our genes), it was the right thing to do.[77]

The worst outcome, then, of a financial crisis is the threat it poses to economic freedom. When citizens are losing their jobs, their first thought (certainly a politician's first thought) is national socialism, the corporate state—where the state protects large industries, purposely creating monopolies that, in exchange for and in appreciation of government having eliminated their competition, do the state's bidding: provide high wages (for union support), pay high taxes (allowing government to provide universal social services —pension, health care, education, unemployment insurance), and create full employment (which has citizen support). Hitler, Mussolini, and Roosevelt came to power promising that citizens would have all the above.[78] In exchange, certainly in Germany, citizens forfeited political freedom, their right to vote, their legislature's right to check or veto leaders. In communist countries, citizens also surrender their right to leave. The corporate state associated with fascism is only minimally different from the communal state associated with communism. In both cases, political and economic restrictions make it impossible for small entrepreneurs, 99.9 percent of all businesses (at least in the U.S.), to lead a creative life of enterprise, launching and managing their own business pursuits. Both cases contradict the freedom and opportunity

---

[77] The Communist Party was infuriated with John Maynard Keynes. Believing Keynes was edging the U.S. toward socialism, the party was disappointed when it realized that his proposals for government intervention served the purpose of preserving capitalism, that he did not mean government intervention to be permanent. This was *the* reasoning for the WPA: employ artists and intellectuals, many of whom called themselves communists, to keep their minds off revolution, off the idea of overthrowing capitalism.

[78] In the U.S., that's how Senator Bernie Sanders (2016, 2020) tried to come to power.

that enabled the prosperity of the United States. The West must not accept such a trade-off. National socialism (the abbreviation of which is NAZI) does not lead to a richer, more equitable society.[79]

V

A modern economy is built on credit. It is built on the confidence of those who extend credit. As a consequence, it is inherently unstable. But the underlying question is, can a modern credit-based economy really be monitored and regulated to make it stable? George Cooper, in *The Origin of Financial Crises*,[80] believes that it can, that monitoring and regulating an economy is as simple as central banks watching the rate at which credit is being created and, when that rate exceeds the rate at which the economy should be growing, reefing the sails, slowing the engine.

Would that address the short-run instability of financial markets? No. If central banks act opaquely, mysteriously, arbitrarily, they may occasionally frighten a market back on track, but rational expectation theory says that unless that is always the case, investors

---

[79] Freedom is at stake when nations drop their hand from the tiller every time a storm arises. European socialism. It is to succumb to anti-capitalist myths that arise every time something goes wrong. With the 2008 financial crisis, the myth was that regulation was too light. Nonsense. The crisis was centered on institutions that were supposedly regulated: investment banks, Fannie Mae, Freddie Mac. Hedge funds weren't regulated, but they weren't the cause of the crisis. They were funded with real money, with pension funds, retirement funds, university endowments. It was banks because of government-ordered subprime mortgages that caused the crisis. That there is not a general consensus as to what caused the 2008 financial bubble—the president ordering Fannie Mae to purchase subprime mortgages, the Fed's monetary policies, foreign investment and foreign lending allowing us to live beyond our means, regulation, deregulation—poses an important question: If we couldn't diagnose the economic environment of 2008, how can we predict the next one? If government regulation is always a response to the last crisis, to how markets circumvented regulation, then regulation will always lay the groundwork for the next crisis.

It is not possible to stop creative financial genius. The founder of AIG, Hank Greenberg, for example, was considered, among people in the insurance industry, to have been one of the most creative insurers of our time. He expanded the nature of insurance by expanding the nature of counterparty insurance. It's irrelevant then that people in insurance consider Hank Greenberg to have been a great miser in that he was slow to pay claims. That may explain why his greed at first fostered creativity but later fostered overexpansion. It does not explain why he, and Alan Greenspan for that matter, was responsible for the 2008 financial crisis. They were its scapegoats.

[80] George Cooper, *The Origins of Financial Crises* (New York: Vintage Books, 2008).

(Wall Street) will always find a way to game the system, to counter any and every central bank move.

Plus, there are technical problems. How should central banks pull the plug, raise interest rates, contract the money supply? If everyone knows in advance that one or both are about to happen, it won't work. Because investors and entrepreneurs anticipate it and duly change how they finance capital projects. One change is to employ an *overall* rate of return: low interest, low payments during periods of economic contraction and higher interest, higher payments later. Another change is to use options—to change terms as conditions change, or to buy or sell in the future. Short of totalitarian tactics, an economy is just too complicated to control. If central banks want to reignite a stalled economy (at a time when it is not ready to be reignited, such as just after a crash), the only thing they can do is pour trillions of dollars into the money supply and hope for the best.

And pouring in trillions of dollars is not an exaggeration. During a recession, in a supply-side economy, an economy run by the owners of the means of production, the only thing that makes producers of goods and services start producing, lenders start lending, is confidence. From a simple injection of cash?[81]

Readers of this essay will realize now that fiscal and monetary policy, even government spending on infrastructure if the purpose is to put cash in the hands of consumers rather than producers (demand-side economics), is not a solution. During the Great

---

[81] Cash is capital, but capital is really surplus production of *real* goods and services. Increased capital then is increased standard of living; free trade of capital is capitalism; capitalism is economic freedom.

During a recession, however, capital is hoarded—why governments print more money. But printed money isn't a real good or service. It easily leads to inflation and is *always* paid for by taxation of the working middle class (who do not have the assets that shelter income). Middle-class taxpayers would be better off retaining $25,000 a year (were the nation's tax rate 10 percent), then paying (at bargain price) for whatever they need (especially health care).* Note: America was originally a nation of responsible adult citizens —why there was no income tax until 1913: and then, merely 1 percent. Let banks and producers who still believe they need an injection of cash borrow from the nation's citizens —and pay *them* back with interest.

*Police, fire, city streets, emergency medical, public schools are not paid from income taxes—they're paid from property taxes.

Depression, that approach, the New Deal, had no effect on employment. Anticipating the economy will get worse, the Ricardian equivalence (or counter) is for consumers and banks to hoard whatever money they receive. If they spend, it is to deleverage their bad loans (pay them off). That is why bailout dollars given to consumers only intensify the liquidity trap, a situation where consumers have money but won't spend it no matter how low interest rates are.[82] The Keynesian solution, putting people to work on public projects as a function of deficit spending by government, doesn't work. It doesn't increase total spending in the economy enough that velocity, the speed at which money changes hands, is increased. Because gross domestic product equals the money supply times its rate of turnover, what economists call velocity, if the money supply is unchanged during a recession, i.e., government borrows rather than prints money (or worse, as in the Great Depression, contracts the money supply), GDP will fall. When GDP falls, employment falls. During a recession, when velocity is down, the only thing government can do is print money.[83]

This is not, however, the moral solution. The moral solution when an economy falls into recession is to let it recover on its own. Still, from the Hobbesian perspective—the perspective of preventing

---

[82] During the 2008 financial crisis, to "jump-start the economy" (an expression a person in business would never use), banks, under pressure to make loans from their bailout funds, made loans only to their richest customers, those with absolutely no need for money but who were convinced to borrow (to refinance business loans, especially real estate) because banks offered them exceedingly low interest rates. A perfect example of markets circumventing government intervention.

[83] According to Irving Fisher, the early 20th century economist who invented the quantity theory of money, monetary forces can produce booms and busts yet produce no change in output (GDP). The theory is Money Supply (MS) x Velocity (V) = National Output (GDP) x Price Level (P). Since velocity does not increase during a recession, money supply must, or GDP will drop (and if GDP drops, employment does too). During periods of economic expansion, because velocity increases, i.e., money changes hands more quickly, money supply can remain constant. This is so because with increased velocity, there is increased demand for money, which in turn raises the price of money (the nominal rate at which money is loaned), which in turn leads to a nominal rise in GDP. Either price level or money supply must rise to raise GDP. During a recession, with interest rates dropping, increasing the money supply is the only option. (During the Great Depression, the money supply was contracted—the worst thing government could have done, the main reason the Depression continued. All economists today agree.)

civil unrest in an interconnected, globalized economy where good businesses are ineluctably dependent upon bad banks, where citizens are dependent upon government for protection from their own human nature and from irrational exuberance and irrational depression at every cyclic expansion or contraction of the economy —there is no moral solution. Populist politicians won't let it happen; their rise to power is dependent upon convincing voters that government is the answer, that there is always a political solution to an economic problem.[84]

Printing money to end a recession causes those who work and save to see their savings wiped out. For those who work and save, who see themselves as moral, who view those who speculate as immoral, economic reality is they are still connected to the world economy, and that once there is an intervening broker, a bank (whose very existence is a function of leverage), all parties are gambling, and when a depression hits, all parties are wiped out.

Even when an economy expands, those who keep their money in savings are wiped out by inflationary price increases (or even from genuine higher demand). Yet, those who spend money they don't have, who borrow profligately to invest in stocks and real estate, which appreciate faster than savings (from 1990 to 2001 at almost 15 percent a year), earn far more. According to Christopher Caldwell in "The Unwisdom of Crowds,"[85] Walter Bagehot (editor of *The Economist* from 1860 to 1877, whose book, *Lombard Street*, is still unmatched for how to deal with economic crises—whose main premise is that, moral or not, the injection of a large amount of capital into a depressed economy is the only way to reverse a contraction) says that every great crisis reveals excessive speculation in ways no one suspected, and if proceeding further than anyone suspected, speculators were "tempted by the daily rise of prices and the surrounding fever." Thus, according to Caldwell,

---

[84] Populist politicians might suggest a bailout superfund, a one-half percent bailout tax on every business transaction. That way, rather than label government bailouts a moral hazard problem, society would call them payoffs on an insurance policy.

[85] Christopher Caldwell, "The Unwisdom of Crowds," *The Weekly Standard* 14, no. 14 (December 22, 2008).

Avaricious people get hurt, but it is the nature of crashes that they are not the ones who get hurt most. A tragic figure present in almost every historic account of speculation and collapse in history is the person who believed, year after year, that the boom was an illusion, and held himself aloof until, at the very last minute, whether out of self-doubt or deference to the opinions of his fellow man, he entered the fray and was (having bought at the top, rather than the bottom of the market) wiped out. What a wicked irony! His punishment is as much for his long and wise forbearance as for his momentary weakness.[86]

In addition to the short-term instability inherent in financial markets (as a result of speculation), there is an inherent cultural contradiction within capitalism itself, namely that although capitalism rewards diligence, which leads to wealth, wealth leads to idleness, idle speculation, which in turn undermines capitalism. Except for those who like to plan their lives, capitalism is the only choice, by providing freedom and opportunity (which, if you were born in a rich capitalist country, you might not appreciate). Even if capitalism has weaknesses, greed is not one of them. Greed is a human defect (if survival of the species is a defect) that manifests itself in any advanced economy.

Does a modern economy have to be built on credit? Yes, because in good times, companies that use leverage have an enormous advantage over those that don't and use that advantage to crush those that don't.

It works like this: one firm invests its own $50,000 to earn $5,000, a 10 percent return. Another firm invests only $10,000 and borrows $40,000 to earn $5,000 less $2,000 (the 5 percent interest it pays to borrow the $40,000), which equals $3,000, a 30 percent return. This second firm will then cut its prices so that its return drops to 15 percent. This price cut will drive the first firm out of business.

---

[86] Caldwell, "Unwisdom."

And it applies to banks. Banks cannot choose not to leverage; they would be competing with banks that do, banks that cut their prices, lower their rates for lending or raise their rates for savings, which is the same thing. Banks steal customers from banks that don't leverage.

This means, then, that speculation and financial bubbles are not primarily a function of greed but a function of leverage and overextension of credit; that financial bubbles are part of a modern economy. Short of communism, there is no way to prevent this. As stated before, overextending credit is natural human behavior; it's borrowers asking for more than they need and lenders not restraining them. In every instance, it is the result of not paying attention to timeless principles of economics and money. It is the result of inexperienced bankers and traders, mostly under the age of 30, none of whom have ever experienced an economic downturn, all competing with each other for higher than market returns. It is the reason behind all economic recessions: overextension of credit. So why don't older traders step in to stop it? Because older traders don't exist; they are the young traders wiped out by the last recession. There is no collective memory on Wall Street!

VI

Conclusion

Perhaps there is collective memory in government. Perhaps central bankers should pull the plug when an economy overexpands. But if one asks two underlying questions: "Are financial markets really so unstable?" and "Can government really regulate an economy?" the answer is no. Financial markets may be unstable in the short run, at the margin, at a particular moment in time, but that does not mean they categorically are unstable. George Cooper believes that financial markets are unstable; that in the short run, they can never be counted on to self-correct to an optimal equilibrium. His *Origin of Financial Crises* is therefore just another book advocating

Keynesian economics and the notion that markets are not efficient. To Cooper, the efficient market hypothesis should be thrown out.[87]

Efficient market hypothesis, however, is the idea that at any moment in time, market price is the right price (no matter how distorted it appears). In the short run, the right price may not be sustainable, but that price didn't come out of nowhere; it was negotiated worldwide, via traders of money and commodities, by millions of buyers and sellers, with no one purposely acting irrationally. To Cooper, these buyers and sellers are unconsciously acting irrationally as the result of powerful unstable forces that

---

[87]To free market advocates (this author), Keynesian economics should be thrown out. In fact, free market advocates, Milton Friedman in particular, believe central banking should be thrown out. Friedman's reasoning is that although central banking stabilizes the credit system, its presence also destabilizes it (by encouraging risky lending). Central banking puts conservative banks—safer, less leveraged banks—at a disadvantage relative to cavalier banks. This means that over time, bad lending practices force out good lending practices, and central banking becomes a race to the bottom (with all banks, in competition with each other, making risky loans). The 1990, 2001 and 2008 financial crises were exactly that.

In the race to the bottom, not only do prudent banks get trampled, but so do prudent borrowers. What about all those borrowers who could have afforded a new home with a subprime mortgage but not a prime mortgage and chose not to buy a home? Or consumers who chose not to max out their credit cards or home equity lines simply to boost consumption beyond their income? Unlike imprudent banks and imprudent borrowers, these people are not being helped. To the contrary, they are being punished. With the Federal Reserve holding interest rates artificially low for the purpose of propping up asset values, home prices for prudent buyers are still artificially higher than they should be, and prices for the prudent mortgage pool investor are still higher than they should be. The immoral bailout, then, is for the profligate. In the race to the bottom, this is the way it is.

True free market advocates would go further. They would argue that if banks issued their own currency backed by their own certificates of deposit (gold or some other inflation-proof asset such as land in downtown Manhattan), they would have every incentive to be careful, as would their customers.* Central banking makes its case under the guise of facilitating credit nationwide, of having sufficient reserves to stop bank runs, of being able to control the exchange rate. But the truth is that central banking is a tool of central government to control banks, to force them to serve a broad spectrum of government policy. For one thing, according to Cooper, government likes to control inflation, usually at 2 percent (rather than 0 percent) per annum. This enables government to avoid the political pressure that arises when workers in dying industries have to face lower wages. With 2 percent inflation, nominal wages can remain the same while real wages painlessly drop 2 percent a year. Second, with nominal interest rates higher than real interest rates (because of inflation), central banking can more easily manage recessions by lowering nominal rates (to encourage borrowing). But most importantly, inflation is the most convenient tax ever designed—a tax that, unbelievably, no one objects to: it raises income taxes because it raises wages and interest income, and it raises capital gains and estate taxes because it raises asset values. With this convenient tax, government has the ability to redistribute wealth—to build a system of unfunded transfer payments and entitlements such as Social Security and Medicare, and now, the Affordable Care Act. (Continued on next page)

permeate financial markets.[88] Cooper believes government must step in and put an end to it.

Why, then, does Cooper, in the Preface to *Origin*, provide his own best counter-argument? He declares that regulation for the last crisis will not prevent the next; "tighter accounting standards [SOX] after the dot-com bubble did nothing to prevent the subsequent housing bubble. To prevent the next crisis, we must look beyond details of today's mortgage bubble to the underlying monetary system which helped facilitate it."[89] In other words, Cooper wants to control the extension of credit via central banking monetary policy. To Cooper, *that* is the core purpose of central banking—not to fight inflation. Unfortunately, as stated earlier, every time there is a financial crisis, those on the Left come forward with the only solution they know: "control the economy, bailout citizens, tax the rich." Seeing themselves as the only ones compassionate about the less fortunate, the only ones worried about the economy, about the

---

(Continued from previous page)

To true free market advocates (and believers in public choice theory), *this* is why we have financial crises—so that government (after having mixed itself into the economy to such a degree that it is at least as responsible as the private sector for recessions) can step in as a savior, reinforcing the necessity of its own existence.**

*In the U.S., private banking ended in the 1860s when President Lincoln financed the Civil War simply by printing money, but this forced him to pull the U.S. charter for all banks that issued their own currency. How is that different than financing the 2008 financial crisis by printing money? To free market advocates, the loss of private banking was a crime, a violation of the Constitution, because it was so fundamental to individual freedom and to early American democracy.

**Inflation Tax

    At 0% inflation and 2% real interest

    (with total government tax at 40%),

    government takes 0.8% and citizens keep 1.2% = real return of 1.2%

    At 2% inflation and 2% real interest,

    government takes 1.6% and citizens keep 2.4% = real return of 0.4%

    At 4% inflation and 2% real interest,

    government takes 2.4% and citizens keep 3.6% = real return of (-0.4%)

[88] The emotional basis for all left-wing ideologies is fear that citizens are victims of sinister forces beyond their control, coupled with the belief that it is the very purpose of a civilized society not to let this happen

[89] Cooper, *The Origin of Financial Crises*, pp. vii–viii.

planet, the Left is willing to spend whatever it takes to relieve their anxiety—even if that sends the world back to the Middle Ages.

What Cooper really believes is that credit expansion should be halted to the same degree that credit contraction is halted: "symmetric monetary policy." If we're not willing to let an economy crash, we should not be willing to let an economy boom. To Cooper, *that* is the role of central banking—in that the cause of economic booms and busts is financial market instability.

False logic. Other than in response to a natural catastrophe, when individuals naturally come together, it is false logic to conclude *that* is how we should behave *all* the time—communally. Life doesn't work that way. A free market economy doesn't work that way. Humans, bees, living organisms in nature all simply pursue their self-interest to survive. Adam Smith (*Wealth of Nations*) believed that citizens individually pursuing their natural interest to survive, automatically, as if led by an invisible hand, produce an incomparably higher level of production *and cooperation* than is possible by design. In advanced industrialized economies, where work is specialized, the economy complex and citizens not economically self-sufficient, socialism is absolutely not an answer. Socialism cannot handle the complexity. Economic freedom is the answer—because only individuals keenly attuned to their personal plans, *via the price system*, are able to pull from that complexity the information they need. (Cf. F.A. Hayek, *The Constitution of Liberty*, for which Hayek received the Nobel).

Also, in a free society, citizens do not generally mistreat each other. Some behave badly, which is why nations institute constitutional government (rule of law), a neutral third party to protect life, liberty and property (to prevent citizens from taking the law into their own hands), but at the heart of morality is Adam Smith's, *The Theory of Moral Sentiments*: no one will associate, let alone do business with those they know to be dishonest. The dishonest, unable to support themselves, fall behind and die.

Governments should not, because they *cannot*, aid the nation's economy. Creative citizens, as in an ongoing chess game, counter government's every move. To create confidence in markets, governments try to create the illusion they are helping—but citizens must not fall for that. Governments cannot do what individuals can only do for themselves (get up in the morning). Out-of-control capitalism will always create financial crises, but governments, beyond an injection of cash, should not intervene. Intervention halts the market's self-correction process, strengthens weak industries, lays the groundwork for the next crisis. The bailout of GM in 2008 prevented forces of creative destruction from eliminating a weak industry (no longer even listed on the Dow Jones Industrial Average).[90]

***

We're not living in Plato's *Republic*. An economy, nay, a free society, is a bottom-up phenomenon. Brilliant leadership is not the cure for the simplicity of populism; *it's the cause*. In a free country, the market, not government, organizes the nation. The deep Left-Right split in America is over a literal versus expansive interpretation of the Constitution—bottom-up or top-down. Why, from 1933 to 1935, the Supreme Court vetoed every legislative act proposed by President Roosevelt. Unconstitutional!

---

[90] Foreign aid fails for the same reason America's public schools fail: government is trying to do something it can't—change the behavior of irresponsible citizens who do not create their own factories and students who do not do their homework.

Aid Trap[1]

When rich nations fall into recession, their governments do what they can—except, after 100 years of socialism, the entire 20th century, those governments know, now, not to intervene in the economy. To prevent a financial crisis, yes, loan money to banks, but otherwise, stay back.

Poor nations haven't learned this. Recession or no, they always look to government. Even when citizens are entrepreneurial, their economies are so regulated, so manipulated by a few families who own the important businesses and resources, that they have to look to government. They have to ask for foreign aid. They *know* their leaders will grab a good portion for themselves yet know they'll also get something—food or employment—because otherwise they'll riot. Their leaders won't let that happen; there'd be no foreign aid. The World Bank, the International Monetary Fund, sovereign wealth funds, private investors—all awash with more capital than they know what to do with—push poor nations into accepting foreign aid, or worse, into making huge loans. The Greek euro crisis. Foreign aid and foreign investment are the absolute *sine qua nons* of their economic existence. Egypt.

A trap. No one can do for others what they must do for themselves. Foreign aid, then, prevents citizens from solving their problems. Aid could go to privately held businesses, but if they don't exist, no foreign aid. Strapped with debt, those nations will be exploited. By China, a nation that has not learned the 20th century's greatest lesson: don't go socialist. Nor the 19th century's greatest lesson: don't go colonialist. *Nouveau riche* China, with no history of democracy, pluralism, or self-control, knows only totalitarianism. If you're a nation receiving aid from China, know that China, a predatory xenophobic lender, cares not one iota about you.

The most successful foreign aid, ever, the U.S. Marshall Plan for Europe after World War II, channeled money directly to businesses, not to governments. That aid was not meant to bolster

---

[1] Published in *Epoch Times*, February 15, 2023.

governments, infrastructure or employment. Understood was that businesses would get the economy going, after which everything else would fall into place. Pure Adam Smith. Marshall Plan money was loaned directly to businesses that repaid the loans to their respective governments, which only then would spend on infrastructure. The Marshall Plan put the horse before the cart. It was genuine foreign aid. Nations were not expected to repay.

The Marshall Plan was a development bank administered by the 1948 Economic Cooperation Administration (ECA) of the U.S. government. Today, that program would be a complete failure because foreign aid today does not go directly to private business.

The purpose of the Marshall Plan was to bring back business, not create business. A new ECA would be another 20th century central decision-making institution handing out money. Progressive socialism. It would be a government agency looking first to protecting its own existence rather than ensuring the success of its projects (which, if it fails, like other government agencies, will simply ask for more money—without realizing the agency was the reason for the failure). With vast financial power to grant or deny loans, an ECA would protect that position by extending its reach. Public choice theory.

The U.S. Federal Reserve is a perfect example. Designed as the lender of last resort with clear guidelines for preventing a financial crisis, i.e., loan money to any and all creditworthy lending institutions that put up real assets as collateral (Cf. *Lombard Street*, by Walter Bagehot), the Fed today is an overreaching powerhouse that creates its own guidelines. To prevent the 2008 recession from deepening, it loaned to any institution it deemed too big to fail, *without* regard to creditworthiness, *without* regard to the quality of underlying collateral. As collateral, the Fed accepted complicated and fraudulent credit security agreements and worthless mortgages. Working with the U.S. Treasury, the Fed today dictates fiscal and monetary policy to the nation.

The new ECA would do the same. Like China, as soon as there is a financial crisis in the lesser-developed world, the ECA would distribute foreign aid to anyone it can find. With the power to grant or deny loans, like the International Monetary Fund, it would dictate foreign policy. Yet just as the Fed did not prevent Fannie Mae from purchasing fraudulent mortgages (to the contrary, it practically ordered Fannie Mae to purchase those subprime mortgages—the very cause of the 2008 financial crisis), so too, the ECA would make fraudulent loans and cause financial crises around the world. Like the Fed, it would solve problems simply by offering money.

The role of the Fed and an ECA is to provide stability—which is completely counterproductive to a dynamic economy. Instability is the essence of creative destruction, the invisible hand's self-correction process, markets self-correcting naturally from an overexpansion of credit. Why, in a recession, nations must wait it out, not stimulate growth; the market is recovering from growth. You don't offer a seven-course meal to someone who just threw up from overeating. In 2008, the Fed threw billions of dollars into the market, which prevented a financial crisis, but it did not stimulate the economy. It flooded the engine—why frightened banks hoarded the money. In a supply-side economy, producers produce only when *they* are confident, not because government gives demanders money. Price stability, the multiplier effect, both, in a recession, are meaningless. They prolong the downturn. (The 2008 recession, over in 2011, lasted until 2018. The 1929 depression, over in 1933, lasted until 1941.)

In a financial crisis, an ECA would act like the Fed. It would stimulate the economies of lesser-developed nations by throwing money at them. But those ECA loans, like Fed loans, would be hoarded. When the ECA runs out of money (because, unlike the Fed, it can't print money), Congress, our foreign policy lender of last resort, would provide more. Except, when those loans are not repaid, to provide more funds, will Congress raise taxes or cut spending? No, it will borrow. *U.S. foreign aid helps no one.* If money solved problems, there wouldn't be problems. (One thing the world doesn't lack is money. The world has more than it can spend—$100 trillion in surplus cash, $1,000 trillion (one quadrillion) in derivatives. Why? Because investors can't find viable capital projects. It is why the New York Stock Exchange is so overpriced: the whole world is competing to invest there. It is why Greece nearly collapsed: the whole world competed to loan it more money than it could handle. With so much money chasing so few viable capital projects, pushing up asset prices and lines of credit, and with most nations not dealing with their debt and unfunded liabilities, the world economy could crash.)

***

Top-down solutions are not an answer. Market economies are a bottom-up phenomenon. They consist of individuals producing goods and services and then trading for other goods and services. A market economy is nature itself, human nature, individuals following their economic instincts. Societies in which individuals are not entrepreneurial, not producing, not saving, not working 12 hours a day, six days a week (because they just *love* making money) will never become Asian Tigers. They'll be gobbled up by China.

Did the Asian Tigers become tigers because their governments funded their industries? No. The world thinks so, but that's not the case. In Japan, government did invest in private industry, but those industries failed. It was industries that the Japanese government did not support, auto and electronics, that saved Japan. Plus, new companies should *not* begin operation on borrowed money; it's the worst thing they can do: it's skipping a step. Companies should start small (so that mistakes are small), then reinvest profit back into the business. That's how to grow a business. *Natura non facit saltum*, Charles Darwin, "Nature makes no leaps." (One of the many serious errors of Soviet communism was that it started too large. Both Apple and Hewlett-Packard started in their garages.)

***

Economic growth is the solution to the world's problems. People with money in their pockets don't need government. Rather, bad governance is the source of the world's problems, especially in poor nations. It's why they have so little economic growth, why America's Founding Fathers practically eliminated government. They wrote a *one-page* Constitution: legislators will be elected, Congress will make law (not government agencies), enumerated governmental power (a post office, a navy, in a very short list): Article 1, Section 8. That's a model that works.

5

SHORT ESSAYS

CUBA AND COLUMBUS

In the course of conversation with John D. Rockefeller, Santayana mentioned Spain's population; and the millionaire [billionaire], after a pause murmured, "I must tell them at the office that they don't sell enough oil in Spain." Here in one sentence leered the ugliness and barrenness of the modern age. "I saw in my mind's eye, " adds Santayana, "the ideal of the monopolist. All nations must consume the same things, in proportion to their population. All mankind will then form a perfect democracy, supplied with rations from a single center of administration, as is for their benefit; since they will then secure everything assigned to them at the lowest possible price." This utilitarian utopia, prophesied by Henry and Brooks Adams as the triumph of the cheapest, starves the realm of spirit and the realm of art as no other dominion can. The culmination of liberalism, the fulfillment of the aspirations of Bentham and Mill, and of the French and American democratic spokesmen, it is also the completion of capitalism. It is communism. Rockefeller and Marx were merely two agents of the same social force—an appetite cruelly inimical to human individuation, by which man has struggled up to reason and art.

—George Santayana[1]

---

[1] Santayana, quote, *Soliloquies in England,* 1922, in Russell Kirk, *The Conservative Mind* (New York: Regnery Publishing, copyright 1985, first published 1953, and again 2001), p. 443.

No person in business speaks like this. Latching on to what they perceive as crude parlance, both Santayana and Kirk (see footnote) completely misunderstand the intuitive process of a creative mind in business. They see only a dystopian attack on spirituality—*a central reproach of classical conservatism*, that business, nay, liberalism, is life without God.

Ayn Rand has a better understanding. In *Atlas Shrugged*, she makes the point that creative industrialists and creative artists are one and the same mind—except that industrialists know it, artists don't.

Artist Diego Rivera felt at ease in the company of industrialist John D. Rockefeller. Sensing a kindred spirit, Rockefeller asked Rivera to paint the interior of Rockefeller Center. Rivera, a communist, was given *carte blanche* to paint a mural at the center of capitalism.

Rockefeller later requested that he take out the portrait of Lenin, saying it was the equivalent of a portrait of Hitler. Frida Kahlo said absolutely not. Let them destroy your work before I let you change your mind—which is what happened. Great art was sacrificed for a principle—that the sun goes around the earth, that communism is the future: see 30 million executed in Russia, 30 million in China, four to five million in North Korea, two million in Cambodia; thousands in Cuba, lined up, shot in the head, one by one (by Che Guevara personally at least 100), with no mercy to home and factory owners who refused to turn over their life's work, their property.

Why Cuba? Cubans are the most entrepreneurial people in Latin America. Had the revolution not turned communist, Cuba, instead of Miami, would today be the financial center of Latin America. Cubans are descendants of Christopher Columbus, an entrepreneurial mind who sailed for commerce, for profit, to cut the cost of importing spices by finding a shortcut from Europe to Indonesia (betting the world was round). Under pressure to repay Spain for those three ships, despite his misgivings about hurting an obviously gentle population, Columbus pressured that population to reveal where they were hiding the gold (which didn't exist). The pressure turned to torture.

Have we judged Columbus too harshly? Queen Elizabeth I came to the throne at a very young age. A daughter of Henry VIII, agents of the pope attempted to kill her. Under pressure and against her nature, she allowed the torturing of plotting traitors and spies to compel them to reveal who else was behind those attempts. In 2003, the U.S. invaded Iraq because Saddam Hussein would not reveal where his nuclear weapons were (which didn't exist). Fearing another 9/11, we again tortured Saudi and Afghani terrorists at Guantanamo Bay prison (Cuba)—to reveal who and where their comrades were, where their nuclear weapons were.

In jettisoning Christopher Columbus, we minimize the importance of the discovery of the New World, a milestone in world history.

***

Great industrialists purchase great art. *Great art is who they are.*

> For if there is a more tragic fool than the businessman who doesn't know that he's an exponent of man's highest creative spirit—it's the artist who thinks that the businessman is his enemy.
>
> —Ayn Rand[2]

> I believe in order to make an American art, a real American art, [it] will be necessary [to have] this blending of the art of the Indian, the Mexican, the Eskimo, with the kind of urge which makes the machine, the inventions in the material side of life, which is also the artistic urge—the same urge primally but in a different form of expression.
>
> —Diego Rivera[3]

---

[2] Ayn Rand, *Atlas Shrugged* (New York: Penguin Group, 2005), p. 784. First published 1957. Still in print—with 300,000 to 500,000 copies sold per year, and 500,000 copies given away annually by the Ayn Rand Institute. The state of Idaho had at one time considered making *Atlas Shrugged* required reading to graduate high school.

[3] In conversation with Dorothy Puccinelli, author of *Diego Rivera: The Story of His Mural at the 1940 Golden Gate International Exposition* (San Francisco: City College of San Francisco, 1940).

> The [Jefferson] memorial is a shrine to a man who during his lifetime owned more than 600 slaves and had at least six children with one of them, Sally Hemings. It's a shrine to a man who wrote "all men are created equal" in the Declaration of Independence . . . yet never did much to make those words come true.[4]

Excuse me, Thomas Jefferson dedicated his life to ensuring that America would be a free nation. At the beginning of the Revolutionary War, it was Jefferson who declared, "we are about to fight a war to create something that exists nowhere on earth: a nation without a king or queen, a nation where every man, regardless of wealth or social status has the vote, a nation whose government is so limited that citizens will barely notice it." It was Jefferson who stated, "if you're afraid of this, afraid to give every man the vote, you're afraid of democracy. If you're afraid, leave!" Many did. They fled to Canada.[5] As John Hancock wrote large his signature on the Constitution, Thomas Jefferson made it known, large, where he lived, Monticello. To the British: "Come on, burn it down." Would the author of the introductory quote really have us take down the Jefferson Memorial? The author obviously has not read what's engraved in the memorial: "God who gave us life gave us liberty . . . Commerce between master and slave is despotism. Nothing is more certainly written in the book of fate than that these people are to be free."[6]

When asked why is it that when one looks closely at those persons one most admires, one always finds something incongruously reprehensible, Aristotle rejoindered with, "They

---

[4] Lucian K. Truscott IV, "I'm a Direct Descendant of Thomas Jefferson. Take Down His Memorial," Op-Ed, *The New York Times*, July 7, 2020, https://www.nytimes.com/2020/07/06/opinion/thomas-jefferson-memorial-truscott.html.

[5] Sixty thousand loyalists fled (and lost their property), although at the end of the war, not the beginning.

[6] When conservative political candidates trail in the polls (2016, 2020 presidential elections), progressive candidates need to stop talking! Certainly not write such articles as "Take Down the Jefferson Memorial."

dropped the ball." They didn't deal with a personal shortcoming. They rationalized, as did Jefferson, working on behalf of the colonies to secure the help of France for the Revolutionary War, on problems of political economy, on botanical studies, who didn't have the energy to deal with slavery.[7] Yet, as a young man, Jefferson wrote *Notes on the State of Virginia*, published in 1785 (written before the war), a report on all activity in Virginia requested by England (which recognized young Jefferson's genius), in which Jefferson warned to have no illusion about slaves: "they are no different from anyone else" (although, yes, older he said the opposite).[8]

Why do we undervalue our Founding Fathers? Their moment in time was a miracle from which the world still benefits—the culmination of the 18th century Age of Enlightenment and its legacy enshrined in the Declaration of Independence, U.S. Constitution, *Federalist Papers*, which explained how and why a democracy works—a rare moment in history that brought the best minds of Europe to America. Searching for freedom and opportunity, fleeing an undemocratic, aristocratic, religiously constrained class-privileged continent, they came to America.[9]

Frederick Douglass in the 19th century, and Clarence Page, a 20th century African American essayist for the PBS *NewsHour*—both stated unequivocally that the Founding Fathers rose to the occasion and transcended their privileged positions to create a

---

[7] Inheriting overwhelming debt from his father, if Jefferson had freed his slaves, he would have been penniless, would have lost Monticello, would have never built the University of Virginia. It's easy to say what he should have done, but disingenuous. It's hypocritical for progressives to say, based on the imperfections of their lives, what *they* would have done if living then.

[8] The Lewis and Clark Expedition was successful largely because Jefferson had been so respectful of American Indians that he obtained their extraordinary cooperation.

[9] The operas of Wolfgang Amadeus Mozart, a Freemason, with librettos by Pierre Beaumarchais, represent Europe's emerging desire for freedom and social equality. Joseph Haydn, Mozart's teacher, with the best orchestra position in Europe, couldn't take it any longer and moved to London. Johann Sebastian Bach's music represents flights of spiritual and personal freedom, but his contemporary, Frideric Handel, for the same reason, moved to London. (Jimi Hendrix, looking for freedom from racial prejudice, living next door to Handel's London house, was an active member of the Handel society.)

document, the U.S. Constitution that they knew was the ticket to emancipation.[10]

***

Yes, Harriet Tubman, for her courage, for her actions to free slaves, deserves a memorial: alongside, but not, as suggested by Truscott, in place of Jefferson. Why do articles that make white Americans feel bad about their country never acknowledge that it was Blacks who rounded up their own people, 50 percent of whom went west (a quarter to North America), 50 percent east? Why is it those articles never acknowledge that Africa (1812 onward) attacked British ships trying to stop the slave trade, that for the previous 900 years had been sub-Saharan Africa's only cash crop, and never once did African countries, Dahomey especially, when they realized how badly slaves were treated, cross the Atlantic to reclaim them, or offer to buy them back?

Why, after living 250 years in America, upon emancipation, did only 20 percent of African Americans run to get an education? Because worldwide, historically, and to this day, that is the percentage that goes to school. Ninety-two percent of African Americans appear to graduate from high school, but that statistic is meaningless: U.S. Department of Education statistics show that only 36 percent of *all* Americans are proficient in reading and mathematics, with African Americans' test scores 26 points lower.[11] Those low test scores are not a legacy of slavery, but of an aural

---

[10] In 1787, with the Revolutionary War just over, America was in no mood to start a civil war. The northern states, needing the southern states to ratify the Constitution, made compromises, yet still kept slavery out of the Constitution. There are no politicians today at the level of vision or competence of our Founding Fathers.

[11] See Average National Assessment of Educational Progress (NAEP) reading and math scores for 4th- and 8th-grade students by race/ethnicity: Selected years, 1992-2017, U.S. Department of Education, National Center for Education Statistics 2019-038.

culture struggling to exist in an advanced industrialized economy, and a legacy of an awful public school system.[12]

---

[12] For example, Marina Middle School in San Francisco, formerly a high-performing neighborhood school, has fallen into chaos (2023). One-third of its staff and its longtime principal left. Academic and behavioral standards dropped so low because teachers and administrators, afraid of being fired for flunking or suspending minority students, just let them wander the halls, videotape themselves beating up students, scream at teachers, throw food at each other.

Teachers were ordered to deal creatively with those problems. State Superintendent Tony Thurmond, in a letter dated August 19, 2021 to school district superintendents, urged education leaders to:

> Replace suspensions with support. Sending a student home from school does not address the root cause of a student's behavior; it removes students from the learning environment; and it has a disproportionate impact on African American students and students with disabilities, among other marginalized groups that are underperforming academically and over-represented in our criminal justice system.*

Weren't these issues resolved in the 1970s? It's pure 1960s political activism, edubabble, the confusion of correlation with causation. It's racist.

There are low-performing schools in San Francisco where students are not misbehaving, but that's because teachers there have excellent classroom management skills. Except, *that* is the reason the schools are low-performing: classroom management, a skill, a career in its own right, a career of creative problem-solving, *is* the trade-off: two jobs at once. Impossible—why in the 1970s and '80s, according to the California Commission on Teacher Credentialing, 50 percent of young, enthusiastic, new teachers quit within three years, 75 percent within five years. Less true today, but it is why teachers quit, why enrollment in San Francisco public schools has dropped, why parents pull their children.

*Tamara Straus, "Discipline in Disarray at Another S.F. Middle School," *San Francisco Examiner*, January 15, 2023, https://www.sfexaminer.com/news/education/another-sf-middle-school-falls-into-disciplinary-chaos/article_468ccbce-9095-11ed-a69c-1b42852679ae.html.

JULY 4

Immigrants die (asphyxiated in unairconditioned trucks in 105-degree heat crossing the border from Mexico) to come to this country.

Why, then, do American schools splice immigrant history and culture into America's core curriculum? They don't want to hear about their country anymore. Teach a multicultural history of the world, and you shorten the time for teaching the history and culture of British and American democracy, whose roots are 5th century Athens, 1st century Rome, 18th century Age of Enlightenment—in elevation, three periods unmatched in the history of mankind, Western civilization, the notion that rights of the individual precede those of the state. The U.S. is the only large nation in the world to have such an ideal—why the world sees America as "the beacon on the hill." For the short time students are in class (six hours less three hours for lunch, PE, art and recess), American schools should focus on teaching what's best about America. There's no time for anything else (plus no one wants to hear it).

Postmodernist critical race theory multiculturalism is destroying what unites this nation: Western civilization—*not* simply one civilization among many. U.S. population in 1800 was 5 million; 200 years later, 300 million; just 20 years later, 330 million: a self-selected citizenry. They came here; they weren't born here. Why can't U.S. multiculturalists appreciate that their parents came to get away from their country and culture? They came for a new life; they came for a better life for their children.

That's why we celebrate the 4th of July: Americans are proud of their country, proud of the Founding Fathers who risked their lives in a revolution (all of whom would have been hung had they lost the war), proud of their parents who risked everything to come here.

***

Veni, Vidi, Vici

—Julius Casear